Measuring the Value of Information Technology

Measuring the Value of Information Technology

John Hares
and
Duncan Royle

JOHN WILEY & SONS
Chichester · New York · Brisbane · Toronto · Singapore

Other Wiley Editorial Offices

John Wiley & Sons, Inc., 605 Third Avenue,
New York, NY 10158-0012, USA

Jacaranda Wiley Ltd, 33 Park Road, Milton,
Queensland 4064, Australia

John Wiley & Sons (Canada) Ltd, 22 Worcester Road,
Rexdale, Ontario M9W 1L1, Canada

John Wiley & Sons (SEA) Pte Ltd, 37 Jalan Pemimpin #05-04,
Block B, Union Industrial Building, Singapore 2057

Library of Congress Cataloging-in-Publication Data

Hares, John S.
   Measuring the value of information technology / John Hares and
Duncan Royle.
      p. cm.
   Includes bibliographical references and index.
   ISBN 0-471-94307-X
   1. Information technology—Finance.   2. Capital investments.
I. Royle, Duncan.   II. Title.
HC79.I55H37   1994
658.15′54—dc20   93-38006
                                                                        CIP

British Library Cataloguing in Publication Data

A catalogue record for this book is available from the British Library

ISBN 0-471-94307-X

Typeset in 10/12 pt Palatino from author's disks by Photo·Graphics, Honiton, Devon
Printed and bound in Great Britain by Biddles Ltd, Guildford, Surrey

Contents

Preface

This book is, as far as the authors are aware, the first attempt to develop a structured method for measuring the financial value of an investment. The valuation techniques used in the method are based on the ideas of others—there is no new thinking on how to ascertain and measure financial value. What is new is that the authors have brought together the erstwhile disparate valuation techniques so that there is a staged structure and sequence in which the techniques are applied. The techniques are therefore able to add value to each other.

There are three parts to this book. The first part is the description of techniques for identifying investment opportunities and ensuring that the opportunities support the business objectives of the organisation. The second part discusses the techniques for valuing the financial investment made in an opportunity and the calculation of the expected returns, taking into account all aspects that affect the return. These two parts are set in the context of an investment appraisal structured method which defines the sequence in which the techniques are to be applied and how the output product of one technique can be used as an input to another technique for further finessing.

The book is designed for the non-accountant and specifically addresses investment in information technology. Notwithstanding the focus on information technology, the techniques of valuation are generic and can be used to measure an investment in anything.

John Hares and Duncan Royle,
Ascot and Manchester, 1994

_____ Acknowledgements

This book is peculiarly the work of others. As already acknowledged the techniques of investment identification and valuation have all been developed by others, the authors merely putting a structured method framework around them. The authors are indebted to these experts.

Particular thanks go to a former colleague of both authors, Gordon Roy. Many of the examples of investment situations are based on the huge array of investment stories Gordon has at his fingertips. Gordon used to lecture with the authors on the method and added immensely to the quality of the course. This quality has been included in the book.

The authors also wish to thank Hugh Eagle who has provided valuable advice regarding the formulas for the Bowater Scott model project valuation technique and on matters general.

Investment Appraisal— What Is It?

This chapter starts by detailing the basis and purpose of the book, which is to describe an investment appraisal method for prioritising and valuing the investments made in projects, particularly information technology projects. The investment appraisal method is much more powerful than the traditional cost/benefit analysis approach. All the considerations that go into an investment decision are described, so that the full array of additional aspects of an investment appraisal as compared with cost/benefit analysis are made clear—aspects such as project risk, event risk and the use of flexibility to offset the risks. The reader is persuaded of the benefits of undertaking a full investment appraisal exercise and the need to apply the investment appraisal techniques in the form of a structured method. The structure of an investment appraisal method is described, along with the relationship of the techniques and their investment valuation deliverables.

1.1 THE BASIS AND PURPOSE OF THE BOOK

This book is about the following:

(1) Identifying opportunities for making investments in projects pertinent to the objectives of a business.

The identification process seeks to ensure that project investments are those that will maximise the financial return *and* the business benefit of the investment to the company. Monetary return is not the sole basis on which investment decisions should be made. If this were the case then investments could be made in a project that does not assist the company as a long term business competitor (because the project is not directly concerned with the business objectives of the company) but in a project which yields the highest return. The ridiculous situation could occur where investing in, say, sports equipment or other non-relevant business activities could be a more profitable investment for a jewellery company than investing in a project concerning the jewellery trade. This is hardly the stuff of business strategy if the intention is to stay in the jewellery trade—good investment yes, good long business no. Both the financial return and the business benefit of a project investment must be based on and assist the strategic objectives of the company.

(2) Measuring the financial value of an investment in a project.

Once the investment opportunities have been assessed and prioritised the actual expenditure on, and revenue monies from, the investment need to be calculated. For an expenditure of £nn, how much revenue will be earned over the lifetime of the project and will this result in a profit?

The monies need to be measured on the basis of today's values, at all times, taking into account all aspects that could alter its value during the lifetime of the project. The monies involved must therefore take into account such things as inflation, the ability to earn interest from alternative competitive investments and the risks that the investments incur—the project could, after all, fail.

(3) Extending the traditional scope of Cost/Benefit Analysis (CBA) into a full investment appraisal.

The boundary between CBA and investment appraisal is open to debate. Some practitioners of the investment valuation process would consider the measurement of the intangible benefits to be part of CBA and others would consider it to be part of investment appraisal. What is not open to debate is that:

- CBA is not a complete science for the full and proper valuation of project investments. There are several components of the valuation process that are not addressed and should be included, such as project and event risk and the ability to offset the costs of risk with flexibility.
- CBA is open to much abuse. It unfortunately includes non-discounting techniques that produce:
  - different and often conflicting results from the same financial information;

- financial results that are not a true value of the investment—projects that actually produce a loss are sometimes made to appear profitable. The book therefore takes that which is valid from CBA and adds additional techniques of valuation to create a comprehensive investment appraisal method.

(4) Integrating all the above into a coherent structured method of investment appraisal.

The current techniques have been developed by many individuals working as independent thinkers on investment strategy and valuation. The result is that the techniques and the valuation deliverables they produce are disjointed and unintegrated.[1] There is considerable overlap in the scope of the techniques, those overlaps leading to wastage of effort. The hitherto standalone application of the techniques has meant the deliverables they produce do not benefit from the information the other deliverables contain. There is no added value from integration. The full and proper value of an investment cannot therefore be measured. The quality of the investment appraisal valuation process would be substantially enhanced through the integration of the techniques and their deliverables into a comprehensive structured method. Only through this integration can the full and proper valuation of an investment be made.

The techniques used in the book for the identification and prioritisation of investment opportunities and for the valuation of the investments are generic to any business. The book is therefore relevant to a wide range of business situations. The first set of techniques are those long practised by strategic business planners and the latter techniques are those long practised by accountants. The problem has been that they have not been brought together even though they both contain information of value to each other—until this book. The strategy techniques enable investments to be made both in support of business objectives and a good financial return. The valuation techniques enable the investments to be measured. The techniques have therefore been adjusted and modified where appropriate by the authors to enable their individual results to be integrated into a structured method of investment appraisal.

Notwithstanding the generic relevance of the techniques, the book focuses on the computer industry. The investment appraisal techniques are

---

[1] The authors wish to stress that any comments made regarding specific techniques and the way that they are used with other techniques are solely in the context of this book and its intention of developing a structured method of investment appraisal. Almost all the techniques considered in the book are included for the very fact that they add value to the understanding of the valuation of an investment. It is the lack of integration in the application of the individual techniques that is the problem, not the techniques themselves.

applied in the context of investing in computer projects that assist the business objectives of a company. All the worked examples of identifying investment opportunities and then valuing the investments are based on experiences of projects that the authors have worked on or are aware of from colleagues similarly involved. The book is based on practical experiences. It discusses the context and theoretical basis of the investment appraisal techniques, but the results are practical examples of what the techniques produce, how they work and how they can be integrated with each other into a structured method. The techniques and the structured method have been applied and found to work. There is nothing significant in this book that is theoretical.

The worked examples are of two kinds—a set of experiences covering a wide range of different business situations and a common case study of one business situation, a container port authority. The port case study shows how the opportunity identification and investment valuation techniques can be applied and be seen to work as a coherent whole to produce a single result—the true value of an investment in support of the company's business objectives.

The book is written in such a manner that non-accountants can understand the investment appraisal process and non-information technology specialists can understand the technology involved. One of the authors is an accountant and one an information technology specialist. Both have worked on each others' contribution to the book with full understanding of what is being described and applied.

The book is therefore targeted at the general person who wants to spend monies on computer projects and who wants to know whether the investment is a wise one, that business will benefit and a profit be made. The readers do not have to be experienced practitioners of investment appraisal or of information technology. They can range from novices to "old timers".

At this point, it is perhaps worth stating what the book is not about. The book is not about the management of the investments, that is planning for and taking actions that are designed to ensure that the calculated costs and benefits are obtained. The management of investments is not addressed.

1.2 CONSIDERATIONS FOR INVESTMENT APPRAISAL

There are a large number of considerations that an investment appraisal structured method needs to address. They are:

(1) That there must be a single unit of measure on which the identification and prioritisation of investment opportunity are based.

The unit is a scoring, the higher the score the greater the opportunity and the higher its priority.

(2) That there must be a single unit of measure on which the monetary valuation of investments is based.

The unit is money. It would be nice to have a common unit of measure for both the identification of investment opportunities and the valuation of the investments but this has not proved possible. The problem with investment opportunities is that monies have not yet been involved. One cannot therefore use monies for this part of the investment appraisal process.

There are four aspects of investment monies to consider—known as the tangible costs and benefits and the intangible costs and benefits. Costs can be considered as expenditure and benefits as revenue/income. The exact boundary between what is a "tangible" and an "intangible" is debatable, but the basic argument is that tangibles are easy to value in monetary terms; they can be identified, counted, priced and valued. This is not the case with the intangibles, both on the cost side and even more so on the benefits side. The tendency, therefore, has been to use money for the valuation of the tangibles and a scoring of some kind for the "valuation" of the intangibles. The problem with this is that there is not a common unit of measure for the valuation, and for projects the proportion of what is tangible and intangible is almost infinitely variable. Where two units of measure are used, proper valuation of and fair comparisons between projects competing for investment monies cannot be made.

This book does not hold to the position of monies for the tangibles and scores for the intangibles. *The position is that all costs and benefits, of whatever type, need to be converted to a monetary value.* Not only is this a common unit of measure but it is the only unit of measure that can calculate the impact of such things as inflation, risk and flexibility on the present day value of investment monies. For project comparison purposes, as well as proper valuation, money has to be the unit of measure.

(3) The need to discount future monies.

The concept that money declines in value over time is one of the factors that leads to the principle of discounting, which is the most fundamental advance in CBA. The technique discounts future cash flows according to a formula which exactly allows for the reduction in money values due to inflation and the risks of the investments. Once this is done fair comparative assessments against alternative investments can be made.

The discounting technique can bring all future expenditure costs and income benefits into present day terms so that costs and benefits can be fairly compared, no matter when they occur in time. This enables decisions to be made about whether the magnitude of benefits in the future is worth the initial investment costs and enables projects of different payback periods to be compared on an equal basis. Discounting removes time from the valuation process, levels the "playing field" for project up-front costs and tail-end benefits—the former are not overvalued and the latter not undervalued—and allows comparison between the project and the basic investment yardstick, the current value of any profit or loss.

When discussing the need to discount future monies, the following issues must be addressed:

- *The impact of inflation on the value of money.*

A problem with measuring investments in money terms is that money does not have a constant value. A pound 20 years ago was worth more than one pound today. The effects of inflation have become particularly significant in the last 30 years and, although its impact is in decline due to lower inflation in the developed countries, it is still of great significance, particularly for projects of long duration. A project can have a life of many years. During that time the inflation of the country in which the project is being undertaken will erode the value of the future monies of the project. The impact of this erosion over time needs to be calculated.

A project which pays back sooner is more attractive than a project which pays back later. Money has more value the sooner it is earned and spent. Intuitively this makes sense, but the problem is to know what allowance to make for the timings of benefits, because of the different timings of the costs and the benefits in the life of a project—the costs occurring before the benefits. The benefits are therefore more vulnerable to declining values over time than the costs. This means that, if the declining value of money is not measured, any project benefits will tend to be overvalued and the project made to appear more profitable than justified.

This varying time delay is also important when comparing different projects. For example, is a project which pays back £1 million in two years time worth more than, less than, or the same as, a project which pays back £1.1 million in three years time? The concept of the 'time value of money' is one of the most important issues when using investment appraisal techniques.

- *Alternative uses that an investment could be put to.*

The investment monies can be invested in a wide variety of ways and not just in a computer project. A would-be investor needs to know whether the financial return on a computer project is at least as great as that which can be earned by any alternative investment, such as bonds or equities. There is a cost in investing monies in a project. One of the costs is the interest lost by not investing the monies in some other investment. These costs need to be measured and taken into account when measuring the true value of the project. The potential for the computer project to produce a profit therefore needs to be assessed and compared with the alternative options. The computer project must compete on the basis of producing a higher return and better business benefit than the other options. Money is not for free.

- *The impact of risk on the value of money.*

Risk is a cost on a project, the extreme case being that the project may fail completely and the entire investment be wasted.

Being a cost risk lowers the value of a project. If there is a 50% chance that the project to be invested in will fail, there is a 50% chance that the benefits to be gained will not be achieved. If the benefits are calculated to be £1 million and there is no risk, then the value of the benefit is £1 million. If the risk is judged to be 50%, then the real value of the benefit is half £1 million. If the project plans include flexibility such that the risk of failure is reduced by half, then the true value of the project goes up by £250 000 minus the cost of the flexibility. If the cost of the flexibility is less than the rise in the value of the project through the reduced risk— that is less than £250 000—then the returns to be expected from the project are increased.

The element of risk is very important in investment. Some investments are more risky than others. This is inevitable given that the projects to be invested in are for different purposes covering different business activities and therefore with different "characteristics". An investment in a utility is not regarded as particularly risky because there will always be a demand for utility services, people always requiring electricity and water, for example. The demand for their services is not so susceptible to business cycles; it is a more stable market. But the business of designing and manufacturing aircraft is a much more risky operation. People do not have to fly and there are large peaks and troughs of demand in the airline industry.

There has always been an understanding that more risky projects are not as financially attractive as less risky projects. The expected returns must therefore be diminished for increasing levels of risk.

Just as there is the problem of calculating an allowance for later cash flows there is a problem of calculating what allowance is to be made for the more risky investments. The usual response has been to use the principle of discounting, but to discount the riskier projects more heavily. The problem has been how to measure the risk and calculate the appropriate discount rate.

Discounting the expected value of investments to allow for risk used to be an arbitrary process. A more "scientific" approach to discounting properly for risk has been needed. The Capital Asset Pricing Model (CAPM)[2] was first put forward in the mid 1960s as a model which quantified the risk–return relationship for individual companies. Each company has a different level of risk due to differing business activities and individual circumstances. The investors expect a higher return from the higher risk companies. The CAPM was the first model to quantify this relationship between a company's risk and the return expected from the company.

The model was built upon observations of stock-market risks and returns over many years. The CAPM was a great advance in CBA techniques. The model provides an algorithm for discounting the expected benefits in accordance with the risk level for a company's shares. If the company's shares varied over time more than the market shares, then the company was a higher risk than the market and a higher return for investing in the company was to be expected.

By grouping all companies in the same industry it is a simple matter to arrive at an average risk and expected return for a given industry type. There would therefore be a risk–return figure for broad industry sectors, such as the utilities and transport, and more detailed breakdowns of each sector, such as water and electricity for the utilities and trains, trucks and aircraft for transport.

Since the CAPM works at the company level and obtains its measure from the variability of company versus market shares, an extension of the CAPM is needed to calculate risk at the project level. Projects are not bought and sold in stock-markets. Projects can be above or below the company average risk. It could be that a utility company (low market risk because the business is stable and certain) is investing in an advanced computer system project (high risk because the technology is new and the design and development skills base limited). It therefore makes sense to adjust the degree of discounting for investments in individual projects. Since the variability of shares cannot be used, another measure of risk is required. The measure is the variability of the projects' cash flows. The more variable the cash flow, the higher the risk. The technique for measuring this risk is the Bowater Scott model. Since projects occur within companies the project risk is incremental to the company risk.

---

[2] Developed by Treynor, Sharpe and Lintner. See: Sharpe, F. W. Capital asset prices: A theory of market equilibrium under conditions of risk, *Journal of Finance*, Sept. 1964, 425–446. Lintner, J. The valuation of risk assets and the selection of risky investments in stock portfolios and capital budgets, *Review of Economics and Statistics*, Feb. 1965, 13–37.

A project can incur change from the original plans due to events occurring during its life. Unanticipated business expansion or decline are perhaps the most common reasons for change. These uncertain events are risks (uncertainty is another form of variability). The impact of these event risks needs to be assessed, as they can change the financial prospects of projects. Shares and cash cannot be used as the events cannot be predicted. Event risk is therefore not based on the CAPM or cash flows but on probabilities, the probabilities reflecting the uncertainty of the uncertain events—the higher the certainty of events occurring the higher the probability. The technique for identifying, measuring and valuing event risk is decision tree analysis.

There are thus several different types of risk that an investment can incur. The full list is market risk, industry risk, company risk, unique risk, project risk and event risk, a kind of risk hierarchy from the most general to the most particular. Each risk has a different negative impact on an investment project, and each risk type must be identified, measured and costed.

(4) The offsetting of risk with the use of flexibility.

Flexibility can be used to offset a risk. Flexibility is the mechanism by which an alternative route to success can be obtained should the preferred route fail because of a risk. Flexibility therefore has the potential for being a benefit to a project and increasing its value.

Projects are not static. There are things which can be done to investments throughout the projects' lives to enhance their value. Projects may be expanded in scale, extended in functionality and generally undergo change. Events can therefore occur during the life of a project that make the original costings and benefits invalid.

If an investment is not able to be flexible then when an event occurs that causes a change the investment is liable to fail. Inflexible investments are therefore more vulnerable. This, of course, lowers the likely return of income from the investment. The investment therefore has a lower value.

The more flexible an investment is, the more the management of a project can take advantage of a beneficial event and offset an adverse event. The investment is therefore of more intrinsic value.

Of all the aspects concerning investment, flexibility is the most difficult to value, but it is a key area of value added in some investments. It must be identified, measured and valued. The adoption of the techniques for the identification and measurement of flexibility has been slow and mainly restricted to only the larger capital projects. The technique is decision tree analysis.

(5) The measurement of the value of intangible benefits of a project.

Intangible benefits make up an increasing proportion of the benefits to be gained from computer systems. It is important therefore to measure the value of the intangibles in monetary terms, with reference to both costs and benefits. Only then can the intangibles be fairly compared with the tangible costs and benefits and a single unit of measure be obtained for all the valuation components of a project. The technique is the quantification technique.

(6) The measurement of the value of the benefits to be gained from projects interacting with each other—project synergy.

Computer application systems initially were developed as standalone applications. Computer technology has evolved on a number of fronts whereby information from different applications can be increasingly combined and become reusable for all the applications of a company. With the advent of database technology all the data can be regarded as a corporate resource. With the recent advent of object oriented technology some 80% of the logic can also be regarded as a corporate resource, as it, like the data, is normalised to the objects/entities of the application system. The wastage of the standalone applications is therefore almost entirely eliminated. Other technical facilities, such as telecommunications, have further enabled previously distinct computer applications to be integrated.

A project may show a positive return (a profit) on a standalone basis but be able to earn even more when integrated with other computer systems. A sales forecasting system can have beneficial repercussions for the planning of the production process, the result being less likelihood of excesses or shortfalls in production. This integration of systems is known as project synergy.

Valuing a project on an isolated standalone basis where project synergy occurs can lead to an underestimation of the value of the investment to the business. This can lead to bad investment decisions in that projects of value may be rejected on a standalone basis as they are assessed as earning a loss, whereas if integrated with other application systems they can earn a profit. The technique for measuring project synergy is the quantification technique.

The aim of investment decisions is to select those projects which maximise the return of the business as a whole. This means being more sophisticated than selecting the individual projects with the highest returns. The approach should be to select the *combination* of projects which maximise the return for the organisation as a whole, taking into due consideration the impacts of those projects on each other. This is known as the portfolio approach.

The portfolio approach to investment appraisal has been appreciated for some time, but it is rarely used in business. The main reasons for this are probably:

- The approach requires cross functional undertanding and co-operation within the business, which may be difficult to achieve or coordinate.
- Analysing all possible combinations of projects may be a large and time consuming task.

Despite these drawbacks business is paying more attention to the portfolio approach. The benefit of the portfolio investment needs to be valued.

1.3 COST/BENEFIT ANALYSIS VERSUS INVESTMENT APPRAISAL

The terms Cost/Benefit Analysis (CBA) and Investment Appraisal (IA) are much used, often interchangeably, to describe the mechanism of valuing projects. There is confusion as to their meaning. As far as this book is concerned, CBA and IA are not the same, although they both try to do the same thing, value a project. The difference is in the scope of the investment techniques applied and the valuation deliverables produced.

CBA measures the tangible costs and tangible benefits, and applies a market discount rate to the future costs and benefit monies to discount them back to present day values. This discount rate is applied to reflect anticipated market risks and national inflation. Techniques for the best possible valuation of the intangibles, for the calculation of project and event risk, for the benefits obtained from the inclusion of flexibility in the project plans and for the benefits from project synergy are not included.

In the excellent series of advice guides for the valuation of projects issued by HM Treasury,[3] a department of state in the UK government, it is stated that there are "factors which cannot be usefully valued in money terms. These may include, for example, . . ., prior commitments, flexibility or general environmental factors. These should be listed, explained, quantified where possible and weighed up". This is an open admission that many extremely expensive government projects may not be properly costed, with the financial value of the alleged intangible benefits missing. The best that can be achieved is a scoring of some kind and then only when the intangibles can be quantified. For reasons explained in Chapter 6 the authors do not hold to this argument, and it will be seen in section 6.1.1 that the intan-

---

[3] The series is, somewhat embarrassingly for the authors, entitled "Investment Appraisal in the Public Sector". H.M. Treasury, ISBN 0-947819-03.

gibles are an increasingly significant portion of the benefits obtained from computing.

There are thus significant components both on the cost and the benefit side that are missing from the CBA techniques for computer projects.

There are two other important omissions from CBA. The first is a set of techniques for the identification and prioritisation of investment opportunities, this of necessity front-ending the investment valuation process. After the investments have been valued it is then necessary to assess whether the claims made about the benefits to be achieved from investing in a project are being achieved in reality. This process is called benefits realisation.

CBA is therefore a "headless" and "tailless" method for a full investment appraisal process. CBA suffers from substantial sins of omission as well as commission. All in all a considerable tale of woe.

This lack of practical utilisation of all aspects of a full IA is a great disappointment and results in a high level of doubt and uncertainty about the validity of investment decisions made. Yet it need not be so. There are techniques to measure all the different types of risk, flexibility and project synergy. Greater effort to use these techniques and push them to the limits can only be good—only then can the full and accurate calculation of an investment be properly made. This is where IA comes in. IA includes all the techniques for the full valuation of projects, including those of CBA. IA includes:

- Investment identification and prioritisation
- Investment measurement:
  - discounting inflation
  - valuing the tangible costs and benefits
  - valuing the intangible costs and benefits
  - discounting company risk
  - discounting project risk
  - consideration of alternative investment opportunities
  - valuing the costs of event risk
  - valuing the benefits of flexibility
  - valuing the benefits of project synergy.
- Benefits realisation.

In summary, the techniques of CBA are well developed in theory but are really only applicable to standalone projects of short duration, if the non-discounted techniques of valuation are used, with few intangibles and of low risk; there are few projects of this kind in today's computer world. The more advanced aspects required for a full IA are not present in CBA. It can support combinations of large projects of long duration, significant intangibles, high risk and great flexibility.

1.4 BUSINESS BENEFIT AND FINANCIAL RETURN

It is important to realise the difference between business benefit and financial return. They are not the same. Business benefit is an operation that enables a company to stay in business, even be competitive against other companies. Business benefit will always provide a financial return. But an investment providing a financial return may not always provide a business benefit. An example will illustrate the point.

A business strategy-led IA may not lead to the investments that give the best financial return. The best returns may be obtained from projects that are of the "housekeeping" type, such as payroll, invoicing and purchasing, although computer systems of the "housekeeping" type do not "add value" to the company—there are no new products or services, no business benefit, no business objectives being satisfied. An example of this is given in Table 2.4 where the housekeeping accounts receivable system provides a better anticipated financial return than the competing production type applications. The traditional very tangible productive business benefits of the production type applications, the food flow package and the computer aided engineering, may be not the best investment strategy. In this case the best investment gave no business benefit.

1.5 WHY BOTHER WITH INVESTMENT APPRAISAL?

The authors are constantly being faced with arguments against the need to undertake full and detailed calculations of the financial value of Information Technology (IT) projects. The arguments used to fall into two broad categories: apathetic due to the disappointing results from computer systems in general, so don't bother; hostile to investment appraisal because the valuation results are not credible and the effort required large, so don't bother.

The "apathetic" arguments that are often used take the following forms:

(1) A general sense that, although computing is now used in almost all walks of business, it has not proved of financial benefit—the payoff has been poor.

Bowen wrote in 1986, "US business has spent hundreds of billions of dollars on computing but the white collar productivity is no higher than it was in the late 1960s".[4] This statement is further confirmed by S. Roach in his report, "A Profile of the Information Economy",[5] where it was shown that the productivity of the information worker (a white collar worker— authors' comment) is some 7% less in 1986 than in 1970. Indeed, investment in IT systems has often proved to be money wasted. A manager of a large printing firm wrote that more money had been wasted by the application of the wrong technology than was ever lost by not investing in information technology at all. Mistakes are so easy to make with IT that the chances of wasting the investment are high. It is high risk technology and the chance of failure that much the greater.

The sense of disappointment has been such that Price Waterhouse noted[6] that there was a drop of some 10% in investment in IT in the late 1980s in terms of the average spend on IT—and this was a time when the UK economy was expanding rapidly under a credit boom. Given this sense of disappointment about the returns that can be obtained from investing in computer systems the enthusiasm to apply the man effort to undertake a full IA for a proposed system was substantially dimmed.

The poor payoff from computing, and hence a lack of encouragement to calculate the financial value of probable "bad news", is a barrier to IA.

(2) "Gut feel" is often the best judge for an investment decision.

An article in "Computing" magazine in 1990 quoted a figure of some 60% of data processing managers deciding to develop a computer system on the basis that "it seems to be a good idea at the time" (author's apostrophes). This is an astonishing figure, both as regards the high percentage of managers making important decisions on this basis and the amount of monies that are involved. Computer systems are not cheap and to use "gut feel" is a sad reflection on the understanding of IA techniques. Gut feel is not the best way to make investment decisions.

Most organisations have taken the view that these investments would be "a good thing", that investment in IT was the way the world was going and so "nodded" the investment through. This approach to investing on a "gut feel" or "act of faith" did not cause much of a problem when the costs of these systems was relatively small compared with the total capital budget of the company; however it cannot succeed in the long term.

There is an invisible force in accounting for the costs and benefits of computer systems. It has already been said that up to 60% of management in the UK decide to invest in computer systems on a "gut feel"—so much

---

[4] *Fortune*, May 1986, "The Puny Payoff of the Office Computer."
[5] Roach, S. "A Profile of the Information Economy".
[6] "Information Technology Review", 1987/88, published by Price Waterhouse.

for the science of CBA. This does not work at the board level, the attendees of which, if the company is publicly quoted on the stock market, have to present themselves to the shareholders on a regular basis. The shareholders are interested in one thing only—the value of the shares. And the value of the shares is directly based on the profit and loss of the company. The higher one goes in the management structure the more "gut feel" will not do. The judgement that a bank's expert system is a "good thing" is all very well lower down the management structure but the policy of a "good thing", if relied upon too many times, would soon make the shareholders wary. Share value is based on money and not on charitable "good things". Sound IA is essential and the readiness of managers to "short cut" the financial decision making process is a barrier to this process.

(3) The decision as to whether to proceed is obvious, the computer system being a prerequisite to do business.

Systems which fall into this category of decision making typically include:

- Accounting and payroll, these being systems necessary for the company to function;
- Airline passenger booking systems, these being systems necessary for the company to compete because its competitors have such a system.

In both cases an investment in computer systems does not have to be justified—just spend the money to stay in business.
    Force majeure is a barrier to proper IA.

(4) The monies involved are not large.

Typical systems in this category include small applications packages, such as word processors and spreadsheets, and their costs are likely to be less than an IA exercise. Low cost projects are a barrier to proper IA.

(5) The business and technical risks are low.

Systems in this category typically include the use of application package software. The certainty that the benefits are going to be achieved and that they outweigh the costs is a barrier to proper IA.

(6) IA has proved to be more difficult for IT than for many other types of investment.

There have been a number of unique features of IT that have adversely affected the application of IA techniques. They include:

- The benefits of IT are already significantly—and will continue to be increasingly—intangible. As stated, it is often difficult to put values on such intangible benefits, some of which are extremely difficult to identify, measure and value, and because of this have often been ignored—it is difficult, the techniques for it are not very good, so don't bother. This aspect of IT is a significant barrier to the application of IA to IT.
- The difficulty of putting boundaries around IT projects:
  - IT technology is now so sophisticated that there is tremendous scope for project integration and interaction. The widespread use of database technology, data communications and, particularly, the recent adoption of object oriented technology, which allows data and logic from previous application systems to be reused, make possible a corporate information base, allowing maximum integration of applications systems. With the above technology we are moving to the era of application independent computer systems to the extent of 100% of the data and 80% of the logic. All this can make unclear the boundary of a proposed computer project as a subject for investment. Should reusable components of previous systems be charged as a cost to the new project and as a benefit to the old system? If so, on what basis and how is it to be done?
  - Hardware and software are undergoing such rapid change that upgrades of both are likely to occur several times during the life of a long term project. How should the costs and benefits of the upgrades be allocated in view of the increasing project/application interactions and corporate information base?
  - IT often influences many areas of a business. The structure of a product database system will affect the efficiency of the sales department, production department, distribution and many others. The cross functional impacts and interactions can be difficult to anticipate or predict, so making appraisal difficult.
  - IT often has a strategic and/or infrastructural element. Many of these investments do not show an immediate return and the time as to when the return will be achieved may be difficult to ascertain. Their real value is that they can open up new business possibilities for the future which are potentially very profitable, but again will the future benefits be identified when they actually occur? It takes a sharp and continuously alert eye to monitor this.

The precise investment appraisal of IT has therefore proved to be difficult. The response to this challenge has been largely to bypass the problem and to do little in the way of proper valuation of the monies being invested.

The "hassle" of investment appraisal for IT has proved a barrier to proper IA.

(7) The techniques of valuation are not equal. The monies involved can be divided into the visible costs and the tangible benefits on the one side, and the hidden costs and the intangible benefits on the other.

It has long been established that the easiest of monies to identify and measure are the visible costs. In simple terms the visible monies are those that appear in one's cheque-book. The next easiest are the tangible benefits to be made through the introduction of computer systems, such as direct labour savings. The identificaiton and measurement of the value of these savings is a simple process of comparing the old situation with the new situation resulting from the introduction of the new computer system (for example, the number of staff required before the new system was installed against the number required after installation), ascertaining the difference and multiplying it by the *per capita* costs of the labour. There is little problem with the first two components of project valuation.

The techniques for the valuation of the hidden costs and the intangible benefits are much less precise, particularly those for the intangible benefits. An example of the hidden costs could be the reorganisation that is required when new technology is introduced. Data processing departments will find this to be the case with the introduciton of object oriented technology, which requires different departmental and project management structures, as well as some new roles and responsibilities. However, hidden costs tend to be of short duration, are usually fewer, more focused and therefore more easily identified, for example while the physical reorganisation of the department is under way, the inevitable learning curves of the retraining and the loss of productivity during the reorganisation and the relearning. The first of the hidden costs is not very hidden (time lost in the move multiplied by the costs of the number of persons moving) and the productivity loss could be calculated on the basis of a reasonable percentage loss for a given period of time for *n* persons multiplied by their costs. If the hidden costs are difficult to identify and measure then the technique for the measurement of the intangible benefits may be required.

Treating the valuation of a project as a potentially "hit and miss affair" is a barrier to IA. Why bother?

(8) Never done it before and we have survived.

This argument is still occasionally heard.

The "head in the ground" ("as it was in the beginning is now and ever shall be") attitude is a barrier to proper IA.

The hostile arguments that are often used are:

(1) Why bother to measure the immeasurable values of IT projects?

Many projects, such as those involving accounting and payroll systems, are of the type where exact values are difficult to identify and measure. Such computer systems, and there are many of them, are designed to support "non-price" application areas, e.g. customer service, that by their nature are of the intangible type.

The old adage "When the going gets tough the tough get going" has applied to this aspect of the investment valuation process.

Difficulty of valuation is a barrier to proper IA.

(2) Where are the techniques to identify the most appropriate investment opportunities for the business?

"OK, I accept the requirement that investments must be such that there is business benefit as well as profit, that the investments must support the business objectives of the company. But the techniques for information system strategy planning are not very impressive and are not complete".

The current techniques for the development of an Information Systems Strategy (ISS) do not, and are not able to, ensure that the portfolio of applications to be developed is based on the optimum potential financial value or business benefit of each application. There should be two components of an ISS—*a value component* that considers the potential financial value of an investment opportunity in a computer system and *an information component* that considers the business need for the information the computer system will support.

ISS techniques today overwhelmingly concentrate on the information component. The information needs of the company are identified and modelled using the standard techniques of the ISS structured methods and a prioritised set of computer application systems is constructed according to the perceived importance of the business applications to the company's business objectives. The systems strategy is thus based on a prioritised information component. The other component of an ISS, the value of the applications, is almost totally ignored, the best offered being a reference to (but no description of) Cost/Benefit Analysis (CBA). All too often the major unit of "financial" measure in the development of an ISS plan is that the proposed systems are subjectively judged ("gut feel" again) to be of business benefit to the company's operations, the "effectiveness" of which are increased. This means that the ability of the computer systems in the strategy plan to add financial value to the company operations and competitiveness are not measured. In this regard the computer systems are developed on the basis of an "act of faith"—provide the information and all will be well.

But even for the information component the situation is not impressive. If one looks at the techniques used by one of the leading ISS methods, the

Strategy Planning method from Learmonth & Burchett Management Systems (LBMS), what is listed and described is a set of different techniques for the identification and modelling of the business information that is required, but there is no mechanism for compiling and interpreting the information gathered as a single coherent unit by the separate techniques and no method for drawing up the best strategy plan. Strategic Planning includes the techniques of the Boston Matrix, Michael Porter's Competitive Forces and Value Chains, Gregory Parson's Business Categorisation, Information Intensity and John Rockart's Critical Success Factors. All good stuff. A great mass of separate information is thereby gathered, but then what? One is left with a set of distinct and uncoordinated products for you, *homo sapiens*, to assess and mentally blend into a coherent plan of IS action.

The situation, fortunately, is the opposite with the other leading ISS planning method, the Information Systems Strategy Planning phase of Information Engineering. Here the information required to support the critical success factors, objectives and goals of the business are identified and modelled. The needs are then scored as to their requirement weight, this being the result of multiplying the importance factor of the need by the satisfaction rating of the need. The importance factor is a ranking of 5 to 1, the higher the number the greater the importance, with the 5 relating to the need supporting a critical success factor, a 4 to a need supporting an objective or goal and the 1 to the need being useful for any other purpose. The satisfaction rating identifies the ability of the current system to support the information need—a 1 indicating full support and a 4 no support. The needs are grouped into business systems, these being the basis of subsequent computer systems. Information Engineering thus includes a technique for bringing the modelled information needs together and prioritising the needs.

But what is missing in Information Engineering are many of the useful techniques used by the LBMS method, such as the Boston Matrix and "value chains".

There are still therefore shortcomings with both methods regarding the information component of ISS and, of course, nothing for the value component.

Hostility born of the inability to have soundly based IS strategies plans is a barrier to proper IA.

(3) Where are the techniques to value projects?

"OK, I accept the need to value the IT projects I am planning, but there are no techniques other than those of CBA to apply, and those techniques I do not regard as credible or complete. You have already advised me that there is much the techniques do not measure and these omissions represent a significant proportion of the total benefits of my computer systems, because of the importance of the non-price factors in the company's business. The costs are easy to calculate, they appear on the cheque that I sign, but the main problem is the benefits. I constantly find that presentations made to my senior managers founder on the lack of credibility regarding financial figures for the benefits claimed for the project". Hostility born of inadequate techniques is a barrier to IA.

(4) Inadequate and non-standardised current accounting practices.

Many of the accounting methods that are used do not support functionally based accounting, so the ability to cost and value particular tasks/processes within a company cannot be easily ascertained. One company that manufactured cross-country vehicles did not have a functionally based accounting system, so the costs and benefits of installing a computerised vehicle paintshop process could not be monitored. The organisationally based accounting systems needed to be modified before the value of the paintshop could be ascertained. (Of course, there is nothing to stop companies organising themselves so that departments are functionally based; the paintshop department could be responsible for painting vehicles). Other accounting methods ignore the departmental infrastructure of a company, so that the effect of operational and organisational change due to new IT systems cannot be easily measured.

The best solution is to have the accounting system support both functions and departments in the account codes.

As regards standards, up to 44 different accounting practices have been identified within the oil industry. One difference was that there were varying write-off periods for investments in IT projects, so that similar projects in one division of an oil company could be profitable with an extended write-off period and non-profitable in another division of the same oil company with a shortened write-off period. There was thus no fair measure of comparison when deciding which project to invest in.

Hostility based on poor current accounting practices is a barrier to IA.

(5) The financial figures can be manipulated and therefore lack credibility.

There are numerous stories about companies that have been fully audited according to the best accounting practices by auditing companies of unquestioned propriety and then a few months later collapsing in a mountain of debt or falling into substantial difficulties. Polly Peck, Bond Corporation, Brent Walker and the Maxwell group of companies are but a few examples. It is not surprising that accounting credibility is lost.

A major electronics company used, quite legitimately, four different accounting procedures covering the sale of its goods. The value of a sale could be accounted for either on receipt of the order, the delivery of the equipment, the commissioning of the equipment or after a set period of acceptance of the equipment. The financial justification of the sales ordering computer system, and the company accounts, would be very different depending on which accounting practice was followed. The first practice would produce a much earlier inwards cash flow than the last practice and would make any financial justification of a computer system easier.

"The Financial Times" on Monday 22 February 1993 reported that a company had recorded an annual loss of something like £70 million but that due to a change in accounting practice would announce a profit of something like £120 million. So much for accounting credibility! Lack of financial credibility is a barrier to IA.

(6) Does value equal financial value?

Computer systems are increasingly being used to assist companies on non-price factors. For example, the travel industry is using computer booking systems not just as a repository of travel timetables and bookings but as an aid to fast customer service.

In an Irish bank a small computer with an expert system has been placed in the reception areas of the major branches. The system could advise existing customers on the likelihood of them being granted a loan, the advice being based on their past creditworthiness and the loan request. Any potential embarrassment of the customer approaching the bank manager and being turned down is avoided. But what is the value of the computer system? The benefit, the saving of embarrassment, is intangible. Certainly the bank is well pleased with the results—customers have used the system and approached the manager only when the expert system advice is positive. Feelings on both sides have improved and there is a general sense of well being. The computer system has been a customer relations success, but there has been no appreciable increase in the bank's business. The valid customers requiring a loan would probably have approached the manager in any case. The only practical result is that "no hopers" for a loan have been discouraged, and embarrassment and wasted time have been avoided. The value of the system was judged to be non-financial, rather a case of creating the right impression about the "up-to-dateness" of the bank and "getting one over" its competitors.

With this example the case could be argued that the value of the system was non-monetary—customers were pleased with the result and hence satisfied with the bank. It is a false argument. If all computer systems were judged on this basis companies would soon go bankrupt. At the end of the day all bills have to be paid. That computer system incurred bills of costs.

It must pay for itself and the value of the benefit revenues it generates to offset the costs must be ascertained. The customer satisfaction should be converted into a measurable—customers retained and new customers gained—and the measurable valued in money terms, i.e. the business brought to the bank by the retained and new customers.

The inability to realise that all values are financial is a barrier to IA, even when the value is an intangible that is very difficult to identify and measure.

(7) The current CBA techniques of valuation and their products overlap, are applied in a standalone manner and are not integrated.

As can be seen in Table 1.1 there are some nine CBA techniques that include valuing the costs of a project. Many of them are widely applied. Each of the techniques is applied standalone from the other techniques, partly because they include different aspects of project valuation and partly for the simple reason that if they are integrated the massive overlap and wastage would become apparent and a rethink of how the techniques should be integrated would be required. This book is, in part, about that rethink.

The wastage of effort in current CBA techniques has proved a barrier to IA.

(8) The benefits claimed for a project are not measured when the project is implemented.

IA is a set of techniques that calculate the profit or loss that is likely to be made on an investment. The money has not been spent yet, merely calculated. Along with the anticipated profit is a monetary expression of a set of claims regarding the benefits to be obtained if the investment is made: "The project will increase productivity by $X\%$ and this will yield £Y". To date little attention has been paid to measuring the actual achievement of the benefits after the investment is completed against the value of the benefits claimed when the investment was planned, that $X\%$ productivity and £Y are obtained.

Benefits realisation, the checking that the claimed benefits are obtained in reality on completion of the project, is now becoming a serious issue and certain bodies, such as the Central Computing and Telecommunications Agency (CCTA) of the UK government Treasury Department, are now addressing how this can be included in the design of computer systems and in the project plans.

The lack of proof that the benefits claimed are benefits achieved has proved a barrier to IA.

These arguments may be excuses, even reasons, for the lack of IA, but,

Table 1.1 The scope overlap of the IA techniques

Variables	Techniques								
	Cost/benefit forecasting	Payback	DCF	Sensitivity analysis	Monte Carlo simulation	Decision tree analysis	Scoring models	Quantification	Portfolio analysis
Costs	▓	▓	▓	▓	▓	▓	▓	▓	▓
Tangible benefits	▓	▓	▓	▓	▓	▓	▓	▓	
Intangible benefits							▓	▓	
Risk				▓	▓	▓			▓
Flexibility			▓	▓	▓	▓			▓
Inflation			▓	▓	▓	▓			
Market return				▓	▓	▓			
Project interaction						▓			▓

except for "the monies involved are not worth the IA effort", they are not a justification. It indicates a sorry state of affairs, both in techniques of valuation that have been applied to date and have bred a cynical attitude towards IA, and even more in the attitude of managers. Something is wrong when the true financial value of large sums of investment monies, even major portions of a company's total investments, cannot be fully and accurately measured and many managers are not too concerned about the situation.

It is probable that the attitudinal aspect is in large measure the result of the absence of adequate techniques for full project valuation. Inadequate IA techniques have been the cause and the effect has been management cynicism.

It is not just in investment identification and valuation that poor techniques have led to reluctance to take any action. There was a considerable reluctance to accept the practice of applying formal structured methods to the modelling of computer system application information until such quality structured methods as SSADM, Information Engineering and MERISE were developed in the late 1970s and early 1980s. These are probably the three leading structured methods for the design and development of computer systems in Europe and other parts of the world. SSADM has been developed by the UK Government's CCTA and is the standard for government projects and many companies in the private sector. It is becoming a *de facto* standard in the UK. Information Engineering is a privately developed method with the James Martin label stamped on it and is the only private method to have obtained wide usage and acceptance. MERISE is a hybrid, being developed with French government assistance and by a consortium of private companies. It is the most widely used method in continental Europe. These information modelling structured methods are now well developed and credible. No self respecting IT manager would now be without one of these leading methods as the standard for information design and development for his/her department. But it has taken a decade of use and improvement to get to this stage. This reluctant attitude regarding IA is therefore understandable. If there was a valid set of comprehensive techniques which were coherently integrated, easy to understand and apply, and which would produce an accurate project valuation, based on all the elements that together define the full value of a project, then it is more than likely that the current cynical attitudes to IA would change in the same way as they did for information design and development. What happened to application information design and development would happen to project valuation.

The major cause of all the current problems with project valuation is therefore judged to be the absence of a comprehensive structured method of investment oppor-

tunity identification and IA. This is confirmed by the Kearney report,[7] which identified that "the greatest barrier to the further use of IT in British industry and commerce is the lack of formal cost/benefit analysis techniques".

This book aims to plug that gap.

1.6 THE CURRENT POSITION ON INVESTMENT APPRAISAL

The current position is not encouraging for the following reasons:

(1) There is widespread ignorance in the IT world of the full range of techniques that are available for the valuation of IT projects. As already mentioned, the manuals of the structured methods for information design mention the need to undertake CBA prior to deciding to design and develop an application. SSADM recommends that CBA is undertaken at three points:
   • In the feasibility stage;
   • When considering different business options with which the application can be scoped;
   • When considering different technical options with which the application can be supported.
   In Information Engineering, CBA is undertaken as part of information strategy planning. With neither of these methods is there any information as to what CBA entails, neither what requires to be done or how to do it. CBA is only mentioned as something to do.
(2) The techniques that are available today are very much used in a standalone manner, obtain no benefit from each other and do not cover all valuation aspects of computer projects.
(3) Some of the techniques are unsoundly based. This is particularly the case with the techniques that do not take into account inflation and market risk, i.e. they are not discount based. As shown in section 3.2 these non-discounted techniques can, and do, produce wrong investment decisions.
(4) Some techniques produce conflicting results. There are several techniques for the calculation of the costs of the projects on a non-discounted basis, such as the cost/benefit ratio, the payback period and the percentage return on investment. Not only are these techniques not soundly based on discounted monies, but they each produce a standalone, different and incompatible result from the same input infor-

---

[7] Kearney, A. T. (1984). *The Barriers and Opportunities of Information Technology—A Management Perspective*, DTI Report.

mation. One technique uses a ratio, one a time period, one a percentage. There is no common yardstick, no common basis by which the techniques can be integrated.

(5) There is much of the valuation process that is still missing:

- *The costs—project and event risk.* Risk is very inadequately covered by the current techniques of project valuation. The current practice, based on the CAPM, from which is calculated the company risk discount rate, uses the expected return formula. This rate is then applied to investments to be made in future years to convert future monies into today's value. But calculating company risk is not enough. There are other risks, such as project risks and event risk, for which an additional discount rate and probabilities of occurrence need to be calculated. Both of these risks further lower the value of a project.

  Given that these risks are not taken into account when valuing projects it is not surprising that the true value of a computer project is often overstated. The cynicism that results when a computer system goes live and fails to perform is all the greater. The disappointment in the value of computing is partly due to the incomplete valuation techniques. The full costs of all the risks are not computed.

- *The benefits—flexibility and the intangibles.* As described earlier, flexibility will, if it costs less than the project risks, increase the benefit value of a computer project. There are now valid techniques to calculate the value of any flexibility applied to a project.

  The benefits that are difficult to identify and measure are usually a substantial portion of the total benefit of a computer system. Computer project investments are increasingly based on non-price and intangible factors for competitive edge rather than cost cutting/efficiency factors. This is confirmed in Figure 6.2 which shows that of the six major benefits obtained from computing, five are non-price related. The intangible of speed of service comes out as the major benefit. The omission of the intangible benefits in the valuation equation can significantly understate the true value of a project.

All in all there is a lot to discourage the potential practitioner of investment appraisal.

1.7 THE GROWING NEED FOR INVESTMENT APPRAISAL FOR IT

1.7.1 The Hindrance from IT

For a long time there has been little incentive to apply CBA and IA techniques to the valuation of computer investments. Indeed, as we shall see, the evolution of IT has been, and still is, discouraging to the process of IA. It is only today that the need is appreciated as imperative. Two influences have forced the hand:

(1) The large volumes of monies now involved.
(2) Given the large monies involved, the investments in IT are now considered as part of the total portfolio of company investments and therefore have to compete with other investment opportunity.

The former influence justifies the time and effort spent in full IA and the latter the need to achieve a common unit of measure for comparison purposes. Each influence reinforces the other. Four interlocking and overlapping phases can be seen in the continued postponement of the justification for IA for IT.

The first phase dates from the earliest use of computers in business. Computers first played a significant role in business in the late 1950s and early 1960s. The applications were typically run on large mainframe systems with batch application programs to process in bulk large volumes of business transactions. These systems were designed for production and administrative type operations where the same process was repeated n times, providing labour savings on very high volume transactions. Typically systems were order, payroll and bank transaction processing. While the costs of such computer systems were high, both as regards the purchasing of the hardware and the development of the software using highly skilled staff, the scale of cost savings was also high through the repetitive operations, each providing only a small saving on their own but a large saving in total. But as a proportion of the total company expenditures, IT spend was still a small component, a few percentage points. This and the productive and obvious tangible benefits being gained encouraged a situation where investments went ahead "on the nod"—"gut feel" indicated that computers were a good thing.

Any CBA appraisal for these systems was also quite straightforward, taking few man hours. The costs were known and the benefits from the labour and product cost savings easy to calculate because they were visible—the labour saved times the costs of the labour, and the lower costs for the production of a product times the number of products produced. Given the type of systems being developed there were very few "intangibles", so these costs and benefits of the investments could be relatively easily analysed using traditional CBA techniques. By and large, investment decisions on computers in those days were *ad hoc* affairs, simple and reasonably easy to make.

The second phase came in the late 1970s and early 1980s. Computer systems became more sophisticated with faster and more capable processors, the introduction of database software and later generations of programming languages facilitated the storage and access of data and the writing of program code, together with the beginnings of structured design methods and CASE tools for the correct logical design specification of the user requirements. At the same time hardware costs were falling and application package software products were becoming available. The added capabilities of software development tools meant that the scope of computer systems to support new types of application was realised, e.g. real-time processing with embedded software controlling machines on the factory floor; active control systems with the ability to ascertain and decide production schedules; and stock replenishment and service support systems. There was a rapid growth in the number of persons and organisations taking on computer systems as well as a growth in the number of applications that each organisation operated.

For the first time systems could provide benefits other than savings on just production and administrative applications. They provided largely intangible benefits, such as service support, better information and better management control. The intangible aspect can best be exemplified by the Management Information Systems (MISs) with their "how much" query languages and Decision Support Systems (DSSs) with more powerful "what if" query languages. Both enabled business improvements and opportunities to be spotted through the provision of better focused and advice seeking queries against the corporate database. But what is the value of this information? What if one manager gets better use out of the same information than another manager? How can you prove that a decision is based on the information in a MIS and DSS report? Not easy. These systems provide a greater challenge to the investment decision makers because a larger proportion of the benefits are difficult to quantify in cash terms—they are intangible. Given the paucity of CBA techniques for the measurement and valuation of intangibles, CBA was not widely applied with the advent of the more sophisticated systems of this second phase.

The mainframe type computers used were cumbersome and the limited capabilities of 3GL and 4GL application program development software meant that responses to user requests for additional functionality from the computer systems took a long time to be achieved. Users became frustated with the delays and many took matters into their own hands. They bought themselves the personal and workstation computers that were appearing on the market. This represents the third phase in the postponement of the justification for IA for IT. The appearance of new and easy to use menu based query languages meant that users could access the data themselves, sometimes in an *ad hoc* manner. A wide range of application package software meant that the required functionality could often be bought off the shelf—no time lost and independent of the DP department. This book has been written on a personal computer with standard application package software and exemplifies this trend. There is no bespoke software in sight. The use of computing became general to the general user.

The cheapness of PCs and the general downsizing of computer systems allowed managers to buy them piecemeal without having to justify them through an expensive CBA exercise—they were probably cheaper than the exercise anyway. PCs were thus regarded as minor and piecemeal capital spend and this, combined with a perceived view that they were an essential tool for senior managers and therefore justified, meant that they were again obtained "on the nod". Appraisal of investments in low cost PC systems was still not considered relevant. The authors have not wasted time doing an IA for the purchase of their PCs for the writing of this book. They applied "gut feel" and bought them. They have not practised what this book preaches. And this has generally been the case elsewhere.

The last phase has evolved gradually with the ability of computer systems to use each other's information. The adoption of database technology has made data a corporate resource, data being common to all the application systems; the use of telecommunications has made it possible for application systems to transfer data between each other; and the use of object oriented technology has made some 80% of logic a corporate resource, being normalised to objects of information just like the data. These three technology thrusts have made the boundary between one application system and the others increasingly difficult to ascertain. Given all this, where is the boundary of a new potential new system in terms of project evaluation. What value is to be placed on the use of an existing infrastructure of telecommunications and reusable data and logic? Again, not easy. For each phase of IT development therefore there have been good reasons for not doing a proper IA. It is either not worth it or it is difficult.

1.7.2 The Evolution of Cost/Benefit Planning and Valuation

There have been two threads of evolution, planning for the investment and valuing the investment. Both have evolved separately.

The techniques of CBA have evolved over the last century and in particular over the last 40 years. The techniques have become more sophisticated as the economics of running a business have become better understood. They are now well developed and have proved particularly successful for investors in the capital markets, for assessing the value of "productive" assets, such as investments in plant and machinery. These activities "produce" deliverables which can be physically seen, counted, priced and valued. The other side of an economy is the service sector. This has always proved to be more of a valuation problem in that the services are not easily "visible" and are therefore more difficult to identify, quantify, price and value. While the bulk of investments were in these capital projects during the early part of this century and managers were concerned more with the performance of the production process than the provision of services, the valuing of the costs and benefits of the investments was a relatively easy, although not fully accurate, affair.

During the last 30 years there has been a shift in the balance of the investment portfolio, because IT has enabled the growth of the service sector. These services included such activities as insurance, wholesale and retail business and distribution. For reasons explained the benefits of the services are not as easy to identify as for the capital projects. And this has very much been the case for many of the investments in computer systems.

Those systems that have been developed to support the production process from the capital investments, such as robotics and manufacturing planning resource systems, have been relatively easy to value. But the computer systems that have been developed to support the service side of business, like the business itself, have been more difficult to value. To date the valuation of the intangible costs and benefits of an investment in service activity and service support computer systems has not been as accurate as it is possible to make it.

In areas where it is difficult to put a cash value on a cost or a benefit there have been attempts to use cash equivalents or "shadow prices". This has been used particularly for government projects, such as the location of an airport or the building of new roads. In projects of this type many of the costs are such things as the increase in noise pollution for local residents and general deterioration in quality of life. The benefits may be time savings for travellers and reductions in deaths on the road. The costs and benefits are easy to recognise, but how do you place a value on them so that you know whether overall the benefits exceed the costs? What cost is put on the increase in noise pollution for residents near a new airport? What benefit is put on a life saved due to a new road bypass being built?

The use of shadow prices is an attempt to put cash values on these intangible costs and benefits. For example, the value of a life saved could be defined as the average earnings that a citizen contributes to GDP over his/her liftetime; divided by half on the assumption that an accident occurs, on average, half way through a person's working life; or alternatively, a life saved could be valued in terms of a payout for a life insurance policy in the event of death, typically in the region of half a million pounds. The cost of increased noise pollution could be measured by the reduction in property prices due to the building of an airport or a new railway line. Attempts at quantifying these intangibles were made from the 1960s onwards. However, difficulties in gaining acceptance for the approach of putting cash values on people's lives and in finding suitable shadow prices have meant that this method has not been widely adopted. There seems to be a reluctance to take these decisions in a "calculated" way and all too often the politics of the situation are the final arbiters of the decision.

Where the calculation of value in cash terms has proved particularly difficult, other techniques for appraising capital investments have tended to involve assessing value in terms other than cash. The most common of these approaches is to use "scoring" or "weighting" models. These models attribute a score to the non-valuable costs and benefits, the scores being weighted according to the assessed "worth" of the benefits and costs. Projects are then ranked and selected according to their monetary value for the tangible costs and benefits, and their total score for the intangible costs and benefits. Assessment of the comparative importance of the monetary value and the numeric score is a matter of judgement.

The attraction of scoring is that it is relatively easy to perform and it gives some prioritisation of costs and benefits that prove difficult, if not impossible, to value. The drawback is that there is no assurance that the project has made a net contribution to the business/organisation, that profit has increased. In addition, investments and the planned for returns are based on cash, not scorings.

Whilst for political reasons it has been difficult to gain acceptance of an approach to valuing intangibles in the public sector, in the private sector the approach for attempting to quantify and value the intangibles is at last becoming more promising. The "quantification" approach described in Chapter 6 is still rare and in the early stages of adoption. It is a powerfully attractive option for fair and full investment decision making because it makes it possible to have all components of the projects measured and valued on a common basis, namely money. This, along with the other techniques to measure and value inflation, alternative investments, risk and flexibility, provide a strong technical basis to modelling a full IA.

Notwithstanding this full set of IA techniques now available it has become apparent that the full potential benefits and financial returns of computer applications systems have been constantly unfulfilled. There has been very little reuse of the information of the business in a corporate way. Integrated systems have been the exception rather than the rule. This was only partly solved with the introduction of database technology. Here the only reusable component between applications was the data in the corporate database. An improvement but not the total answer. The expensive overheads entailed in the separate development of application programs were still being borne because of the very limited ability to reuse software previously coded. The development of telecommunications and object orientation has at last and above all provided the final facilities to enable system integration. The standalone nature of applications development is perpetuated by the fact that there is still often no overall strategic systems development plan matching the business plan and objectives of the company. The applications are all too often disjointed. The applications systems are thus not oriented to providing the maximum business benefit to the company. Investment in IT is not being wisely spent. This lack of a coordinated system development plan will be shown in Chapter 2 to be the biggest hindrance to getting good value for money for IT investment.

The pressure has therefore mounted to make greater efforts to appraise IT investments properly so that:

- The investments are made in support of a coherent ISS plan;
- The investment decisions can be made on the basis of accurate calculation of the monies involved and only monies;
- The true financial and business benefits from an investment can be measured.

This combination of four technical and two business trends have forced this beneficial situation. They have caused computer systems to become much larger, more integrated and more expensive, to the extent that the expenditures on computing are now a significant proportion of a company's total investments. This has created the necessity for proper appraisal and justification of the heavy investment required. Given the valuation techniques described in this book, this can now be undertaken.

1.8 WHY DO WE NEED A STRUCTURED METHOD FOR IA?

Why do we not continue with CBA as we have done in the past? The techniques work and have produced adequate results. Yes, the techniques work, but they are not complete and have not been integrated; therefore the results (the valuation of the investment) are not the best that can be obtained.

The valuation of the investment can be improved in two ways:

(1) Use a full set of investment identification and planning techniques followed by a full set of valuation techniques to take into account all the issues that affect the value of a project.
(2) Apply the techniques in an order such that the deliverables incrementally add value to each other. The information contained in a set of integrated techniques and their deliverables is more than the techniques and deliverables alone. The whole is more than the sum of its parts. This is true whether the method is for modelling information, valuing projects, designing ships or whatever.

A structured method is composed of many things, which can be categorised under two interrelated headings—structure and deliverables. The deliverables are produced from the application of the techniques and provide information germane to the problem to be solved. The structure ensures that the deliverables are produced in an order that enables them to be integrated, the output from deliverable A being input into deliverable B and so on.

Given that there are many aspects to the solution of the identification and valuation problem, no one deliverable is adequate. It is usual practice that a deliverable covers one aspect of the solution. With computer system information design there is a technique and associated deliverable showing the static structure of the data, another for the access to the data, another for the processing of the data and another for the man/machine interface presentation of this data. With IA there should likewise be a technique/deliverable for measuring market risk, one for measuring project risk, one for measuring event risk and so on.

Without a structure these currently standalone deliverables would remain just that, standalone. And be the poorer for it. Structure therefore includes a sequence of modules, steps and tasks that ensure the techniques are so applied that their deliverables are integrated, that the output of one deliverable is the input to another deliverable. The output of the deliverable that shows market risk is one of the inputs to the deliverable that shows company risk, which is one of the inputs to the deliverable that shows project risk, which in turn is the input to the deliverable that shows event risk and flexibility. This sequence reflects the fact that flexibility can be used to offset an adverse event or to take advantage of a beneficial event, events can affect a project during its life and that the project functions within the scope of the market the company operates in. The deliverables therefore require order/sequence, hence a structure for the application of the techniques that produce the deliverables.

Structured methods are relatively new as a formal mechanism of work. Perhaps the first area to use them was the computing industry, but even here they have obtained widespread acceptance only within the last decade. There was initially considerable reluctance in certain quarters—they discourage "flair" in the design of information and computer systems. The argument that they would discourage "flair" in the calculation of the value of a project is not likely to be heard for IA, because one is dealing in numbers, not design options. Once the benefit of the ordered techniques and integrated deliverables was seen, the initial reluctance in the IT industry to adopt structured methods has been replaced by a wholesale recognition of their long term advantages. This should also be the case for IA. This book aims to speed the process.

1.9 WHAT IS REQUIRED OF A STRUCTURED METHOD?

A structured method is an ordered set of techniques and supporting procedures with a resultant set of integrated deliverables and supporting documentation. The structure should comprise:

(1) Modules, within which there are techniques to apply for the production of the deliverables serving a common objective.

Techniques, procedures and documentation are not the building blocks of a method. Techniques, procedures and documents are but the means to an end—the production of deliverables. It is the deliverables that are the building blocks of a structured method. The structure of the method is therefore based on the sequence in which the deliverables require to be produced and the way in which the outputs of one deliverable are input into another.

Where the IA deliverables relate to an objective of the IA method—the two main ones being the identification and planning of investment opportunities of potential projects and the calculation of the values of actual projects—the associated techniques, procedures and documentation can be grouped. The tasks and related techniques and skills for each of the objectives form a distinct and separate whole, each with a different set of skills. The objectives are thus the perfect basis of the modules of a method.

Within the domain of valuing the costs and benefits to be obtained from investing in computers, a module could be to identify the opportunities that offer the greatest scope for profit. The final deliverable from this is a prioritised portfolio of computer applications to develop. Within the module the individual deliverables will reflect a set of common but distinct skills as exemplified in the techniques, procedures and documents to be applied, all related, in this case, to identifying investment opportunities. The skills for producing the deliverables of a module may be sufficiently distinct to require a different set of persons from those producing deliverables from another module.

For the IA method it could be, for example, that business analysts should be used for the module concerned with identification and planning of investment opportunities, that people with accountancy training should be used for the module concerned with the calculation of the project value and that the project manager should be used for the module concerned with benefits realisation.

Being commonly related in objective techniques, skills and deliverables, the modules can be regarded as self-contained blocks of work that can be contracted out to company staff or outside contractors.

(2) A sequence of steps and tasks which ensure that the techniques are applied in a proper order, so that the deliverables are integrated and add value to each other as appropriate.

The sequencing of the techniques means that, as the techniques are applied, the resultant deliverables are progressively merged and reduced in number, with the aim of ultimately producing a final and single deliverable that combines all the strengths of the previous deliverables. The plethora of deliverables produced at the beginning of a structured method are progressively "hardened up" with greater degrees of precision and accuracy by the succeeding deliverables adding value through the merging process. Each subsequent deliverable becomes more focused and based on more definitive and more thoroughly designed information. This is illustrated in Figure 1.1 and is the ideal situation at the end of each module of the method.

For an IA method, the final deliverable of an investment identification, measurement and planning module is the portfolio of applications to be developed. As described in Chapter 2, the inputs to this final deliverable are a set of five deliverables, the outputs of which are merged into a single matrix table showing the compound investment opportunity scorings of the applications in the portfolio—the higher the score the greater the investment opportunity. From the IA modules, the final deliverable is the total project value for each application in the portfolio. The input to the IA module is, for each application in the portfolio, a set of techniques for measuring and valuing the different aspects of the costs and benefits of projects to be invested in, the final output being the value of the project. The input to the benefits realisation module comprises all the claimed benefits to be

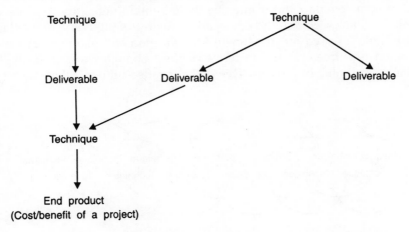

Figure 1.1 Interrelationships of techniques and deliverables

obtained from the investment—the company value to be followed by the project value to be followed by risk value to be followed by . . . . The output is an indication as to which of the benefits are being realised.

Having discussed the "structure" of a structured method, two points should be noted regarding the set of deliverables:

(1) The deliverables are produced by the application of techniques. The effectiveness of the deliverables, in terms of the ease with which they are produced and the quality of the information they present, is considerably enhanced if they are diagrammatic. Diagrams are much easier for the user to understand and interpret. It is also much easier to learn the technique that produces them.
(2) The description of the deliverables must also contain the quality criteria that ensure the deliverables are completed to the standard required, both in the information they contain and the accuracy of that information. The quality criteria need to be in the form of:
 • The inputs and outputs to and from deliverables;
 • The information, its level of detail and presentation form.

There are other features that indicate a method is well thought out. One such feature is that the method is "lean and fit", without unnecessary overlap in the scope of the deliverables. Figure 1.2 is a perfect example of what a structured method should not be like, with n techniques producing n deliverables, each of which has a high degree of information overlap. It is another representation of the situation in Table 1.1, this showing that to date CBA has not been "lean and fit".

Given that the deliverables need to interlink in a sequenced manner there has to be some overlap, but it must be the minimum necessary to achieve the link. It will be seen that there is a certain degree of unnecessary overlap in the techniques used for investment identification and planning, but the IA method is extremely "fit" in terms of the techniques concerned with calculating the value of projects. This perhaps reflects the fact that strategy

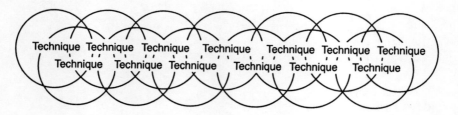

Figure 1.2 What a structured method should not be like

techniques are by their nature broader in perspective than prescriptive techniques for the calculation of monies.

1.10 WHAT KIND OF IA METHOD?

When presenting the IA method at seminars and workshops it is often asked why there are two parts to the method—the identification and planning of investment opportunities and the calculation of the value of the investments. Surely IA is only about the latter aspect? The question is valid—and indeed IA is more about the calculation of the value of an investment than the identification and planning for an investment. But the decision to include the identification, measurement and planning of investment opportunities is deliberate and based on a sound position.

The sense of disappointment in the financial benefits of computers identified earlier is in part based on the fact that the true value of computing has been difficult to calculate. Everybody agrees that computers add value to a company. Few companies today could survive without them. Computers are not only "a good thing" and help a company to be competitive but are essential to the very running of the business. They are operational as well as competitive facilitators. But the problem is that nobody knows how much of a good thing, how much computers add value to a company.

This value aspect, or lack of it, is not the only factor behind the sense of disappointment. The Kobler Unit at Imperial College London has found that the main reason for the lack of long term success in the use of computers for the benefit of companies has been the matching lack of a business, information systems and IT strategy.[8] The absence of a business and information systems strategy leads to piecemeal and uncoordinated investments, to the Alice in Wonderland situation that "if you don't know where you are going then any old route will do". It has been calculated by Kearney that if there is no strategy, up to 20% of the money spent on computers is wasted: "Investment on a piecemeal basis . . . is no guarantee of business success and, in fact, can slow a company down and hamper its profit performance".[9] The hallmarks of a lack of strategy include the duplication of data, functional overlap of the applications programs and different and incompatible hardware and software. All result in additional expenditure in the development of the applications and in the purchasing of the equipment, with long term increases in the maintenance costs. And there can be gaps in the information supported. Sins of omission as well as sins of

---

[8] The Kobler Unit (1988). *Does Information Technology Slow You Down?*, Department of Computing, Imperial College, London.
[9] Kearney, A. T. (1984). *The Barriers and Opportunities of Information Technology—A Management Perspective*, DTI Report.

commission. And the sins of omission inevitably result in lower benefits. You cannot obtain benefit from something that isn't there.

Business strategy is not considered in the IA structured method. Business strategy is the first stage of the information life cycle and as such precedes the information systems strategy stage. It is inevitably at a high level of ideas and broad statements of business direction, regarding which deliverables and services are to be supported by the company for which sectors of the market. At this level there is no concept of specific applications and potential computer systems to be invested in. It is therefore outside the scope and focus of the IA method and this book.

The next lower and more precise level of strategy granularity is the Information Systems Strategy (ISS). It is more detailed in its considerations as it moves towards the identification of distinct business applications and their information requirements to be developed. The exact boundary between business and ISS is not precise or even agreed, to the extent that some of the techniques used by business strategists are also used by information systems strategists—the Boston Matrix being an example. The boundary is not important provided the appropriate deliverables from the strategies are obtained: a deliverable, service and market sector business direction from the business strategy and the sequenced portfolio of investment opportunities and planned computer applications to develop that are matched to the business objectives of the company from the ISS.

The techniques that are included within the financial value component of an ISS within the IA method are those that enable the potential financial value of an application system to be ascertained. Only one of the five techniques does not use money as the measure of value, using a scoring mechanism of some kind instead. But the four other techniques base their scores on crude CBA monetary estimates. It has to be appreciated that, at this stage in the investment decision making cycle, the monies to be allocated to application projects have not yet been calculated. Precise monetary figures are therefore not possible. But these scoring techniques are brought together at the end to produce a compound application score that is based on monetary estimates. The techniques have also been chosen on the basis that they model the information that is required to support the business. The IA method therefore includes both the value and the information components of ISS. *This, as far as the authors are aware, is unique.* It is therefore possible to prioritise the sequencing of the applications on the basis of the "value for money" measure as well as the "information required".

The IA method is therefore business based, the valuation techniques only being applied to investment opportunities judged to be of significant potential in adding value to the company. Business analysts are required prior to those with accounting skills.

1.11 THE IA METHOD STRUCTURE AND DELIVERABLES

The method includes:

(1) A set of integrated techniques that identify opportunities for investment related to the business needs for information. The opportunities and needs together are the foundation of a strategic application development plan, a plan that is based on the concept of "value for money" and "business information required". The value results of the IA method are merged with the information results to produce a strategy plan of application system developments prioritised on the merged results. The two components of IS are brought together.

 The IA method described in this book concentrates on the value component for the simple reason that the existing methods for ISS already have valid techniques for modelling the information component and prioritising them into information needs.

(2) A further set of integrated techniques that calculate the total financial value of each application/project in the strategy plan, and specifically of:
  • The visible and hidden costs;
  • The tangible and intangibles benefits;
  • The different types of risk—market, project and event;
  • Offsetting the costs of risk with flexibility;
  • The benefits to be obtained from project synergy.

(3) A mechanism by which the actual benefits claimed for a proposed computer application system can be measured when the system is implemented.

The Kearney report goes on to say that the second major barrier "is the constraint imposed by previous investments". We shall see numerous examples in the book where the refusal of managers to ignore previous investments that have been sunk/written off/paid back is a major hindrance to investing in new applications. An American delegate at one of the seminars being presented by the authors described the British as a risk averse nation (this discouraging a forward looking attitude to investment) with a hoarding instinct (this producing the backward looking attitude that old assets will only be got rid of if they no longer work or cannot compete with the worst of competitors). We only invest when we have to. The book will therefore also provide advice as to good accounting practices for the investment decision making process.

 The structure of the IA method is shown in Figure 1.3. The method is composed of four modules, numbered deliberately 0 to 3, the 0 indicating

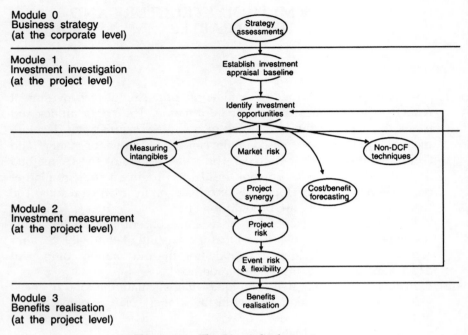

Figure 1.3 The IA method structure

that no techniques are applied. Each module serves an objective of the method. The title of the module is descriptive of the objective of the module.

Each module is composed of a set of "bubbles", each bubble representing, as described, a major aspect of the module objective. Within each bubble there may be, and usually is, a set of techniques for producing the deliverables that together model the aspect being addressed. The grouping of the techniques into bubbles in the investment measurement module concerned with valuing projects is illustrated in Figure 1.4. It can be seen that there are two techniques for the calculation of the discount rate, one for the market rate and one for the project rate, and three for the valuation of the benefits of flexibility. The intention is that where there are multiple techniques and deliverables produced covering a single aspect of the method, then the deliverables will be integrated as far as possible, so that each deliverable can add value to the information contained in another deliverable, thus producing an aggregate result. This can be done for the discount rate, with the project rate being added to the market rate. Sometimes this is not possible, as is the case for the valuation of the intangible benefits. Where this is the case all the techniques will be described and the one recommended as the most suitable will be used. The other techniques can be used by the reader of this book if so desired.

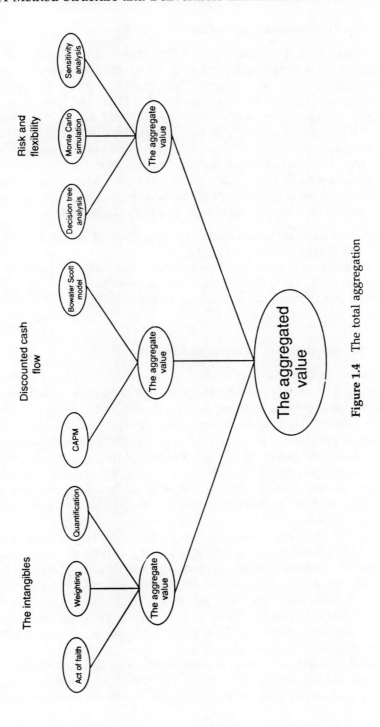

Figure 1.4 The total aggregation

1.11.1 The Business Strategy Module

The first module is "business strategy". The objective is to define a business strategy for the enterprise, the strategy being the provision of specified goods and services for specified sectors of the marketplace. The techniques that are applied for this are not considered further. The reason for this is that IA is not concerned with defining a business strategy but with the result of the business strategy, because it is the results that are the basis of investment opportunities and plans. The numbering of the module as module 0 is an indication that this module is "empty" of techniques and deliverables, but included in the method as a means of indicating that investments must be within the scope and aid the achievement of the business strategy.

The deliverables from a business strategy should include:

- A mission statement of the company's objectives in terms of the deliverables and services to be provided;
- The market sector to be addressed in the short and long term;
- The goals as to when the objectives are to be achieved;
- A broad statement of the investment portfolio.

1.11.2 The Investment Investigation Module

The Investment Investigation module is concerned with the identification and planning of investment opportunities, that is projects which should be developed on the basis that they are financially viable as well as contain the information that enables the business objectives to be achieved. The greater the opportunity, the greater the priority for the development of the project. Given that precisely calculated monies have not yet been allocated for expenditure, all the techniques use a scoring mechanism of some kind to assess the investment opportunity, and all but one also use broad cost/benefit analysed monies alongside the scores. The scores are therefore monetary based.

The module starts by defining four steps that must be taken before undertaking IA. The baseline on which the IA is to be applied must be agreed with senior business and financial managers, otherwise the financial projections made for the proposed computer systems will not be accepted when presented for consideration. Once the IA baseline has been agreed it is then possible to begin to identify the opportunities in which to invest. Once the opportunities are identified their relative merits can be ascertained and an investment portfolio can be prepared.

The module addresses the information as well as the opportunity/value component of investment. The strategic value analysis techniques use dataflow diagramming as a central part of the technique, the processes and data information contained being the source for an entity model of the business. The techniques of information modelling are not described in this book. They are contained in the many structured methods for the analysis and design of computerised application systems.

This merging of the opportunity/value and information components enables the investment investigation module to be properly considered as a genuinely full ISS method in its own right, uniquely with both opportunity/value and information components as a combined priority score for computer systems planning.

1.11.3 The Investment Measurement Module

The Investment Investigation module is the major part of the method. It is concerned with the measurement of the financial value of the application projects planned from the previous module.

The module contains the techniques traditionally associated with CBA, the identification of the market discount rate to be applied to the project monies to bring any future monies to present day values. The market discount rate is based on the assessed risk that the company planning an investment is likely to incur by being in the type of business the company is in, set by the business strategy. The market risk includes the effects of inflation. The techniques for measuring market risk are within the bubble "market risk". Also used in CBA are the non-discounted techniques, such as "payback period" and "return on investment".

The non-discounted techniques do not include the debilitating effects of inflation and market risk on the value of the project monies over time. These techniques have been included in the IA method with some reluctance, not because they are considered worthy of merit (they are not), but because they are there and widely used. They are described, their deficiencies identified and then discarded. Their redundant place in the method is shown in Figure 1.5. They correspond to the "dead end" arrow in Figure 1.1. Also redundant is the application of scoring techniques used by other methods claiming to value projects, these techniques being applied where the costs or the benefit is difficult to measure. Scores cannot be compared with monies. Fair comparisons between alternative investments cannot be made.

The bubble entitled "cost/benefit forecasting" is a hybrid in that it contains advice for good accounting practices when making investment decisions rather than a set of techniques. It does not produce any deliverable as such. The different role of this part of the method explains that the bubble is not part of the sequence of IA deliverables and is therefore, notwithstanding its usefulness, a dead-end in the method.

Figure 1.6 shows the techniques used in the IA method that are not

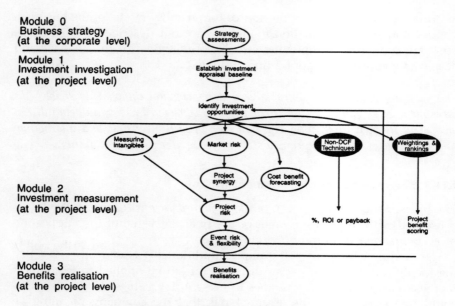

Figure 1.5 The IA method—techniques not included

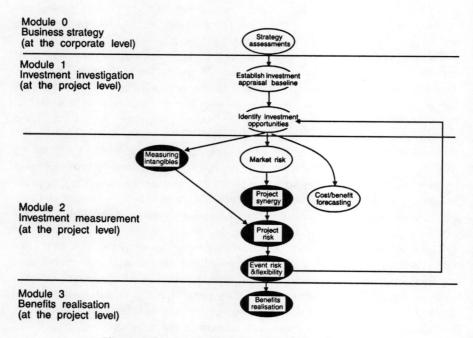

Figure 1.6 The IA method—the new techniques

regarded as part of CBA. *These techniques apply to the valuation of project investments which is the added value component of this book regarding the subject of IA. It is with these techniques that this book takes CBA forward to full IA.*

A separate group of techniques are used for the identification and measurement of the intangible benefits that computer systems can provide. The techniques are applied at an early part of the module so that the results, the value of the intangible benefits, can be included in the discounting to be applied to the project monies.

Another early measure is that computer applications do not run in isolation from one other. The advent of database and object oriented technology means that data and logic are now corporate resources, so that projects can gain from the information that they each add to and access from the database. Logic, like data, will thus be designed and used as a corporate resource. An obvious benefit will be the ability to reduce software as well as data maintenance (the major benefit of object orientation is the ability to reuse existing data and logic). With this and other emerging technologies such as new powerful query languages that can access information by topic ("Get me all the information on elephants", the elephant being the topic) and perspective ("Get me all the information on elephants as perceived by Joe Bloggs", Joe's perception of elephants being different from that of John Smith) in a totally non-procedural way—the scope for applications/projects to gain benefit from each other's information will be much larger.

Given these healthy technical trends the value to be obtained from the linking of computer applications together is much larger. These trends come under the heading of "project synergy". The positive value of project synergy needs to be measured and included in the project monies to be discounted.

Once the discount rate for the market is ascertained and added to the inflation rate to produce the overall market discount rate, the project risks are calculated. The risks are converted into a discount rate that is added to the market rate. The combined market and project rates make up the total discount rate to be applied to the project monies.

Events may occur that could affect the original project plans. These events are risks that could affect the viability of the project as initially conceived. The market may expand or contract more than anticipated, new technology may emerge that requires the design of the system to change and new business requirements may necessitate added functionality to the original system. The probability of these events/risks occurring and the way they affect the costs and benefits needs to be measured. Where the event risks are judged to lower the value of the project, the project plans can be changed to offset the risks (flexibility), thus alternatives need to be identified and their costs and benefits similarly measured.

1.11.4 The Benefits Realisation Module

The final module of the method is "benefits realisation", which assesses whether the benefits claimed for the project are being achieved once the computer system is installed. The project total value has been calculated and the current and future costs and benefits presented as a net present value. The benefits claimed require to be designed into the computer application. This enables the operational running of the computer system to be the source of the benefits realisation. The financial benefits profile of the project investment plans can be obtained as management reports. Remedial action plans can be drawn up where the actual profile is different from the planned profile.

1.12 CHAPTER SUMMARY

Chapter 1 addresses two main issues—the need to apply the full array of IA techniques rather than the much more limited set of CBA techniques and the form and structure of an IA structured method.

The traditional CBA approach to valuing project investments is to apply either a non-discounted technique or a market based discount rate to the project cash flows. Other techniques used include the valuing of intangible benefits, but without detailing particular methods for doing this.

But CBA techniques do not address many other aspects that affect the cash flow of a project. They do not take into account the following facts:

- That investments need to be made in the context of a company's business strategy;
- That an investment in an IT project has to compete with alternative projects;
- That projects have risks that are additional to the market risks;
- That events during the life of a project can affect the riskiness and hence the value of the project;
- That flexibility can be used to offset the cost implications of risk.

All in all, traditional CBA has long failed to take into account all the aspects that affect the value of a project.

The structured method of IA is essentially in two parts—the identification of investment opportunities and the valuing of investments in projects once the decision to invest has been made. Investments need to be made on the basis of a well thought out and prioritised plan designed to support the company's business objectives. The techniques for doing this are not based on monies (and such monies that are addressed are only on the costs side, benefits being ignored), so a scoring mechanism for prioritisation is used. The techniques of project valuation are based only on monies. There is a strict sequence in which the techniques are to be applied, the calculation of the market discount rate being followed by the calculation of the project discount rate, then the assessment of the event risks to be followed by flexibility. The non-discounted techniques are ignored as far as project valuation are concerned.

Investment Investigation

This chapter considers the identification and planning of investment opportunities.

There is much to be gained by ensuring that the IA is conducted against a clear strategy plan of projects that are judged to be worthy of investment. Any IA should be applied according to a strategy plan for investment.

There have long been techniques for the development of a prioritised list of investments, particularly for IT projects. Various ISS methods have been developed for doing this task. The problem is that the prioritised list of IT projects to invest in and develop are based solely on the information component. No consideration is given in these methods to the financial benefit the project is likely to give to the company. Ultimately projects are invested in because they offer value for money. There is, therefore, a need for a value component *as well as* an information component to investment plans for IT projects.

This chapter pays particular attention to the techniques that identify the likely financial benefit to be gained from investing in an IT project. The information component is well addressed by the methods of ISS planning already existing. The chapter also shows how the value and information components can be combined to create an integrated score of the total benefit that investing in any particular IT project is likely to give to a company as compared with other projects.

2.1 THE MISSING VALUE COMPONENT

The general view is that CBA is usually undertaken for one of two reasons—either to show that the proposed computer application benefits outweigh the costs over the lifetime of the project or to show that the pay-back period for the investment (the time when the benefits outweigh the costs) can be met. Both reasons are valid. But they are not enough. The problem is that CBA, as shown in section 1.3, is not a complete science for the measurement of the benefits against the costs and the concept of the payback period is seriously flawed if used as the basis of an investment decision, for reasons discussed in section 3.3.

There is a tendency to use the payback period as the basis of an invest-ment decision in a time of economic hardship. For example, the UK econ-omy is going through extremely hard times (early 1990s) and there have been announcements by the financial directors of several large companies that projects will be temporally judged on the basis of a payback period of, say, three years. If the costs are not paid back within the specified time the project will not be invested in. As explained in Chapter 5 the payback period mitigates against long term projects—and long term projects in a time of deep recession require an act of considerable management courage. The preferred approach of net present value was abandoned in these cases.

Modern IA techniques offer more than a dozen ways, many complemen-tary to each other, of viewing IT investments. The problem is that the tech-niques are of an accountancy type in that they calculate and measure finan-cial figures on a project by project basis only. To date there has been no built-in mechanism to ensure that financial investments are made in the context of the company's business strategy plans. Techniques to identify the plans and match the opportunities to invest in computer applications to the plans have not been part of the IA approach.

To attempt to remedy this and other problems, several companies have developed ISS methods—companies such as James Martin & Associates with the Information Systems Planning (ISP) stage of the Information Engineering structured method and Learmonth & Burchett Management Systems (LBMS) and their Strategic Planning method.

At this point, the difference between an ISS and an IT strategy needs to be explained. Many vendors seem confused on this matter and claim to supply an IT strategy method whereas they are, in fact, supplying an ISS method. An ISS is a set of techniques that produce a prioritised portfolio of application systems to develop, irrespective of hardware and software considerations. The portfolio is logical in that physical technology is not included. An IT strategy comprises a separate, distinct and different set of techniques that identifies and models a set of hardware and software technology architecture options by product type to support the ISS and selects the optimum product set to run on the selected architecture.

The problem with ISS methods is that they consider only the information component. The information that is needed to support the business plans is identified and modelled at a "high level" and a portfolio of computer applications that can support the information (prioritised according to the need for the information) is constructed. The information modelling techniques are well established and stable; they include entity modelling, dataflow modelling and process decomposition. The prioritisation of the applications is based on techniques that model the perceived importance of the information need—on such proactive factors as where information can support new business opportunities and such reactive factors as where the response to customer queries can be improved, costs can be saved and known areas where the existing applications are technically and functionally weak enhanced.

But the techniques of affinity analysis/process decomposition and requirements weighting are information based—and only information based. The production of an application portfolio of business systems to develop is therefore based only on the information component of an ISS.

These traditional ISS methods pay no attention to the financial value of the applications to a company. There may be good information need and technical reasons for the sequence in which the information systems need to be developed, but the sequence should also take account of the monetary value of the applications.

Computer systems are developed because they provide operational and management information to enable a company to increase profitability, because they can add value to the processes the business goes through in the production of its goods and services, as well as store and access information for presentation to management for them to take appropriate decisions regarding operational and financial improvement. *There is thus a value component to computer systems as well as an information component.* The computer systems incur expenditure and generate revenue. Monies are therefore involved. This aspect needs to be measured.

The above requires that there are two components in an ISS method—the information modelling component and the investment identification and planning component—each to benefit the other.

As indicated, the information component is already well covered by the IS information modelling techniques long used in current methods for ISS planning and includes the static structure of the required data in the form of a logical data model and the dynamic flow and processing of the data in the form of dataflow/process decomposition/process dependency diagrams. This book does not re-describe these techniques.

The purpose of this chapter is to add the financial component to the information component. It will show how opportunities to invest in applications that have the best scope of providing a good financial return as well as providing the information to support the business plan can be identified and measured. The techniques that model products and measure the investment opportunities will be described. The resultant opportunity score is merged with the requirement weight of the business systems to produce a portfolio of computer applications that give a combined "value and information return" to the company.

2.2 SCOPING APPLICATION SYSTEMS

A problem that requires to be resolved is how do you identify the business scope of a computer project in which you may want to invest?

The technique of "affinity analysis" is used in the Information Engineering method for the identification of business applications or business systems as they are called. Affinity analysis ascertains the similarities of information objects/entities and processes, and the need for them to be grouped together. The affinity is based on such criteria as the number of processes that access an entity, the "involvement" of the processes with the entities. The problem with this approach lies with the information that is accessed infrequently (where do you put it?) and the fact that data is not limited to specific business applications but is corporate and open to access by anyone so entitled.

For example, stratigraphical information obtained from oil exploration is very static and may only be accessed infrequently by the oil analysis system, but the users of the oil analysis, geological and drilling and other such systems will not be too pleased to find stratigraphy excluded from general corporate access. There is little affinity in that the number of business processes that access the data is not large and that the users are from n application areas. To which application/business system should the information therefore be allocated? To all of them, of course. OK, given this, where is the boundary of the application system(s)? There are many occasions where affinity analysis does not provide a clear boundary to a business system.

An alternative approach is that of process decomposition to identify functional areas as advised by the user and to use them as the basis of business applications. A functional area has been described as a grouping of "logically related events", that is events concerned with a common business "thing to do", such as invoicing, purchasing and stock control. It is a long used and valid approach for business system identification. The user can view the process decomposition diagrams and draw a boundary around the business processes of an application/business system.

2.3 MEASURING THE IMPORTANCE OF INFORMATION

Information Engineering assesses the application business system development priorities based on whether the information of operational use to the business supports the critical success factors and business objectives (weightings 5–1), the degree to which there is functional support provided by the current system (weightings 1–4) and multiplies the two to produce a compond "requirement weight". These information needs are grouped into the business systems resulting from the affinity analysis or process decomposition. The combined requirement weight of the information needs within the business systems determines the priority of the business systems for development.

This is a much better approach, as it recognises that the basic reason for the development of computer systems is not so much to support the operational running of a company but to answer crucial management queries about the areas of the company that must be successful and be meeting objectives, and from this enable the operational running of the company to be competitive.

2.4 INVESTMENT STRATEGY WITH INFORMATION STRATEGY

This section describes the techniques and their products in the "investment investigation" module of the IA method. The ultimate purpose of the module is exactly the same as an ISS, that is the creation of a portfolio of business applications to be developed as computer systems to enable a company to operate competitively. But the portfolio is based on value.

However, the IA method also shows how the value component can be added to and merged with the traditional information modelling component of current ISS planning methods. The combined result is much more powerful than the ISSs described in Information Engineering's ISP Strategic Planning and Strategic Planner from LBMS—the application development plan is value plus information based.

This linking of the value techniques to the information modelling and prioritis-ation techniques transforms the IA method from the previous accountancy led, defensive/reactive use of the financial modelling to a proactive, corporate wide and positive financial planning management tool. The identification of investment opportunities, preferably before the competitors, enables other managers to force events to react to their plans and not the other way around. This proactive approach also lowers risk—for how to calculate the benefits of this see Chapter 3.

It is a lower risk situation when others are responding to your actions rather than you reacting to theirs. Your plans are not subject to the whims of others, for the simple reason that it is you in proactive control and your competitors are reacting to you. The likelihood of untoward and unplanned events occurring to put your project investments at risk is reduced—and reduced risk raises the value of a project.

As stated in Chapter 1, a clear statement of direction in the company's mission statement and business plans, and their conversion into ISS plans, have been identified as the key factors relating to the "success" of computer systems. Without IS and IT strategies any old route to the development of applications and hardware/software architectures will do, with all the dangers of departmental systems, standalone systems, systems that do not support the business objectives of the company and systems that are not compatible with each other. All lower the value of a project.

One example of this "any old route will do" approach was with an oil company that had produced separate systems for monitoring the flow of fluids up and down the pipes of oil and gas wells. Yet the systems were the same in terms of data and function. The pipes were the conduits for the flow of oil, gas, mud, water, steam and lubricants to moisten viscous oil and chemicals. Yet seven different computer systems were developed, which ran on three different and incompatible architectures. When the data of these systems was modelled the result was the same—a single data model of the fluids of a different type flowing up and down the pipes. A single system replaced the seven systems.

The Kobler report quantified the danger of the "any old route" approach as accounting for up to 20% of the wasted expenditure on IT where there was no strategy. In the case just described, 20% was a very conservative figure.

The structure of the "investment investigation" module of the IA method is shown in Figure 2.1. The relationships and overlap of the value and the information components can be seen. What is significant is that:

- "Critical success factors" are the ultimate source of all information in the company's computer systems and hence form the basis of the logical data model.
- "Strategic value analysis" is the one technique that includes both the information and the value components in assessing the business benefit of a potential computer system. The information component is modelled with dataflow diagrams and the value component is based on the costs of the proposed system. The two components are therefore genuinely intertwined, with the value component adding value (no pun intended) to the information component. They are not separate and distinct.
- The "value chain analysis" technique is a "dead end" technique producing a deliverable that is not compatible with the deliverables of any other technique. This is addressed later in the chapter. It means that the output of the technique cannot be input into the total combined score from the applications scoring technique.

The output of all the techniques but one can be pulled together to produce a

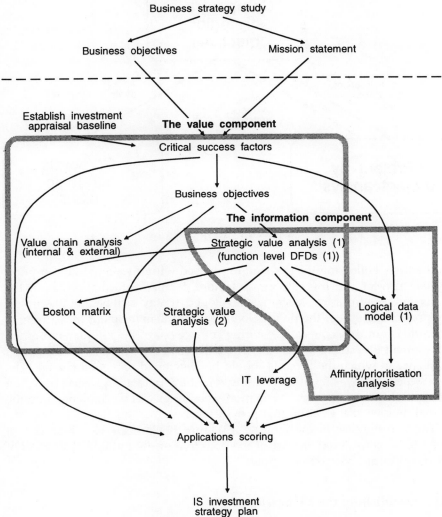

Figure 2.1 Investment investigation

total combined score of the "benefit value" of the project to the competitive operation of the organisation.

The structure in Figure 2.1 needs to be set in the context of Figure 2.2, which shows that the strategic plans are not set in concrete. They can be challenged. The strategy plans are based on the best information available

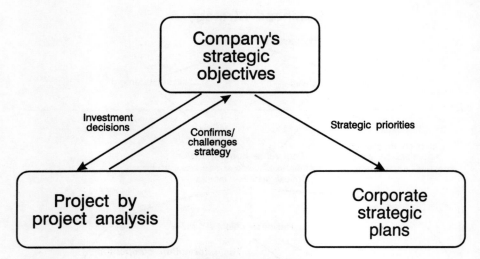

Figure 2.2   IA overview

at the time. Following the decision to proceed with investing in a computer system project and the gathering of more detailed information about the costs and benefits as the system is developed, it may well be that the project by project analysis of the financial value from the investment measurement module is not the same as the scoring component of the ISS plans from the investment investigation module. The balance of argument as to the correct sequence in which the projects should be developed may well change. The assessment of investment opportunity of all the potential projects based on opportunity scorings and information weightings can be challenged by the actual monies at the individual project level.

The two bubbles in the module in Figure 1.3 indicate two aspects that need to be considered as part of the objective of the module. The tasks of each aspect are considered below.

2.4.1 Establishing the IA Baselines

There is a set of tasks that must be carried out prior to undertaking any IA exercise. They are:

- Set the investment baseline;
- Set the investor's baseline;
- Tune the baselines to reflect opportunities;
- Establish threats that can skew the baseline.

Establishing the investment baselines needs to be done with the board of the company, as it is the board members who are the ultimate arbiters of investment decisions. There is little point in presenting the figures about a potential investment if the board does not agree with the way the figures, be they the "scoring value" or the "financial value" figures, are obtained and calculated.

The first thing to establish is the investment policy, the basis on which a decision to proceed or not to proceed is made. There are basically five possible policies for defining the "financial value" of a project:

(1) A payback period (the project must pay for its costs within x years).
(2) A return on investment (the project must obtain an $x\%$ return on the investment during the lifetime of the project—and the lifetime must be established in advance of the investment, not an easy thing to do).
(3) A cost/benefit ratio (the benefits of the project must be greater than the costs by a factor of x).
(4) The net present value must be greater than zero (the project must make a profit of x in current money terms).
(5) An internal rate of return (the project must obtain a certain discount rate in terms of the profits gained).

The figures for the investment in a project must be presented in a manner that reflects the investment policy.

The second thing to establish is the techniques to be used for the identification of investment opportunities (some of the techniques produce dubious results for a lot of work) and for the valuation of the projects (as shown in Table 1.1 there are a lot of techniques that overlap in their scope, and some of the techniques are considered controversial). Opinions are likely to differ on their merits. It may be that the business strategy manager does not like the Boston Matrix technique for the identification of business opportunity—and, as we shall see, there is good reason for dislike. It may be that the financial director does not like the technique of Monte Carlo Simulation for the measurement of event risk as compared with the decision tree analysis technique. If you want your figures relating to the scoring and financial values of projects to be accepted then don't use the Boston Matrix or Monte Carlo Simulation techniques. For project risk, the directors like the approach of the Bowater Scott model rather than sensitivity analysis. Use the Bowater Scott model.

It may be necessary to do some "education" of the directors as to the techniques available for opportunity and financial measurement, and their relative merits.

Having established the investment baseline and the techniques to be used it is necessary to establish the returns that can be obtained from alternative sources of investment. The proposed computer system must beat all competitive investment opportunities. The most basic alternative is a riskless investment. For those who are risk averse, one can invest in a building society or government stocks. If one can obtain, say, a 7% return on monies invested through these investment media then a computer project must obtain at least that return. Given that computer projects by their nature incur risk, the greater the adjudged risk the greater the returns there must be over the riskless investment. The returns to be obtained from a riskless investment are based in large measure on the difference between the inflation rate and the government established public interest rates. If the gap between the two is large—inflation is 3% and the general public interest rates 12%—then the return on a riskless investment is greater than if the inflation rate is 3% and the interest rates only 8%. The computer project must "work harder" for a greater return.

There may be avenues of investment other than the riskless kind. One could invest in buildings, in aircraft or whatever, rather than a computer system. The attractiveness of these other forms of investment must be established so that the baseline of minimum return which the computer systems must better can be ascertained. If the proposed computer system cannot match that investment baseline it has little chance of being accepted.

Opportunities affect the investment baseline. All projects have a certain "character". Some projects are such that the proportion of variable cash flows to the fixed cash flow is great whereas with other projects the balance is the other way around. Fixed cash flow is riskless—one knows the expenditure and the revenue. If there is no variability in the project cash flows, there is no risk. Management will tend to opt for projects with fixed cash flows. If the variable cash flow is a high proportion of the total cash flow, such that the risk element is greater, it may be necessary to introduce flexibility to the project plans to minimise the risks of the variable cash flows. It may also be that the business application the computer system supports uses information already created by existing systems. Project synergy becomes an issue. As will be explained in Chapter 4, project synergy is an issue of growing importance.

The "character" of the "overall riskiness" of the project needs to be established as much as possible at this early stage, because the higher the risk the greater the required return when using monies in an open and free market. An open and free market is one where monies can be borrowed and lent on a competitive basis without outside interference. The classic example of "beneficial" interference is the UK government's Export Guarantee Scheme, which ensures that companies doing business with countries and companies with low credit ratings can cover themselves via the scheme for payments that may not be made for the services rendered/products sold. This scheme distorts the market, as projects that should be rejected because the required return is too high become "artificially" financially viable.

The final aspect that needs to be examined concerns threats and events external to the project. There are any number of external and internal threats to a project. An obvious source of external threat is changes in government policy on such matters as taxation and loans for regional development. A non-governmental threat is represented by the competitive marketplace, where competitors may come out with new products or services that could render the computer system redundant. All these threats need to be compiled and assessed as to their impact on the project. From this, plans of action can be prepared to offset these threats—these plans reflecting flexibility. How this is done is considered in Chapter 5.

The one aspect that should never be considered is the unknowns. Nothing can be planned for these. One cannot plan for such unknowns as company takeovers and mergers. There have been several large computer projects that have been stopped in their tracks halfway through development because the company they were being developed for has been subject to a hostile or one-sided takeover and the projects it was investing in have become redundant. Just write off the monies expended to "the hand of fate"!

2.4.2 The Techniques for Planning Investment Opportunities

There are seven such techniques. They have all been developed independently of each other and each addresses some different part of investment identification and planning. It has proved necessary to modify and add to the techniques so as to be able to merge their findings and from this produce a single coherent applications development portfolio that includes both the value and the information components. Note that the techniques for the modelling of information are not considered; these are principally logical data modelling and dataflow diagramming. They are well described in the methods that include ISS planning, such as Information Engineering and Strategic Planning. The seven techniques for planning investment opportunities are described according to the sequence in which they are produced in Figure 2.1.

2.4.2.1 Critical Success Factors

This technique has been devised by John Rockart.[1] The definition of a Critical Success Factor (CSF) is "The limited number of areas in which satisfactory results will ensure successful competitive performance for the individual, department or organisation". In short, CSFs are indicators of one's business health *vis-à-vis* one's competitors' at whatever level within the business.

---

[1] *The Information Strategy Planning Handbook*. James Martin Associates Ltd, 1987.

The importance of CSFs as a technique is much underrated in terms of the design and development of computer systems. *CSFs are the ultimate source of all the information in a computer system.*

Computer systems are developed to support a company's business objectives as defined in the business strategy. These objectives need to be measured so as to ascertain the company's success or otherwise. CSFs need to be defined within the context of the company's business objectives. Rockart analyses the business objectives and for each identifies their CSFs. A CSF could be "The proportion of the market our company has captured in the last month for our products/services". Another could be "Has the minimum percentage of the customer satisfaction been achieved and is the percentage rising?"

The CSFs are the measure of a company's success—the factor that makes life difficult for the company's competitors. But what about the opposite of CSFs, the inhibiting factors that make life difficult for a company—the external inhibitors, namely competitors, and the internal inhibitors, namely bottlenecks? They also need to be identified and recorded in like manner. An external inhibitor could be "The number, quality and price of our competitor(s) product(s)/service(s)". An internal inhibitor could be "The areas of the production process causing holdups".

As defined above, the CSFs and the inhibitors seem innocuous enough— the managers receive reports on their desks detailing the market share by volume and value respecting their own and competitor companies' products/services, with explanations as to why their share is going up or down or whatever. That on the face of it is the end of it. Not so, behind these usually few and seemingly simple requests for management information is a great mass of supporting raw data. For the two CSFs identified above the information requirements are enormous—the products and services provided by the company and competitor companies, information about their quality and price, the size, type and geographical spread of the market for the product/service, any significant and total orders received this month by the company and competitors by region and type of customer, and the number of customer complaints. . . . Each CSF and inhibitor can thus describe a substantial part of the database data.

There is yet more to CSFs and inhibitors than voracious information needs. Each level of management requires to identify their CSFs and inhibitors. All management reports retrieving information about the measurement and causal explanation of their success or failure to meet an objective, or objectives, are re-expressions of the CSFs and inhibitors. All management data retrieval business requirements should therefore be reports that are CSF and inhibitor based.

The only business requirements that need not be so based are those for the day-to-day operational running of the company. Yet even these business requirements have their ultimate origins in business objectives and their associated CSFs and inhibitors. The day-to-day operations of a company are organised to support the CSFs.

The information to support the management and operational data retrieval business requirements has to be put into the database. Data cannot be retrieved unless it has been previously inserted into the database. This, of course, is only achieved through data maintenance business requirements. It therefore follows that CSFs and inhibitors are also the ultimate source of data maintenance business requirements. Each CSF and inhibitor is thus the source of a corporation's database, is a data retrieval business requirement in its own right, the father of other more detailed data retrieval business requirements and of all the data maintenance business requirements. At the end of the day all data maintenance and data retrieval business requirements are the progeny of CSFs.

All information in computer systems should be CSF and inhibitor based.

CSFs and inhibitors are also an excellent mechanism for tracing company strategy to its physical implementation as a computer system in that the data in the database can support CSF and inhibitor queries.

The task for identifying and measuring investment opportunity is to ascertain the significance of the CSFs in relation to each other and the functional areas of the business that provide the information the CSFs need. This can be done by the use of cross-matrices, the functional areas on one axis and their CSFs on the other. For each meeting of the functional area and the CSF allocate a score to reflect the deemed importance of the CSF and the ability of the function to support the CSF. An example produced by a broking company dealing in chemicals is given in Figure 2.3. The

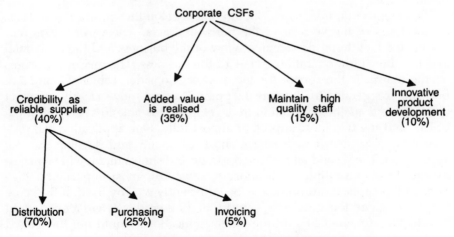

Figure 2.3 Weighted CSF selection

company had a turnover of some £300 million with some 100 employees. The hierarchy of the CSFs is given in Table 2.1 and the CSFs are typical of a broking type operation. The company has been fortunate in that invoicing is only rated at 5% importance. Presumably the company's clients pay their bills on time. The path of the most important CSFs is that to the left, ending up in "distribution", the importance being based on the percentage figure given.

Each layer of the CSF hierarchy needs to have a matrix diagram produced. An example of the top layer is given in Table 2.1. The numbers in the cross-sections linking the CSF to the functions represent an assessment of the capability of the function to support the CSF as given by individual assessors. In the example the number of assessors is three—and they need to be of the same seniority in order to ensure the equal significance of the score. To ascertain the overall importance of the functionally based computer systems to the significance of the CSF it is a simple case of multiplying the average score of the boxes on the vertical and horizontal planes with the percentage figure of the CSF. If one takes the horizontal significance of the functional areas then the "trading and logistics" system scores 6.76 ($40\% \times 8$ (the average of 10,6,8) + ($35\% \times 9.3$) + ($10\% \times 0.53$)), "product development" scores 3.46 and so forth. On this basis, "trading and logistics" scores higher than "product development" and should be developed first. One can apply the same mechanism on the vertical axis. The scores for the CSF of "credibility as a supplier" would rate a score of 6.4 and "added value demonstrated" a score of 10.97. On this basis the systems supporting the "added value demonstrated" CSF should be developed first. Although "credibility as a supplier" is a more important CSF, the computer systems are not able to satisfy the requirements as well as the CSF "added value demonstrated".

The obvious question arises. Should one develop the application systems on the basis of the vertical or the horizontal axis? The vertical axis represents the long term management view of the business and the horizontal axis the short term operational view of the business. The mix of the scores on the matrix is the source for the answer. Consider Tables 2.2 and 2.3. Both are exaggerated to illustrate the point. The first shows clearly "product development" as the application to develop as it is able to satisfy multiple CSFs—and the two most important almost fully. One application can provide many CSF answers. Take the short term view and develop the one application. The second table is the opposite and shows that it will be necessary to develop multiple applications to satisfy the most important CSF— none of the applications doing the job sufficiently well by itself. If the score for "trading and logistics" was, say, 10, 10, 10 then this sytem alone would be adequate for the CSF and the other applications would not be needed for this purpose. Given the scores shown and the 40% importance of the

Table 2.1 Broking company CSF/functional matrix

Functions/CSFs	Credibility as a supplier	Added value demonstrated 35%	Maintain high quality staff 15%	Innovate product development 10%	Score
Trading and logistics	10,6,8	10,8,8		4,6,6	6.76
Product development		8,8,6		10,8,2	3.46
Market intelligence		10,6,6		6,10,6	3.3
Contracts management	8,8,8	6,8,8			5.77
Personnel management			4,4,6		0.7
Score	6.4	10.97	0.7	1.92	19.99

Table 2.2 Broking company CSF/functional matrix different CSFs for the same example (1)

Functions/CSFs	Credibility as a supplier 40%	Added value demonstrated 35	Maintain high quality staff 15%	Innovate product development 10%
Trading and logistics	10,6,6			
Product development	10,8,6	10,8,4	6,6,8	6,4,2
Market intelligence		4,4,4		
Contracts management				
Personnel management			10,6,6	

Conclusion—take a short term view and invest in product development

Table 2.3 Broking company CSF/functional matrix—different CSFs for the same example (2)

Functions/CSFs	Credibility as a supplier 40%	Added value demonstrated 35%	Maintain high quality staff 15%	Innovate product development 10%
Trading and logistics	2,4,2			
Product development	6,4,2			4,2,6
Market intelligence	2,4,4	4,4,4		
Contracts management	6,2,2			
Personnel management	2,4,2		1,6,2	

Conclusion—take a long term view and invest in multiple systems simultaneously

CSF, there is a need to take the long term view and develop the five applications together. The long term view with the situation in the second table clearly entails high cost.

The action taken by the broking company was to develop the "trading and logistics" first, as this application obtained the highest score on the horizontal axis, followed by the "product development", "market intelligence" and "contracts management" as these together obtained the highest score on the vertical axis. A short term view was thus initially taken. This fortunately had the advantage that two of the most important CSFs were satisfied to a high degree as well as a third CSF to a lesser degree, so that a long term effect was achieved at the same time. Once the immediate requirements of the short term were satisfied a long term view of systems development was taken. It was a happy compromise.

The technique is simple to operate and can achieve a most useful result without much effort. The hidden benefit of building information systems on the basis of the correct information needs of the company is also gained. The obvious downside is that there is no financial basis to the technique.

2.4.2.2 The Business Objectives

These are identified and used in the next technique, Strategic Value Analysis. The business objectives need to relate to the CSFs identified in the above technique.

2.4.2.3 Strategic Value Analysis

This technique has been developed by R. M. Curtice and is explained in detail in the book "Strategic Value Analysis".[2] The technique is a weighting based approach, but has the benefits that it also includes financial information, IT systems capability and business objectives, the information for which is modelled as dataflow diagrams. The technique has much to recommend it, as the sequence of tasks are in line with the requirements of a business strategy, an ISS and an IT strategy. Of all the techniques for the identification of investment opportunities this is the best—it is the most comprehensive in scope, including the matching of the technical capabilities of the computer systems with the ability of the systems to satisfy the business objectives. It then relates the resultant scorings to the monies involved, to come up with a financially based technical capability score. The technique is well thought out, with the information and value components nicely integrated. It is the only investment opportunity identification technique to do so.

Strategic Value Analysis (SVA) starts by listing the business objectives of the company and allocates a percentage score to them according to their perceived importance. These objectives need to support the CSFs. An example of the matching could be an objective that the company is to obtain 30% share of the marketplace. (In the Information Engineering method a goal is an objective with a time limit, such as to obtain 30% market share within two years). The CSF of this could be more loosely worded, such as

---

[2] Curtice, R. M. (1985). *Strategic Value Analysis*, Prentice Hall.

"The customer perception of our products and services is such that the customers purchasing the same products and services feel inclined to purchase from us again". Given the definition of a CSF, customer perception is the all important factor—all other issues are irrelevant. Efficient marketing, production and distribution are all wasted if there is no customer perception of satisfaction. If the customers do not perceive the product or service as meritorious then the purchases will not be made. *CSFs are therefore within objectives.*

The objectives and their importance score for a food manufacturing company could be:

- Improve customer response—45%;
- Maintain product quality—20%;
- Improve cost position—15%;
- Increase share of the food processing market—15%;
- Exploit applications knowledge—10%.

These high level business objectives are then decomposed into their functional parts. The objective of improving customer response can be decomposed into two parts—designing products and marketing products, with a score of 35% and 65% allocated to them. The design of products can then be decomposed into reducing food processing and design lead times, with respective scores of 35% and 15%. This total score at level 2 is within the score of 45% at the top level 1. The task of decomposing the processes continues to the event level of the individual business requirements, because it is at this event/business requirement level that the computer systems operate. Each of the processes at each level of decomposition is allocated a percentage score within the score of the higher level of decomposition.

The technique for decomposing the business objectives into their constituent business processes is the standard dataflow diagramming technique. Thus a beneficial by-product of this technique, designed as it was for identifying the investment opportunities of IT, in that it also includes the information modelling component of an ISS. Not only can the structure of the dynamic flow of the data around a business be modelled but the dataflow diagrams can easily be used as the source of the information to build a static structure of the company's data in the form of a logical data model.

Once the business requirements have been identified the capabilities of potential technical solutions are assessed and matched against the business requirements they can support—and so on up the decomposition model. Figure 2.4 is a simplified example of the model. The proposed computer system is a Computer Aided Design (CAD) package, which has the capability of getting 10 out of 10 in supporting the requirements for supporting

Table 2.4 Strategic value analysis (SVA)

System	Score	Cost £	"Score" per £000
** Vendor database	Prerequisite	140 000	—
Computer aided design	*(77 100)	90 000	857
Computer aided engineering	180 000	80 000	2250
Food flow model package	165 000	45 000	3666
Client-server technology	13 000	140 000	93
Accounts receivable	18 500	4500	4111

* $(10 \times 35 \times 2 \times 45) + (10 \times 15 \times 4 \times 45) + (10 \times 15 \times 4 \times 15)$
$+ (8 \times 10 \times 4 \times 15) = 77 100$
** mission critical, so suggest do not bother with IA on the benefits side

the reduction of the food processing and design lead times, but only 8 out of 10 for lowering the industrial costs. And so on up the model.

The next step is to put the scores of the IT capabilities against the business objectives on a financial footing. This is done in Table 2.4. The score of 77 100 for the CAD system is the compound result of all the scores up the hierarchy of Figure 2.4. Notice that there is no score for the vendor database as the database is a prerequisite, being the repository on which the corporate data is to be held. The "hassle" of applying SVA for this technical *sine qua non* would be wasted. The application with the highest score in this example would be developed first after the prerequisite systems, this being the Computer Aided Engineering (CAE) package, with a score of 180 000. However, when the costs of the system are taken into account a different

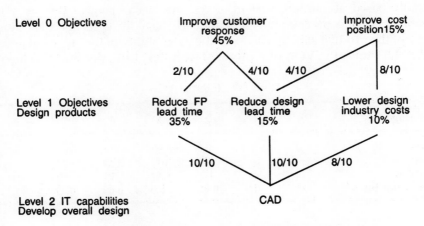

Figure 2.4 Strategic Value Analysis (SVA)

picture emerges. (Unfortunately the technique does not consider the income from the benefits of the system.) The score per £000 costs shows that the system with the highest score is not the CAE package but the "food flow model" package. On the basis of "£ buck per capability bang" go for this package first, followed by humble "accounts receivable". This has a high value score because, although it is not very useful for satisfying the company's business objectives, indeed, it has the lowest score for this measure, the computer system is a cheap application package. It is a good value for money purchase. The CAE solution comes some way down the list of applications to be developed, even though it is best at satisfying the business objectives. The problem is that it is rather expensive.

2.4.2.4 Value Chain Analysis

Value chains are a concept developed by Michael Porter and described in his book "Competitive Advantage".[3] The concept recognises the added value given to a product as it goes through each stage of the production process. This staged monitoring of the production process means that the Value Chain Analysis (VCA) technique is also based on the concept of time. It is the only time based technique in module 1 of the IA method and as such it is difficult to integrate its findings with the other techniques, which are not time based. Which stage of the production process do you use for investment opportunity identification? The great strength of VCA is that it is the only technique of investment identification and planning that is based solely on monetary values and is therefore doubly useful for the value component of investment strategy planning.

The purpose of VCA is to ascertain the profit and loss of producing a product at each stage of the production process. As such it requires a functionally based accounting system, given that each stage of the life production cycle is a process/function. For each stage the costs and the selling price of the product are recorded and the profitability of the stage obtained. Table 2.5 shows the VCA of a product, with the "bang per buck" value of

Table 2.5 Internal VCA

Life stages	1	2	3	4	5
Price	1	40	50	130	200
Cost	10	25	100	120	150
Net value	−9	15	−50	10	50
"Bang per buck"	**−0.9**	**0.66**	**−0.5**	**0.08**	**0.33**

[3] Macmillan, 1985.

the profitability of each stage of production—this being the net value divided by the costs. The figure shows that for £1 invested in stage 2 the product can be sold for £1.66.

The interpretation of the results of the exercise is simple. If it is a case of merely obtaining the biggest return per £ invested then sell the product in stage 2 of the production life cycle. Computer systems require to be developed only to support up to stage 2 of the production life cycle.

But there are other factors in the interpretation process than merely the "bang per buck" and the associated computer systems. For example, if a product being manufactured/produced is sold in a stage earlier than stage 5 then the product is not in a completed state. As such it cannot be sold to the general public—the largest market of all and the one that obtains public profile for the company. One of the ways of marketing goods and services is to be in the public eye—remember the saying "out of sight out of mind". There is therefore a hidden cost in selling a product prior to its being finished.

Then there is the volume of monies involved. Stage one of the internal value chain shows a very substantial loss on a ratio of the monies input and the monies obtained. But the issue is not serious. The monies involved on both price and costs side are small—so why bother? It is much more serious in stage 3 where there is a much smaller loss on the price/cost ratio but the absolute volumes of money are much larger. One should concentrate more on stage 3 than on stage 1—yet at first glance the message from the VCA figures is the other way around.

But assessing the value chain in Table 2.5, useful though it is, is not enough. It is an internal value chain and therefore does not consider whether you are efficient in comparison with the market. The full value of the technique can only be realised when the company product/service value chain is compared with the competitors'. This is the purpose of Table 2.6. It shows that the company is not doing well at all in any of the stages. It is very clear that the biggest problem is at stages 2, 4 and 5, where the returns for each £1 invested are only one third of the competitors'. This is a very different message from the assessment of the internal value chain analysis, where the message is pretty much the exact opposite, sell at stages 2 and 5. In this example very different solutions and computer systems would have been developed depending on whether the VCA was applied only to internal information or compared with external information.

The major problem with external VCA is obtaining accurate information about competitors, given the sensitive nature of company information. The problem is particularly acute in the UK, where the laws regarding publicly available information are limited. In the US the law requires much more information to be made public. One of the less reputable ways of gathering the information is to recruit persons who are working in the production

Table 2.6 VCA (external comparison)

Life stages		1	2	3	4	5
Internal VCA	Price	1	40	50	130	200
	Cost	10	25	100	120	150
	Net value	−9	15	−50	10	50
	"Bang per bang"	**−0.9**	**0.66**	**−0.5**	**0.08**	**0.33**
Competitor 1	Price	2	45	60	150	270
	Cost	9	20	90	100	130
	Net value	−7	25	−30	50	140
	"Bang per buck"	**−0.7**	**1.25**	**−0.33**	**0.5**	**1.07**
Competitor 2	Price	1	40	50	130	250
	Cost	7	15	80	90	120
	Net value	−6	25	−30	40	130
	"Bang per buck"	**−0.7**	**1.66**	**−0.35**	**0.44**	**1.08**

process of competitive organisations and obtain from them the information about production costs and practices that is proper. This practice is not unknown.

The structure of stage 1 of the method shows that the VCA technique produces a "dead end" product, which is not then used as the input into another product as one would wish with an integrated structured method. As explained, VCA is based on the concept of time and is therefore not possible to integrate with the other non-timed techniques of this stage. It is advised that the findings of the product be considered on the lines described above and the judgement included with the findings of the application scorings technique that brings the other products together—see section 2.2.2.7—and come to a combined judgement of which applications require to be developed in which order.

If it is considered essential to integrate the findings of VCA with the other stage 1 products the best that can be achieved is to take one stage, and thereby take out the aspect of time, and include the result of the stage in the bringing together of the products in the application scorings technique. It is suggested that the stage most requiring the development of computer systems be the selected stage.

2.4.2.5 The Boston Matrix

The name Boston Matrix reflects the origins of the technique, that is the Boston Consultancy Group. This technique is also known as the Portfolio Matrix.

The purpose of the technique is to model the ability of an application to earn revenues for a company both now and in the future. A matrix, as in Figure 2.5, is produced. If a product/service can provide high revenue both now and in the future it is classified as a "star"—the opposite of this being a "dead dog".

The normal life of a product/service is that it starts out as a somewhat experimental "wild cat", earning little current revenue but with potential in the future. It becomes established as "star" with current and long term revenue earning potential. In due time it becomes dated, but continues to earn good current revenues as a "cash cow", and finally dies a death as a "dead dog". The trick is to prolong the life while it is a "star" and to reinvigorate it while it is a "cash cow". The perfect example of this was the Beetle car from Volkswagen, which was constantly being upgraded. Its life in the "star"/"cash cow" categories was astonishingly long.

The purpose of the technique in the context of computer systems is to assess where investment IT can assist in the process of prolongation and reinvigoration.

Before a potential application can be allocated to a square in the matrix it is necessary to do some CBA. The application cannot be allocated to a square until the revenues to be obtained both now and at some future point

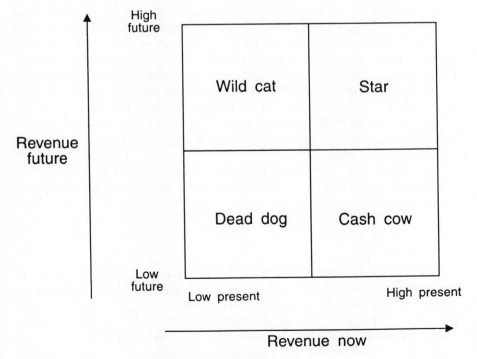

Figure 2.5   Boston Matrix

in time are ascertained. A formula relating the ratio of the revenues to the costs and a weighting to the "wild cat", "star", "cash cow" and "dead dog" categories needs to be constructed before the results of CBA can be allocated to the Boston Matrix. A suggested formula could be:

Ratio E : R		Weighting
1 : < 1	dead dog	1
1 : 1–3	wild cat	2
1 : 3–5	cash cow	6
1 : > 5	star	10

The formula can be anywhere between risk averse and risk taking towards investing in computer systems. The above formula is towards risk taking in that the weightings are more spread out than the ratios of the expenditure to the revenue. The weightings encourage investment.

The Boston Matrix as described above is not an impressive technique. There is no information component and the value results are crude and require much work to obtain. Each of the applications requires two CBAs, one for the current revenue versus costs and one for the future revenue versus costs. And the only thing that the matrix displays is the placement of the application in a box on the matrix—a pictographic representation of the CBA results. The results are crude in that no relationships are established between the applications other than their placement in the matrix. There is no consideration, for example, as to whether the life span of an application in the "cash cow" box is longer and therefore more valuable than a possible "flash in the pan" type application in the "star" category. Neither is the size of the revenue assessed, merely a ratio. As seen for the value chain, the single basis of measure, a ratio, is not the total view to take on an investment.

None of the other techniques are limited to a single unit of measure. The Boston Matrix is the most vulnerable of all the techniques in module 1 of the IA method.

2.4.2.6 IT Leverage

This technique has been developed by D. Hyland, formerly of Ernst & Young. What is described here is a slightly modified version, as the article describing the technique leaves certain tasks and products not fully explained. It has also proved necessary to make some modifications to enable the results of the technique to be merged with the other techniques in the application scoring product. The technique is based on answering three questions:

(1) Is the company getting value for money from the IT systems?
(2) Is the IT being applied to maximum effect?
(3) Is IT providing competitive advantage?

In short, is IT providing business leverage?

The technique was designed to function on the value chain concept described earlier. The technique therefore:

- Identifies the processes;
- Determines the current and potential added value within each process;
- Identifies the IT support actually given and that which could be given to the process;
- Identifies the costs of each of the IT systems.

It is thus possible to compare the applicability of the support with the costs of provision and arrive at answers to the questions posed.

The technique uses a management voting mechanism on a paired comparison of all the processes, the voting question being "If you had to invest in only one of this pair of processes, which would give the best leverage to the business?". The answer to the question is judgemental. The result is a process ranking of the potential added value the processes provided. A similar ranking is also obtained in relation to the views of the suppliers and the customers, so as to ascertain competitive advantage. The suppliers' and buyers' views remove any internal bias from the earlier exercise.

The steps of the techniques are:

(1) Identify the processes; this is based on the functional decomposition approach as used in Information Engineering.
(2) Assess the business impact of the processes; this is based on the paired ranking of the processes.
(3) Map the current IT systems to the processes; this is achieved by a questionnaire to the user and the IT manager regarding the:
    - Support intended for each process by the system;
    - Effectiveneess of the system in providing the intended support;
    - Running costs of the system.
(4) Model the results; the results of the above are modelled on the basis of:
    - Business impact of each system;
    - Intended support provided by each system;
    - Actual system support for each process;
    - Running costs of support for each process.
(5) The results—the assessment of IT on the company; this is based on, for each system:
    - Business impact versus intended support;
    - Business impact versus actual support;
    - Business impact versus cost of support;

Table 2.7 Example of possible results using IT leverage

System	Business impact	Support	Actual running costs	Number of processes	Proposed action
A	High	High	High	5	Cost reduction
B	High	High	Low	3	None
C	High	Low	Low	3	Increased support
D	Low	Low	High	6	Cost reduction and increased support

- Actual support versus cost of support.

The results show which systems require enhancement and which areas of the business require additional support. The results are recorded as shown in Table 2.7.

The results of the modelling are plotted as shown in Figures 2.6 and 2.7. Only two out of four of the models are shown, those which show the most stark findings. These show the results of applying IT leverage for the individual applications. On the horizontal axis is the ranking of the processes

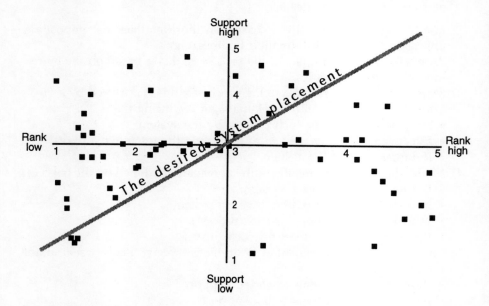

Figure 2.6 IT leverage—intended support by business impact

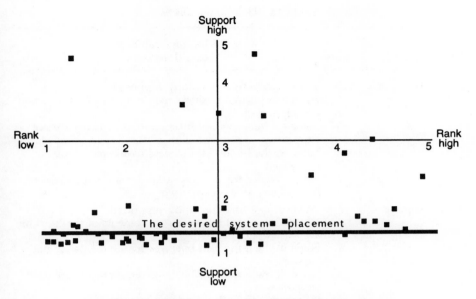

Figure 2.7 IT leverage—costs by business impact

according to their business leverage impact and on the vertical axis the degree of support and costs, each axis assessed on the basis of a score of 1–5. The classification of the boundaries between the categories of high and low on the vertical axis requires clarification, something not explained in the Hyland article describing the technique. A suggested approach is given in Table 2.8.

The models are easy to interpret. Consider Figure 2.6. One would wish to see a line of systems from the bottom left to the top right. The systems to the bottom right need corrective action—they reflect poor analysis of the user requirements, are functionally deficient and reflect missed oppor-tunities. The systems on the top left reflect wasted monies. By contrast, in Figure 2.7 the match of what one would wish to see and the evidence is satisfying. One could refine this and say that the systems providing low support should have lower costs than those providing higher support. It is nice to see that the systems with high costs are those providing the most business leverage. The system in the top left needs urgent consideration. It is not providing value for money.

The information in these figures shows the work that needs to be done to which computer system to meet the current cost and functional needs of the company. The IT leverage technique therefore has the advantages that:

- It supports both the investment identification planning and information modelling components of an ISS;

Table 2.8 IT leverage scores

The question	Score	IT leverage rankings Score description
Support intended	5	The business functions fully supported
	4	All the important business requirements of the function are supported
	3	Some of the important business requirements are not supported
	2	None of the important business requirements are supported
	1	Only some of the less important business requirements of the function are supported
Actual support	5	The business functions fully supported
	4	All the important business requirements of the function are supported
	3	Some of the important business requirements are not supported
	2	None of the important business requirements are supported
	1	Only some of the less important business requirements of the function are supported
Cost of support	1	The annual running costs are 10% of the development costs
	2	The annual running costs are 20% of the development costs
	3	The annual running costs are 30% of the development costs
	4	The annual running costs are 40% of the development costs
	5	The annual running costs are 50% of the development costs

- The four models provide management with an extremely effective over-view of both the problem and successful IT systems. The technique is able to show what proportion of the IT expenditure goes on high impact systems (well spent monies) and on low impact systems (monies badly spent). A plan of exploitive and corrective action can therefore be drawn up. IT leverage is well suited to the investment investigation module of the IA method. There is much to recommend the technique.

There are some problems which need consideration. To be fair, they are not significant and can easily be catered for. The value component is based only on the expenditure side. No attention is paid to the revenue that the computer systems produce for the company. There is therefore a danger that systems which have high costs but also produce high revenues may not be given a fair judgement—except in terms of business impact. Also, the information component is limited to the processes and not the data. In the context of the development of the technique, data was not a criteria at issue and is therefore sensibly not included; given the other techniques used in the investment investigation module this information omission is not serious.

The most serious problem is that the technique is backwards looking. The computer systems assessed are already in operation. The value of the method is therefore short term.

2.4.2.7 Application Scorings

This is a new technique specifically designed by the authors to overcome the main deficiencies of all the current methods for the identification of which application systems in which to invest. Those main deficiencies are:

(1) The current situation is that the techniques described in this chapter have all been developed in an uncoordinated manner by separate individuals. The products they produce are thus standalone, each addressing different aspects of investment identification and planning. The results they produce need to be merged so as to obtain an overall picture of those IT applications which will give the best value and information returns to a company.

(2) Some ISS methods, such as Information Engineering Information Strategy Planning, include techniques like requirements weighting and affinity analysis to create a corporate development plan for IT applications, but these techniques are based on the information component only. No attention is paid to whether the resultant computer systems add value to the company's profit and loss or how much that value will be. There is an implied "act of faith" in these information based prioritisation techniques on this issue.

Management should not have to consider the different results from a plethora of products but have a single overall view of all the information and what it means. The application scorings technique therefore brings together the findings of the products for the information and value components. It produces a single combined overview, on the basis of multiplying together the score of each business application considered worthy of investment by the previously described techniques. A very simple solution.

2.5 A WORKED EXAMPLE OF PLANNING INVESTMENT OPPORTUNITIES

The worked example is based on a container port authority concerned with the planning for and movement of containers. The example will apply each of the techniques described in section 2.2.2.

The common link between the techniques and their products is the applications systems for which the potential merits of investment are being assessed. These potential systems are based directly on the major functional business areas of the port. The functional areas were identified by the technique of dataflow diagramming that is used in SVA. They are vessel scheduling, yard planning, container movement, sales and marketing, finance and harbour maintenance. In most cases the titles of the functions are self-explanatory. Yard planning is the process of grouping the containers within the port (they have been unloaded but not yet loaded) in the optimum sequence according to the vessel, train, truck or barge they are to be loaded onto.

2.5.1 The CSFs

The CSFs for the port were:

(1) The perception by the shipping companies that the port provided fast and reliable turnaround of the vessels.

Shipping companies do not like a situation where a vessel is not moving and is not loaded with containers. A static vessel is one that cannot earn any revenue. The movement of the vessel therefore requires careful planning, so that in a typical journey where the vessel loads and unloads containers at a number of ports the vessel spends as little time in each port as possible. Any significant delay means that the schedule to other ports still to be visited is affected, with a possible chain effect of further delay.

Since a single vessel can be carrying several hundred containers, possibly all of which require unloading and another batch reloading, this is considerable business to the container port. Shipping companies' perceptions of the efficiency and reliability of the port are therefore important. There is little loyalty of the shipping companies to a port. It is very easy for the vessels to turn left or right and go another port and, if the service of the other port is impressive, to take their business to the other port. Turnaround time is a major component in this perception of efficiency.

(2) That the container port could provide more sophisticated vessel scheduling and vessel cargo redistribution facilities than the competitors.

A vessel may need to unload and reload many containers. This is a highly complicated task, particularly if there is a need to rearrange the allocation of the containers in the vessel cells when the suite of other container ports still to be visited has been altered. And the loading of the containers must be such that the integrity and buoyancy of the vessel are preserved. If the port could offer a first class service to the shipping companies, such that the shipping companies could have flexible sailing plans, the container port would be judged a success.

(3) The marketing of the port was to be assessed as professional by both the water-side customers and the landside customers.

Waterside customers constituted shipping companies and barge owners (the container port was at the estuary of a large river). Landside customers constituted truck and train operators.

(4) The scheduling of the trucks to be optimised towards trucking companies with large fleets.

Trucking companies have a similar business importance as the shipping companies, and, although the loading and unloading of containers is a much simpler task with trucks than with vessels, the scheduling is likewise a complicated process. This has to be judged as a success by the trucking companies.

(5) The number of container movements from the unloading of a container to the loading of a container to be reduced from seven to five.

The only charges that can be made on the container movement companies are for the loading and unloading of containers. Any movement of containers within the port are burdens to be carried by the port itself.

These CSFs all meet the requirements of a CSF, that is they had to be obtainable, measurable and within one's control. To be measurable, numbers have to be defined and allocated to the CSFs.

In the Information Systems Planning phase of the Information Engineering structured method the CSFs are defined as "a factor that has a major influence on whether the enterprise will achieve an objective or goal", an objective as "a broad long term result that the enterprise wishes to achieve to support its mission" and a goal as "a specific target the enterprise wishes to achieve at a specific point in time".[4] The numbers are allocated to the goals rather than to the CSFs.

---

[4] *The Information Strategy Planning Handbook.* James Martin Associates Ltd, 1987.

The results of the technique are shown in Table 2.9. Each of the CSFs are given an importance percentage, with three persons of similar grades assessing the ability of the major business functions of the port to support the CSFs. An average of the assessments was produced and multiplied by the percentage score and added up on the horizontal and vertical axes. The results are then interpreted.

Table 2.9 shows that the yard planning and vessel scheduling business functions score very highly, yard planning with a higher score on the basis that it functionally precedes vessel scheduling. The intangible benefit of customer service (fast and reliable turnaround) wins as far as the CSFs are concerned; the reduction in container movements is of equal importance as excessive container movements represent wasted effort and therefore substantial cost to the port. The message is clear—go for the short term investment and develop the yard planning and vessel scheduling systems first. Not only are the most important of the customer service benefits obtained but the two applications also support all the other CSFs, and with high assessment ratings. Many birds (the CSFs) can be killed with two stones (the application systems).

Given that the short term investment approach (the horizontal view of the CSF matrix) is to be used, the scores for the application systems (the horizontal axis scores) are added to the Container Port Application Scoring Matrix.

2.5.2 SVA

The SVA technique was applied and produced the results shown in Figure 2.8 and Table 2.10. The business objectives relate to the CSFs and were defined as:

- To be able to satisfy 95% of the vessel turnaround requests from the shipping companies when their vessel visits are planned;
- To ensure that 95% of the vessels depart on the date and tide agreed in the original vessel schedule;
- The vessel container scheduling to be able to calculate the optimum unloading and loading sequences, taking into account the other ports to be visited by the vessel and the integrity and buoyancy of the vessel;
- The trucking scheduling to be able to schedule the loading and unloading of containers for fleet operators; (Note that no numbers are included in the definition of the above two objectives. This is because the answer to the objective is a yes or no situation. The objective is or is not achieved—there are no degrees of achievement).
- To reduce the number of container movements within the port from a vessel unload to a vessel load from seven to five.

Table 2.9   Container port CSFs

Function/CSF	Fast service (16%)	Reliable service (16%)	Vessel scheduling (16%)	Cargo distribution (10%)	Marketing (15%)	Fleet truck scheduling (10%)	Reduce container movements (17%)	Score
Vessel scheduling	8,8,10	8,8,8	8,8,10	6,6,4			2,4,2	5.02
Yard planning	6,8,10	6,8,10	4,4,6			6,6,4	10,10,10	5.52
Container movement	2,6,4	2,6,6					6,8,8	2.62
Sales and marketing					8,8,8			1.2
Finance system								Prerequisite
Harbour maintenance	2,2,2	2,2,2						0.64
	3.62	3.62	2.12	0.52	1.2	0.52	3.4	7.82

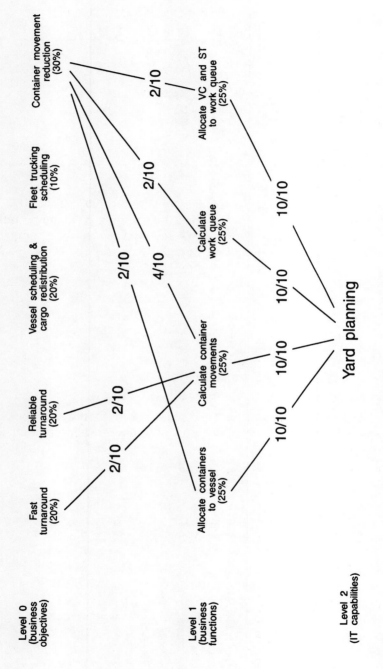

Figure 2.8 Container port SVA—IT capability to objectives

Table 2.10   Container port SVA scores

System	Score	Cost £	"Score" per £000
Yard planning	95 000*	170 000	559
Vessel scheduling	72 500	350 000	207
Sales and marketing	45 000	80 000	562
Harbour maintenance	8000	60 000	133
Finance system	62 000	120 000	517
Container movement	68 000	250 000	272

* $(10 \times 25 \times 2 \times 30) + (10 \times 25 \times 2\ 20) + (10 \times 25 \times 2 \times 20) +$
$(10 \times 25 \times 4 \times 30) + (10 \times 25 \times 2 \times 30) + (10 \times 25 \times 2 \times 30) = 95\,000$

The objectives were given a percentage weighting of 20%, 20%, 20%, 10% and 30%. The 60% allocated to "pleasing the shipping companies" reflects their tremendous buying power as compared with the trucking companies. There are few shipping companies compared with the number of trucking companies. The significant 30% for the reduction of internal container movement reflects that any internal movement is not revenue earning.

The standard dataflow diagrams were produced and the processes decomposed from the high level, business objective level processes, to the function processes level, to the event/business requirement level. The functional areas were identified and an assessment made of the type of system that could support their processes. The functional areas were those mentioned earlier. It was decided that the following computer systems would be most appropriate:

- Vessel scheduling, yard planning, container movement—a bespoke solution with a graphics package (to show in realtime where the individual containers are located in a vessel or a "ground spot" in the port);
- Finance and sales and marketing—a package solution;
- Harbour maintenance—a bespoke solution.

The ability of the computer systems to support the functions and the functions the business objectives is then mapped, one map being produced for each system. The yard planning "map" is illustrated in Figure 2.8. It shows, as one would expect with a bespoke system, that the business functions are able to support the business objectives, in this case the reduction in the container movements within the container port between the unloading and loading of a vessel. As regards the measured ability of the system to support the functions for which it is designed, it can be seen that it gets 10/10 for each function. The capability of the functions to support the other business objectives is less complete, again as one would expect. A single function by itself is not likely to support a broad business objective. The 2/10

represents the ability of the functional process "calculate container movement" to support the processing required of the business objective "fast
turnaround". It can be seen that all the functions of the yard planning system are able to support the business objective of reducing the container
movements in the port, together producing a score of 10/10. The function
"calculate container movement" is also relevant to the business objective
of "fast and reliable turnarounds". The function is judged to be relevant to
2/10ths of the processing for the turnaround objective.

The scoring is calculated as follows. Yard planning is able to get 10 out
of 10 in the support for the four functions in Figure 2.8. The functions are
able to support in part three business objectives, with one of the objectives
(container movement reduction) supported in full by all the functions. Each
path of support from the business functions to the business objectives needs
to be calculated, working back to the systems that support the functions.
Thus for yard planning the path to the function "allocate containers to vessel" gets a value of 10, the function has an importance weighting of 25%,
and is able to support the business objective "container movement
reduction" with a score of 2 out of 10, and the business objective has an
importance weighting of 30%. The formula for this can be seen in the bottom of Table 2.10. The same calculation is done for each of the paths from
yard planning—and there is a bracketed formula of all the paths in Table
2.10. The total of the formulae for yard planning is 95 000 points.

The same exercise is applied for each of the functional areas of the port
authority's business. Their scores are shown in Table 2.10. From these scores
it can be seen that yard planning, sales and marketing and the finance
systems are rated the highest. This is a very different picture from that
drawn by the CSFs technique. The reason for this is partly the fact that the
scores are based on the financial costs (note there is no consideration of the
business benefits to be gained from the systems) of the applications as well
as the ability of the application systems to support the business functions
and objectives. The scores therefore reflect "£ buck for a capability bang"
and not just critical business need.

The scores for the application systems are added to the container port
application scoring matrix.

2.5.3 Value Chain Analysis

Value chain analysis was not a very relevant technique to the port. The
only added value in the port operations is the unloading and the loading
of the containers and, although there can be several movements of the containers within the port, and therefore several stages in the "production life"
of the containers, there is no return to the port. If one applied the technique

Table 2.11 Container port VCA

Life stages	Unload container	Container movement 1	Container movement 2	Container movement 3	Container movement 4	Load container
Price	100	—	—	—	—	200
Cost	70	20	20	20	20	70
Net value	30	—	—	—	—	150
"Bang per buck"	0.42	—	—	—	—	2.14

one would have the strange situation illustrated in Table 2.11, where there is no "bang per buck" for a stage.

2.5.4 The Boston Matrix

The Boston Matrix for the container port/application systems is shown in Figure 2.9.

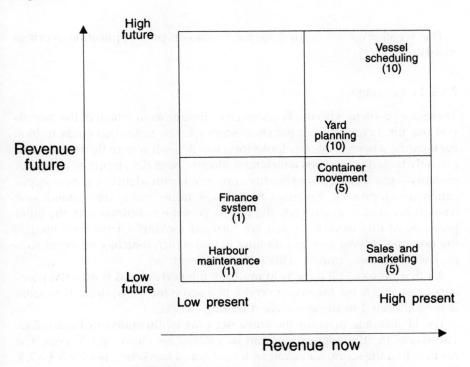

Figure 2.9 Container port Boston Matrix

CBA for the functional areas was as detailed in Table 2.12. The weightings added to the applications were therefore, 1, 1, 2, 2, 10, 10 on the basis that if the short and long term costs to revenues/benefits ratio is less than 1 the weighting is 1, the ratio between 1 and 3 the weighting is 2, and the ratio is more than 5 the weighting is 10.

Table 2.12 Container port CBA for the functional areas

	Current/future costs	Current/future benefits	Current/future C/B ratio
Finance system	£120 000	£40 000	1:0.33
Harbour maintenance	£60 000	£50 000	1:0.83
Sales and marketing	£80 000	£150 000	1:1.87
Container movement	£250 000	£320 000	1:1.28
Yard planning	£170 000	£1.2 m.	1:7.05
Vessel scheduling	£350 000	£2.45 m.	1:7

The weightings are added to the container port application scorings matrix.

2.5.5 IT Leverage

There is a problem with the IT leverage technique as to which of the models you use for inclusion in application scorings. The technique tends to look backwards, whereas strategy looks forward. By their nature the four models can only include processes which have already been developed as computer systems—and strategy is primarily concerned with identifying new application developments. Excellent though the technique is on a standalone basis, it is not easy to integrate the products of the technique with the other products of this module, which are forward looking. Of the four models the one that is most forward looking is that which matches intended support with business impact. This is the one used.

All that needs to be done is to multiply the vertical and horizontal numbers of each process together to come to a score for the system. This score is then allocated to the application scoring matrix.

The IT leverage map for the container port is illustrated in Figure 2.10. The scores for the applications can be plotted on the X and Y axes. The result is that the score, for example, for sales and marketing is $1.7 \times 3.4 = 7.5$. The scores are added to the container port application scorings matrix.

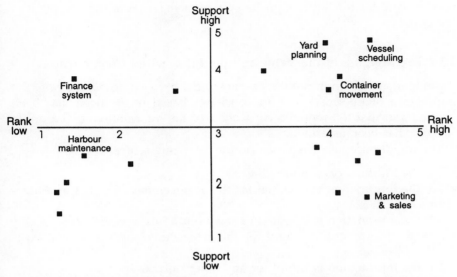

Figure 2.10 Container port IT leverage—intended support by business impact

2.5.6 The Container Port Application Scoring Matrix

The container port application scoring matrix is now ready for construction. It is a simple process of multiplying the application scores together to come to a combined "statement of opportunity value". The result is illustrated in Table 2.13. The total scores show that the yard planning is handsomely the "winner" with the vessel scheduling application also comfortably ahead of the other applications. The finance system is not given a score because there was no score for the application in the CSF technique. It does not

Table 2.13 Container port application scoring matrix

System	Combined "statement of opportunity value" CSF score × SVA score × IT leverage score × Boston Matrix score	Total score
Finance		Prerequisite
Harbour maintenance	$0.64 \times 133 \times 3.75 \times 1$	319
Yard planning	$5.52 \times 559 \times 19 \times 10$	586 279
Container movement	$2.62 \times 272 \times 16.4 \times 5$	58 436
Sales and marketing	$1.2 \times 5.62 \times 7.5 \times 5$	25 290
Vessel scheduling	$5.02 \times 207 \times 21.6 \times 10$	224 454

need a score for it is a prerequisite system, being vital to the operation of the port.

2.5.7 The Merging of the Value and the Information Components

Assume that the Information Engineering approach to identifying the importance of information to the business, based on its need, has been applied and that the requirement weight of the information, based on its support, has been ascertained.

The importance factor is based on the following scores:

- 5 if the information supports a CSF;
- 4 if the information is essential for the achievement of a goal or a business objective;
- 3 if the information is essential to carry out a business activity;
- 2 if the information is useful for the achievement of a goal or a business objective;
- 1 if the information is useful for any other purpose.

The satisfaction rating is based on the following scores:

- 1 if the information need is fully supported by the current systems;
- 2 if the information need is moderately supported by the current systems;
- 3 if the information need is poorly supported by the current systems;
- 4 if the information need is not supported by the current systems.

The requirement weight is the multiplication of the information need and the satisfaction rating.

The importance factor for the finance system was 3 in that it supported business activities only, with no support for critical functions and objectives of the container port. Its satisfaction rating was 2. The importance factor of harbour maintenance was 1 and the satisfaction rating was 4. Scores for sales and marketing were 4 (no CSFs were supported) and 3. The import-

Table 2.14   Container port requirement weightings

The information need	The importance factor	The satisfaction rating	The requirement weight
Finance system	3	2	6
Harbour maintenance	1	4	4
Sales and marketing	4	3	12
Container movement	5	2	10
Yard planning	5	4	20
Vessel scheduling	5	3	15

ance factors of the last three systems were crucial in that CSFs were supported in abundance while the satisfaction rating varied from good to adequate support. The requirement weightings results are shown in Table 2.14.

All that requires to be done now is to multiply the requirement weightings by the opportunity scores to produce the final portfolio result, a result that matches the investment potential with the business benefit to be gained from the information contained in the computer application system. The value and information components of investment identification and planning are now achieved. The final scores are shown in Table 2.15.

The leading applications to be selected on the basis of the above scores are clearly yard planning and vessel scheduling, followed by container movement. This nicely matches the business situation, where the moving of containers requires the scheduling of the vessels and the scheduling of the vessels impacts on the yard planning process.

2.6 CHAPTER SUMMARY

There is a large number of techniques that can be used for identifying IT projects that are likely to give benefit to a company. Most can be integrated to give added value to results they each produce.

One of the techniques, value chain analysis, cannot be integrated. The reason for this is that it is based on the concept of time, with the financial returns for each stage of the value chain varying over time. All the other techniques produce a unit of measure of the benefit to be gained from investing in the project at a single point in time.

Some of the other techniques are judged not to be worth the effort expended. The main culprit here is the Boston Matrix/portfolio approach. This requires all the projects being considered for investment to undergo CBA, the results of which are plotted in a matrix to show current cash flow and future cash flow. The information contained in the matrix is merely a

Table 2.15 Container port final scores

Application	Opportunity score	Requirement weight	Total score
Finance system	Prerequisite	6	0
Harbour maintenance	319	4	1276
Yard planning	586 279	12	7.07 m.
Container movement	58 436	10	584 436
Sales and marketing	25 290	20	505 800
Vessel scheduling	224 454	15	3.36 m.

pictorial representation of the project cash flows—there is nothing new and the effort required to produce this matrix is enormous.

Much the best technique to use is SVA. This combines both the information and the value components.

Much the most important technique, however, is the CSF technique. It is not often realised that computer systems have no value unless they retrieve information and present that information in a way that is meaningful to the user of the system. It is the data retrieval business requirements that add value to a computer system, not the business requirements that put data into the system. Such data maintenance business requirements are necessary, but they add no value. CSFs are the ultimate data retrieval business requirement in that they identify the information that the company needs to ensure that it is in a good state of commercial health. At the end of the day all the information in a computer system needs to be based on the CSFs.

All the techniques used for the identification of investment opportunities use a scoring mechanism of some kind. In order to gain an overall picture of the benefits the projects can give to a company it is necessary to combine the scores of the techniques together. This is done with the application scoring technique. This technique combines the scores for the value and information components for each application system considered. This produces a single total scoring of projects to be invested in, the higher the score the greater the likely long term benefit of investing in the project.

Chapter 3

Investment Measurement I

This chapter goes to the heart of the techniques for measuring the value of investing in projects. It describes the first of the techniques, and much the most important of the techniques, for the correct valuation of investment monies. The technique is discounting.

The chapter shows how the two formulae that go into discounting are calculated, these formulae being the "expected return formula" and the "net present value formula". The need for the net present value formula has long been understood and applied by the CBA approach to the valuation of investments. It is only more recently that the expected return formula has been well understood and is now being applied in CBA. The major difficulty has been how to calculate the discount rate to offset inflation, opportunities to earn interest, and the risks of the investment. This is now much better understood.

Discounting is applicable to the risks of investing in the market, in a company and in a project. It is not applicable to the risks of unanticipated events that can affect a project during its life or to offsetting the event risks by flexibility. These require a different approach and are discussed in Chapter 5.

3.1 THE DISAPPOINTMENT WITH CBA

CBA techniques are concerned with the measurement of cash flows into and out of a company or a specific project. Projects are the lowest level of cash flow measurement, the company cash flows being the summation of the individual project cash flows in appropriate combinations.

The reason that markets, industry types and companies are not considered in CBA techniques is that one, from a project perspective, does not invest in markets, industry types and companies; as far as CBA is concerned one invests in projects. This book will show that this view of the investment world is too "parochial". The project invested in is actually within a company, which itself functions in a particular type of industry, which in turn operates within a market. Each offers opportunities for alternative investment. The precise reasons for putting a project in the context of a company, industry type and market will be explained later—suffice it to say at this stage that these more general considerations of investment affect the discount rate to be applied to the project monies. The riskiness of the market, the industry and company affect the discount rate to be applied to the investment monies in the project. One could also invest in the shares of the company, any company, rather than in the project, one could invest in the shares of companies of a similar industry type or one could spread one's investment across a portfolio of companies operating in a variety of industries, this being investment at the market level. These alternatives need to be known and measured so as to ensure that investing in a computer system project offers the best investment opportunity.

The taking of a "parochial" project view of the world, a view that ignores the alternative investments and outside influences that affect that value of a project, puts the accurate measurement of the true value of a project investment at risk. This book also operates at the project level, but puts the project in the context of the company making the investment and its industry type, all within the context of the national market. (This book does not attempt to consider the techniques for measuring the cash flows of international projects).

The result of the valuation of a project may challenge the results of the investment investigation module of the IA method. The investment plans from the investment investigation module are based on a set of points-scoring based techniques with a modicum of speculatively estimated costs—considerably better than nothing but still vulnerable to detailed financial analysis. The detailed financial analysis is what happens in the investment measurement module. The much more accurately measured project monies will often challenge the estimated project points.

An example of this is illustrated in Figure 3.1. The situation arose within a public service sector organisation in the UK, where there was little or no liaison between the business strategists and those concerned with the public purse. Thirty-seven projects were accepted for development on the basis that they were relevant to the business objectives of the organisation and were included in the ISS. Over the same time period 24 projects were accepted and developed on the basis that they would yield a net present value profit on the basis of discounted monies. Notwithstanding all this careful analysis, satisfaction with the benefits obtained from the IT systems

Example: Projects in a public sector organisation

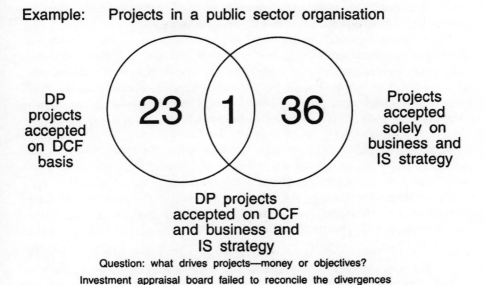

Figure 3.1   Relevance of DCF

was not high—either they were providing the users with what they wanted but were not adding much to the bottom line of the organisation's profits or they were adding to the bottom line but were not being much used by the users. It was only when the two sets of projects were examined in relation to one another that it was ascertained that only one project provided a significant profit as well as supporting the business objectives. It was not surprising that the organisation was dissatisfied with the financial value obtained from 36 of its DP systems and the business benefit obtained from 23 DP systems. This sorry state of affairs was solely due to the fact that the two departments did not liaise with each other. The solution was a simple matter of better coordination, thus enabling the IA results to challenge the strategic investment plans.

What was needed was to use the results of the techniques of investment opportunity identification as described in the previous chapter, then to value the projects using the techniques to be described in this and the next chapters, and finally to relate the business value and the financial value together in order to reach a judgement as to the best projects to invest in. If one merely measured projects on the basis of the largest net present value profit, one would choose the 24 projects in Figure 3.1. If one chose projects solely on the likely business benefit, the 37 projects would be chosen. What is really required is a judgement in matching the projects with the highest net present value and the projects with the highest points scoring from the business benefit viewpoint. The investment in IT projects would then be on the basis of the overall profit/business benefit.

The value of a project is measured in terms of net cash. Net cash is the difference between cash flow in and cash flow out, the cash flows in hopefully exceeding the cash flows out. The costs are seen as flows of cash out of the project or negative cash flows, whilst benefits are seen as flows of cash into the project or positive cash flows. The costs and benefits of projects are thus estimated as a series of cash outflows and inflows period by period, usually at yearly intervals, over the life of a project.

There are many CBA techniques for measuring the cash flow and the resultant financial return of an investment. The techniques have been widely applied for many years and are well understood, tried and tested.

Nevertheless accounting professionals have long expressed their dissatisfaction at the consistent failure to capture adequately the full and true worth of a project. The main problems are due to the following facts:

- there are too many techniques, with the inevitable result that they overlap in what they are trying to measure and, worse, in some cases conflict in that they provide different results (and therefore messages for investment making decisions) from the same financial information;

  Figure 1.1 shows the many cases of overlap in what the techniques measure. Examples of conflict can be obtained from a number of sources. One example is that if non-discounted techniques are applied projects may well be shown to be profitable, whereas if the cash flows are discounted to offset inflation and risk during the life of the project then the project may well be unprofitable. An example of this is given in sections 3.3 and 3.4.1, where the non-discounted value of the project is a profit of £1000 and the discounted loss is –£27.

- some of the techniques do not adequately account for inflation and the riskiness of the investment;

  This is particularly true of the non-discounted techniques.

- the techniques have not been integrated to provide added value to each other. The techniques are applied and interpreted in a standalone manner, so that the different information they contain and provide cannot be used to construct a coherent and comprehensive "picture" of a project investment. The output from the non-discounted technique of the payback period technique is not used as an input to any other technique. The payback period technique is standalone, its value isolated.

A structured method of financial measurement is missing.

But the most serious failing of all is not to do something in a deficient manner, as in the above, that's bad enough, but not to attempt to do anything at all regarding an aspect that is important to the valuation equation:

- CBA techniques have been reduced in usefulness because of the failure to measure the monetary value of the intangible benefits of certain investments, or to measure event risk and flexibility. The seriousness of this is based on the fact that a large and increasing portion of the benefits from computing are intangible, as will be seen in section 6.1.1.

This is a long list of serious deficiencies.

Yet the CBA techniques are, and will continue to be, used widely. Some writers on accounting techniques and practices, such as Hodder and Riggs,[1] claim that the fault lies not so much in the techniques themselves but in their misuse. These writers consider that the non-discounted cash flow techniques can give meaningful results, the fault lying with *"Homo sapiens"* that uses them. As will be shown later in this chapter and in Chapter 4 the complaint has some justification.

Both the wide usage and the considered view of such knowledgeable persons show that there is life in CBA techniques. They just need improvement. To this end, this chapter is about describing the discounted techniques, explaining their proper uses, how the techniques can be integrated and therefore add value to each other, and how to avoid the pitfalls that have given some of the techniques a "bad name". If certain rules and good practices are followed then the techniques can yield useful and meaningful results, and become a valued part of the IA process. The CBA discounted techniques are therefore put into context for the full and proper valuation of an investment.

This chapter also shows the limitations of the non-discounted techniques, and therefore also describes the circumstances where and when other discounted techniques are required. CBA techniques are classified into two categories: non-discounted cash flow and discounted cash flow.

3.2 THE NON-DISCOUNTED TECHNIQUES

There are three popularly used techniques for calculating the non-discounted value of a project:

(1) *The payback period (with net cash flow)*. This is the period of time for the benefits to exceed the costs. A decision has been made to buy a personal computer. The purchase cost of the PC plus extras comes to £5000, this

[1] J. Hodder and A. Riggs (1985). "Managing as if tomorrow matters", *Harvard Business Review*. Harvard University Press.

being modelled as a negative cash flow in year 0. ("Today" is often taken by convention as year zero. The next year is year 1.) Assume that the PC has a four year life and it is predicted that the use of the PC will yield real savings of £2000 after the year of installation, producing the following cash flow:

	Year 0	Year 1	Year 2	Year 3
Cash flow	−5000	+2000	+2000	+2000

From this simple analysis it can be seen that over the whole life of the project the net cash flow is +£1000, that is the benefits exceed the costs by £1000. This analysis can also be used to determine the time taken for the benefits to recoup the initial investment. In this case the PC pays for itself after 2.5 years, this period of time being known as the payback period.

(2) *Cost/benefit ratio*. This ratio is the ratio of benefits to costs (yes, the two are confusingly inverted, the title of the technique being "cost/benefit ratio" whereas, in fact, it is the other way around). Using the same figures as for the purchase of the PC, the ratio is 6/5, the £6000 of benefits to the £5000 of costs. Obviously, the higher the ratio of benefits to the costs the better the project.

(3) *Return on Investment*. Another popular measure is to calculate the Return on Investment (RoI), which is merely the sum of the benefits, divided by the costs and expressed as an annual percentage, as shown below:

$$\text{RoI} = 6000/(5000 \times 3 \text{ years}) \times 100 = 40\%$$

These three examples of the measurement of a project's value can be used for making decisions about selecting projects for investment. In one survey of the automotive components industry it was found that 40% of companies use the payback period results as the basis of making their investment decisions. This figure tends to rise in a time of recession, where it is under-standable that a rapid return is required. Investments must bring in a posi-tive cash flow in a short time, and for a short period of time inflation and risk are regarded as non-issues. In this context, so goes the argument, the weaknesses of the non-discounted approach can be discounted (no pun intended). The finance director of a major international airline that had been using a broad portfolio of IA techniques for the valuation of projects recently announced that all investments would until further notice be based on the payback period—back from the sophisticated IA valuation to the simplistic CBA approach.

However, these techniques suffer from a number of serious deficiencies.

First of all they produce radically different results from the same input information, the first producing a period of time, the second a ratio and the third a percentage. Which of the results should management use for the decision making process as regards an investment? The 'best' project for investment will depend upon the criteria chosen. For example, the project with the quickest payback may not be the project with the biggest return. A project may pay back £100 000 over two years but only have further benefits of £50 000. A second project may take four years to pay back its initial investment of £500 000 but yield benefits of £1 000 000 in the subsequent years. In this case the payback measure would be misleading. With the same financial input figures and the varying financial results, different projects may be selected by different managers depending on which of the techniques is preferred. Astonishing!

But more importantly these techniques do not discount cash flows to reflect their timings. Obviously a cash flow of £1m. in five years' time is worth less than a cash flow of £1m. today. Any technique which fails to recognise this will overstate the value of future costs and benefits. This is particularly important for investments in computer systems, because the costs tend to be incurred up front in the life of a project and the benefits materialise later on.

The element of risk also affects a cash flow's value. Two expected cash flows of £1m. with identical timings but different risks are not identical in value. The more risky cash flow will be worth less than the safer cash flow because the project is more likely to fail. The value of a risky cash flow must be discounted with a higher discount rate to reflect the degree of risk. This is another failing of the non-discounted cash flow—all cash flows are valued equally regardless of risk.

> The non-discounted techniques fail to consider the crucially important concept of discounting for declining money values or risky monies. They are crucially flawed for anything but the shortest term and the safest investments.

3.3 DISCOUNTING

3.3.1 The Principles of Discounting

The principle of discounting is the basis on which all true values of monies are founded—it is the most important and fundamental principle of finance, much like Newton's first law of motion is to physics.

> The principle argues that £1 in the future is worth less than £1 today because there is an opportunity to earn interest.

Suppose interest can be earned at a rate of 10% per annum then £1 will be worth £1.10 in one year's time. In other words an investor would be indifferent to an opportunity to earn between £1 today and £1.10 in one year's time. The two are equivalent.

Consider the possibilities if the two were not equivalent. Suppose an investor was allowed to choose between £1 today and £1.09 in one year's time. The wise investor would choose the £1 today and invest it at 10% and so earn £1.10 to make a penny profit. Thus £1 today is worth more than £1.09 in one year's time. A similar argument shows that £1.11 in one year's time is worth more than £1 today. From this it can be shown that there is an equivalence between cash in the future and cash in present day terms. This equivalence can be expressed by the formula:

Cash value (year 1) = Cash value (year 0) × (1 + interest rate)

Or, more importantly from an investment point of view, the equation can be rearranged to express the future cash value in "today's" terms (that is in Year 0 terms):

Cash value (year 0) = Cash value (year 1) / (1 + interest rate)

The cash value in "today's" terms is known as the present value. By using the above equation it is possible to express a future cash flow in present value terms. For example £100 in one year's time is worth £100/1.1 or £90.91 in present value terms with a rate of 10%.

It is important to note that the interest rate covers the impacts of inflation. For example, if the current rates of interest are 10% and the current rate of inflation is 4% then investors know that 4% of their earnings from interest will be eroded by inflation. Thus the real return will be 10% less the 4% inflation.

The rates of interest are based upon investors' expectations of inflation and the return the investors expect to earn above the rate of inflation. For example, if inflation is 8% and the interest rates are 12% then the real return that investors expect to earn above and beyond inflation is:

$$\text{Real return} = \frac{1.12}{1.08} = 1.037 \text{ or } 3.7\%$$

This 3.7% is the return that investors get for lending their capital after inflation has been accounted for. Interest rates therefore allow for the effects of inflation and the real return that investors expect to earn for lending their capital. The basic relationship between these rates is:

(1 + interest rate) = (1 + inflation rate) × (1 + real interest rate)

or as the above example shows:

$$1.12 = 1.08 \times 1.037$$

The causes of inflation are beyond the scope and are not relevant to the purpose of this book and are therefore not discussed. The reason for this disinterest is that the book is about investment and there is nothing that the investor can do about inflation from one investment opportunity to another investment opportunity. If the investor decides to invest in some other project the same inflation is still there. The important point to remember is that the interest rate contains an allowance for inflation and as such all future costs and benefits should be inflated at the expected rates of inflation. Failure to do so would lead to cash flows being undervalued—severely undervalued in times of high inflation or for long term projects.

The interest rate is usually replaced by another rate known as the discount rate. It is given this term because it is used to discount (i.e. diminish the value of) future cash flows so that they are brought into present value terms.

It needs to be appreciated that the discount rate may not necessarily be the same as the prevailing interest rate, which is that set by the national government and on which the rates charged to business are based. The reason is that there may be some other similar investment opportunity with a different rate of return, which may be a more appropriate benchmark or target for the investment decision. There may be an opportunity to earn 12% on an investment whilst the interest rate may be 11%. One could invest in a risk free investment project that yields 12% rate of return. In such a case an investor would use 12% as the discount rate because he has the opportunity to earn 12% on his capital. One could invest in the market by buying a wide portfolio of company shares, this yielding some 15%. Perhaps this higher rate of return would be more appropriate to use as the discount rate. This is a matter for the managers of the company to decide. The issue is discussed at length below, as it is one of the most crucial disciplines of CBA. However, it follows that the discount rate for measuring the true value of a project investment will never be lower than the interest rate and must be equal to or higher than the highest similar alternative opportunity to earn interest elsewhere. The discount rate therefore includes inflation and the opportunity to earn profits elsewhere. The selection of the appropriate yardstick for the opportunity to earn profits elsewhere is detailed in section 3.4.

This now gives a more general formula for discounting a cash flow in the future:

Present value (PV) = cash flow (year 1) / (1 + discount rate)

The principle can also be extended to multiple time periods. For example, suppose over two years there is an opportunity to earn interest at 10%. The interest on £100 will earn:

Capital + interest = £100 × 1.1 × 1.1 = £121

The result is that £121 in two years' time is equivalent to £100 in today's terms. Discount rates are therefore compounded on an annual basis. By rearranging the equation as before, the present value of a cash flow two years from hence can be found:

PV = cash value (year 2) / (1 + discount rate)^2

PV = £121/1.1^2 = £100

This can be expressed more generally to the case of n time periods as:

PV = cash flow (year n) / (1 + discount rate)^n

This simple formula is at the heart of the principle of discounting.

Whilst cash values are not constant from year to year, the principle of discounting enables cash flows at different points in time to be brought into equivalent value terms—that is present value terms. The result is that a level comparison is made between different investment opportunities covering different time spans, the level playing field being today's values; the time aspect is removed.

The laborious task of discounting cash flows can be lessened by the use of tables of discount factors. A discount factor is calculated by:

Discount factor = 1 / (1 + discount rate)^n

The discount factors vary for both rate and the number of years. As n increases, that is the project life gets longer, the discount factor increases. Table 3.1 shows factors for years 0 to 3 for discount rates of 10% and 15%. By using these factors the present value of future cash flows can be simply calculated by multiplying the cash flow by the appropriate discount factor. For example a cash flow of £5000 in two years' time discounted at a 15% rate is worth:

PV = £5000/1.32 = £3780 (the equivalent of (£5000/1.15)/1.15)

Table 3.1 The discount factors for years 0 to 3 for discount rates of 10% and 15%

Year, n	Factor (rate 10%)	Factor (rate 15%)	$1/(1.1)^n$	$1/(1.15)^n$
0	1.0	1.0	1.0	1.0
1	1.10	1.15	0.9091	0.8696
2	1.21	1.32	0.8264	0.7561
3	1.331	1.52	0.7513	0.6575

As may be seen from Tables 3.1 and 3.2 the cash flows are discounted more as the rate increases and as time increases. For example the present value of a cash flow in three years' time is worth 75.13% (100/1.331) of its nominal value at a 10% rate and only 65.75% at a 15% rate (100/1.52). This is a basic property of the discounting of cash flows. The higher the rate of discounting and the later the cash flows of an investment then the greater the diminution of the value of that cash flow.

The failure to take interest and inflation into account when measuring the value of money means that techniques which treat all cash flows as having the same nominal value, regardless of timing, will yield misleading results, the present values of future monies being inflated. The simple decision criteria of non-discounted cash flow techniques are flawed. This is why Discounted Cash Flow (DCF) techniques are so important.

The DCF techniques can be applied to the example of purchasing a PC, which was analysed using non-discounted techniques earlier. This is done by determining the cash flows of the investment year by year as with the non-DCF techniques. The next step is to discount the cash flow for each period by the appropriate discount factor. In this case a rate of 10% has been assumed. The DCF figures are shown in Table 3.2.

Table 3.2 Sample DCF figures for PC purchase

	Year 0	Year 1	Year 2	Year 3	Total
Cash flow	−5000	+2000	+2000	+2000	+1000
Discount factor	1.0	1.1	1.21	1.331	
PV	−5000	+1818	+1652	+1503	−27

The total present value of the project is −£27. This shows that the investments actually lose money for the investor, once the effects of inflation, risk and the investor's opportunity to earn interest elsewhere are taken into account. An investor would be £27 better off by putting the money into an investment which yielded 10% per annum. This is a very different result from that given by the non-DCF techniques, which indicated that the project would earn £1000 profit.

3.2 The Application of the Discount Rate

There are two techniques for the application of discounts to investment monies. These are detailed and compared in the next three sections.

3.3.2.1 Net Present Value

The Net Present Value, or NPV as it is commonly known, is simply the net sum of all the discounted cash flows over the life of the investment. The significance of the NPV is that if it has a positive value then the discounted cash inflows (i.e. the benefits) exceed the discounted cash outflows (i.e. the costs). An investment would be worthwhile if the project yielded a positive NPV. This positive NPV is not just that the costs are exceeded by the benefits in an absolute sense (the costs are £100 and the benefits are £110 so there is a net benefit to the company) but that the benefits exceed the costs even taking into account inflation and all the anticipated risks that can adversely affect the project during its life. If the NPV were negative then the discounted costs would exceed the discounted benefits, hence the investment would not be worthwhile. In the example quoted in section 3.3.1, the NPV is –£27, so the PC investment is not worthwhile.

The magnitude of the result, in this case –£27, also has more meaning, which can be explained as follows. An NPV result of zero means that the benefits discounted at 10% equal the initial outlay. In other words if the NPV were zero the project would repay the initial outlay and provide a return which is exactly equivalent to 10% compound interest. If one compares the PC investment with the opportunity to earn interest at a compound rate of 10%, then the conclusion of this technique is that the investor would be £27 worse off by investing in the PC. The NPV measure therefore also shows the value of the project relative to investing in an alternative interest bearing investment.

It is this aspect of the NPV technique that is so useful. *It demonstrates the financial performance of a project relative to some alternative financial investment, as well as taking into account the inflation and risk.* It is of crucial importance in investment decisions because it indicates where capital funds are best invested.

This is a very different message from that obtained from the non-discounting of the monies. For this PC example the non-discounted approach indicates a positive net cash flow of £1000, whereas the discounted approach indicates a negative cash flow of –£27. With the non-discounted approach the investor would go ahead and buy the computer thinking there is a good profit to be made. In reality the opposite is the case. The investor would be better off investing the money in some government bonds which yield 10%. If this was repeated n times in a company/organisation it would soon have no shareholders, there being better investment opportunities elsewhere.

As indicated in Chapter 1 and above it is necessary for the financial returns from a computer project to be competitive with other alternative forms of investment, otherwise it is better to put the investment monies into these higher returns opportunities. By bringing future monies into current values the DCF technique provides:

- a fair comparison between alternative investments which may have different time profiles of incoming and outgoing cash flows;
- a true measure of the current value of long term investments.

DCF is therefore *the* yardstick by which the benefits of investments can be measured. If all the current and future costs and benefits of a project can be predicted and converted into cash flows then the DCF technique will tell investors whether they are better off investing in the given computer project or whether it is best to invest in some other interest bearing investment with a greater degree of confidence.

Of course, the important *caveat* is being able to place cash values on all costs and benefits. This has proved to be the biggest problem in the past. The problem is that many of the benefits may be difficult to value because they are intangible, but this is a failure in measurement not in DCF techniques. However, benefits that are classified as intangible can now be quantified with an increased degree of completeness and accuracy, and as such can now be analysed by DCF techniques. There is thus no reason why all the costs and benefits of an investment evaluation cannot be included in the DCF techniques.

3.3.2.2 Discounting to Internal Rate of Return

There is a second popular DCF technique known as the Internal Rate of Return (IRR). Other names used for this technique include "yield rate", "DCF yield", "marginal efficiency of capital", "trial and error" (not very flattering), "discounted yield" and "actuarial rate of return". The IRR is defined as that discount rate which gives a net present value of zero, where the discounted costs are the same as the discounted benefits. As stated earlier, when the NPV of a project is zero the project repays the initial outlay plus a return equivalent to the discount rate used. The IRR is simply this equivalent rate. An example will help to illustrate the point.

Suppose a PC investment has a four year life and the cash flows for the project are:

	Year 0	Year 1	Year 2	Year 3	Year 4
Cash flow	−5000	−4000	+9000	+6000	+4000

At a discount rate of 10% the NPV is +£6042, that is this particular investment will yield £6042 more than an interest bearing account of 10%. The IRR technique asks—to what rate of compound interest does the return equate? In order to calculate this, the rate has to be guessed at initially and arrived at by graphical interpolation or by calculation. For example, at a discount rate of 30% the NPV for this investment is +£1382 and at 35% the NPV is £617. By linear extrapolation the rate at which the NPV is zero must be just under 40%. In other words this PC investment is equivalent to an interest bearing investment of almost 40% per annum. The linear extrapolation of this can be shown graphically in Figure 3.2.

3.3.2.3 NPV versus IRR—Which Is Best?

There is often some debate as to which technique is the better—the NPV or the IRR. For the purposes of measuring the financial value of an investment, or the financial value of a project, the conclusion is clear-cut and decisive. The NPV technique is the better because:

- It is easier to calculate and use (the result has meaning and is in money terms);
- The discount rate that is used is that which the type of investment should obtain when compared with the expectations of investors in the general marketplace for investment being made. The company or project you are investing in will produce a competitive return;
- It produces a monetary value; one invests monies, and monies, not discount rates, are the basis of management action;
- The IRR technique can give more than one answer when the sign of the cash flows reverses more than once. In the project below there are two IRR values of 12.7% and 787.3%, whilst at a discount rate of 15% the project shows a NPV of +£134 216.

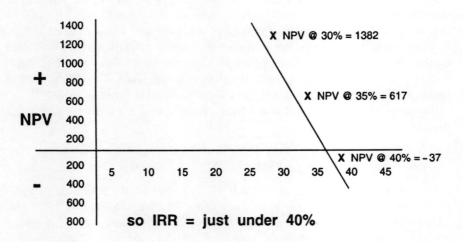

Figure 3.2 Internal rate of return

Year	0	1	2
Cash flow	−£1000	+£10 000	−£10 000

The rates are correct because:

$$-£1000 + \frac{£10\ 000}{1.127017} - \frac{£10\ 000}{(1.127017)^2} = \text{Nil (to within £10)}$$

and

$$-£1000 + \frac{£10\ 000}{8.8729} - \frac{£10\ 000}{(8.8729)^2} = \text{Nil (to within £10)}$$

In these situations which rate is correct? The IRR technique does not help in these cases, it confuses.

- The selection of projects based solely on IRR versus NPV can give conflicting results. It is possible for project A to have a higher NPV than project B but for project B to have a higher IRR than project A. Which project is best? Again, the IRR measure can produce conflicting results that cloud the issue of ascertaining the best project investment.

Use the NPV technique—it has practical relevance and unambiguous meaning. The IRR should be used with care.

3.3.3 The Reasons for Discounting

There are three aspects of any investment that form the basis of the discounting technique. They are discussed below.

(1) An investment suffers inflation.

A project may well last over several, even many, years. During this time there is inflation, this lowering the value of future monies. The cash flow of the project n years from now may well be set against a very different financial scenario from that prevailing today. It is necessary to bring the value of these future project monies to current day terms. Inflation needs to be discounted for—the higher the inflation rate the higher the discount rate.

(2) An investment incurs risk.

From the point of view of investors risk is variability, be it in the returns in the shares of a company or in the cash flow of a project. If there is no variability there is no risk.

Risk lowers the value of an investment for the simple reason that the greater the risk the more likely it is that the project will fail. The invested

monies could lose part or all of their value. Investors need to be compen-
sated for this increased risk with a higher interest return on the invested
monies. The risk needs to be discounted for—the higher the risk the higher
the discount rate.

Risk is composed of two things—the probability of an event occurring
and the variability of the event when it occurs. An obvious example of this
is the probability of car owners crashing their cars (which they do once
every three years) and the seriousness of the accident when it occurs (the
cars are write-offs and two persons are injured in such a manner that a
claim can be made against the insurance policy).

Risk is measured by what is called the *beta* factor—the higher the risk
the greater the *beta* factor.

For the purposes of project IA there are five types of *beta* factor:

(1) Market risk;
(2) Industry risk;
(3) Company risk;
(4) Project risk;
(5) Event risk.

There is also another risk, called "unique risk", but, as we shall see, this
is ignored.

It can be appreciated that this list of risks goes from the general risk
affecting many projects to more particular risks that are specific to a particular project. The most general risk is the "market" and the most particular
risk is the "event". The market *beta* factor is always set to a value of 1 and
the more particular *betas* are given a value relative to 1 to indicate the riskiness of the investment in relation to the market average.

But surely there is a more general risk than the market, and that is
investing at the national level? It seems strange, therefore, that there is no
national *beta* factor for comparing the riskiness of investing in different
countries, those countries that are politically unstable and hostile to capitalism being more risky than those that are stable and favour capitalism.
The Balkans are currently unstable and Cuba is hostile and would therefore
have a higher national *beta* value than Germany and Japan, for example.
One would expect a league table of national *beta* values of countries according to their attractiveness for investment at the national level and then
league tables of the market, industry, company and project risks to function
within the national risk. An article in *The Times* newspaper in 1992 did
publish such a league table and put New Zealand at the top for low national
risk. But that league table was unofficial. Such a national *beta* factor would
be most useful for projects that span international boundaries. Unfortunately for the national league table of risk the techniques for measuring
beta values start by measuring the correlation of the returns on an asset (a

project for example) as compared with the returns of the stock-market as a whole, and each stock-market is for the market in one particular country. This obviously limits the measure to within national boundaries. It therefore raises the question as to whether there is a more international measure of risk. There isn't.

The problem is that within a national economy there is one unit of currency and so returns are measured in the same unit of money for all investments in that currency. At the international level, however, each nation has its own currency, so there are different units of measure between countries. Not only that but the value of the currencies in relation to each other is constantly changing, the units of measure varying in relation to each other. This means that returns can be radically altered by swings in exchange rates. Identical projects with identical business risks in two different countries would have very different risks from the point of view of an international investor if one project was in a country with a very stable exchange rate and the other was in a country with a widely fluctuating exchange rate.

Investment in another country adds exchange risks on top of the underlying market, company and project risks. If the investor is from a country with an exchange rate that is stable relative to the currencies of the rest of the world then the risk would be less than the one from a country with a volatile exchange rate. This constant variability of exchange rates makes the measurement of the value of investments in international projects extremely difficult. For the purpose of this book what is of prime importance to an investor is the exchange rate of his "home" government. This book does not address the issue of exchange rates in project investments. It is a nightmare. The solution is to measure projects on a national basis and then compare.

The market risk is the average of the stock-market risk for a country as a whole. It is set to create a common baseline for the *beta* factors of the industry types, companies and projects. The figure is weighted in that due consideration is given to large companies as compared with small companies based on the number of shares and their values.

The industry *beta* is the weighted average of all the company *betas* which are in the type of industry being measured. Assume that the industry type is telecommunications and there are three companies with weighted *beta* values of 0.750, 0.861 and 0.697 (the lower than 1 *beta* factor showing that telecommunications is a lower risk industry type than the stock-market average). This produces an industry *beta* value for telecommunications of 0.769.

The company *beta* value is the risk of individual companies and is obtained from the Capital Assets Pricing model (CAPM), discussed later. The company *beta* risk is obtained by plotting the variability of the company shares compared with the variability of the shares of the market as a whole, variability being judged the basis of risk—if there is no variability there is no risk. *The greater the variability of the company shares over time compared with the market shares the greater the company beta value*—the company is more risky than the market because the value of the company shares is more variable than a broad portfolio of company shares in the market. If the company shares are more variable than the market shares then the company *beta* value is greater than 1, if it is less than the variability of the market shares then the *beta* value is less than 1 as with the three telecommunications companies above.

One works back from the company *beta* to calculate the weighted averages for the industry and the market *betas*—all the company *betas* in an industry together forming the industry *beta* and all the industry *betas* together forming the market *betas*. The important baseline *beta* is the company *beta*, as projects are invested in at the company level.

The CAPM for company risk is based on the principle of the variability of the company shares in relational to the market shares.

Some *beta* factors for individual companies for the middle of 1992 (they can vary from day to day) were:

- A building society = 0.929;
- A food manufacturer = 0.530;
- A water company = 0.777;
- An airline = 1.352;
- A drug manufacturer = 0.894;
- An aero-engine manufacturer = 1.136;
- A telephone company = 1.236.

The highest *beta* factor was 1.511 and the lowest was 0.530. These figures were all for publicly quoted companies. If a company is a private concern then it is best to use a proxy *beta* factor from a competitive company of similar size.

The project risk is that of a project within a company. One can have any combination of high risk or low risk companies investing in high or low risk projects. It could be that a project is more risky than the company which is investing in the project, so that the project *beta* would be a higher value than that for the company. It could be that one of the above companies is investing in prototyping the latest technology for telecommunications and there is a high risk of failure—and the resultant *beta* for the project is 1.66. These project *beta* values are calculated by the Bowater Scott model technique, this technique being based on the CAPM but refined for the specific requirements of investing in projects. It is not possible to use the CAPM as the sole basis for measuring project risk. This is because one is not dealing in the shares of projects—projects have cash flow, not shares. Projects are not bought and sold in stock-markets. What is possible, however, is the adoption of the same approach to the measurement of risk as used by the CAPM, i.e. that the variability of a unit of measure is the measure of risk. In this case the variability of the project cash flow is the risk, not shares.

The event risk is a happening that affects the outcome of a particular project. It could be that the size of the business market the project is designed to exploit does not expand as much as anticipated due to a particular event, such as a collapse of confidence in the market or a war.

Event risk is the one risk that does not have a *beta* factor. It is unique in this regard for the simple reason that many events are of the unexpected type and cannot therefore be planned for and measured by a *beta* factor. And events do not have shares or cash. The techniques of CAPM and Bowater Scott are therefore not suitable. Event risks are handled by another mechanism, the mechanism of probability, and are calculated in the Decision Tree Analysis technique. Once the event has occurred its impact on the project cash flow is assessed and the net present value of the project is adjusted accordingly.

The unique risk is (in theory at least) immaterial to investors. The reason for this is that such risks can be diversified away. For example, if an investor is considering investing in several companies in the food processing sector each company will have risks which are unique to itself. For instance, company A may have industrial relations problems and so high risk of losses due to strikes, company B may have an expensive lawsuit pending, company C may have a fire which completely destroys one of its important factories. All these risks are unique to each individual company and will affect each company's returns. However, if an investor spreads his investments over several companies then he is hedged against the individual risks of each company. The swings and roundabouts of each individual company's results will be smoothed out. The risk unique to each company will become negligible. Say there is a strike in company A and sales are lost, the investor doesn't care because sales will go to companies B and C in which investments have also been made. As the number of different shares held increases, so the portfolio will approximate to investing in the industry type as a whole and not to the individual companies. In this way the investor diversifies away unique risks so that they no longer matter.

Unique risk is discussed further in section 3.4.4.

(3) An investment can earn interest elsewhere.

The monies that are invested in a project could equally easily be invested in some other form of interest bearing investment, be it a fixed interest bond or another project. For each investor there is a range of investment opportunities. Once the Net Present Value (NPV) of a project is calculated, based on a discount rate adjusted for inflation and risk, then any positive monies in the project NPV value represent profit *over and above* the expected return to cater for inflation, market risk, company risk and project risk. Projects can now be compared on an equal basis, based on two measures— the discount rate of the expected return and the amount of the NPV profit. If two projects have a similar NPV, would one invest in the project with the higher discount rate as this project provides a higher return, taking into account inflation and all the risks? If two projects have similar discount rates one would invest in the project with the higher NPV. But how do you judge two projects, one with a high discount rate but low NPV and the other with a low discount rate and a high NPV?

The answer is simple. The higher discount rate is purely to cover the higher risk in a given inflation and risk scenario. Other projects in a common inflation situation have different discount rates to cover different risks. The different discount rate between projects is therefore a compensation factor for the additional risks of the projects. It is not the deciding factor as to which projects to invest in. *It is the NPV which is the decider*. Select the project with the highest NPV, as this is profit over and above the dangers of general inflation and the various risks of the project. If one project has a NPV of £10 and another a NPV of £15 select the project with the NPV of £15.

It is up to each investor to determine which rate of return and NPV is the most appropriate. Whatever discount rate is selected for the project the rate must be appropriate to the inflation and market, company and project risks in order to bring future cash flows into true present value terms for that particular investor. If the intention is for the investment in computer systems to be based on fair competition with alternative opportunities of investment, the computer project must not be "subsidised" with an artificially low discount rate, this providing a greater positive NPV and the "appearance" of being the best investment opportunity.

If the alternative investment is not within the company (invest in such and such a building in the City of London as prices are rocketing, notwithstanding that the company's business is food wholesaling) then investing the company's monies in the alternative increases the company's long term positive cash flow but does not enable the company to better its competitive position, such as being more productive through purchasing new equipment or improving its marketing publications.

The alternative investments should be those that can be made *within* the company. The alternatives from the point of view of the information system investment opportunities are purchasing new equipment (gives a 16% return) and improving the marketing publications (gives a 12% return).

With this situation the return to be expected from investing in IT should be greater than 16%.

Given that investing in company IT systems is an investment within the company it is only fair that IT investments are compared with other investment opportunities within a company. This provides a level playing field of comparison.

If the intention is merely to obtain a reasonable rate of return above inflation and risk then you do not need to consider the rate of return from other investment opportunities.

3.3.4 Actual versus Real Discount Rates

There is a relationship between actual discount rates, real discount rates and inflation. This is expressed below:

(1 + real discount rate) = (1 + discount rate) / (1 + inflation rate)

The real discount rate in this example is given by:

(1 + real discount rate) = 1.1 / 1.04 = 1.05769

The real discount rate is therefore about 5.8%. This is the return above and beyond the impact of inflation.

This opens up two possibilities for discounting. Either the actual rate of 10% can be used and all costs and benefits can be inflated by the expected inflation rate, or the real rate of 5.8% can be used and all future cash flows can be treated as inflation free. Both approaches will give the same result.

It is important to remember this point because it is often forgotten or not understood by many users of DCF techniques. The actual and real rates are often confused. To avoid further confusion the actual discount rate will be used in this book. (The treatment of inflation is discussed further in section 4.3).

3.4 DISCOUNTING—MARKET RISK

3.4.1 The Calculation of the Discount Rate

The greatest improvement to the use of DCF techniques would be the widespread use of the correct discount rate for each investment. The question, of course, is—what should the discount rate be? How is it calculated? This section shows how the discount rate is calculated.

There are three techniques of relevance to these DCFs:

(1) The Expected Return. This is used to calculate the discount rate for an investment for a time period, usually for a financial year.

The return is that to be expected for a given investment in a particular company or project under prevailing inflationary and risk conditions. Investment projects can then be compared fairly on the basis of their discount rate, those with a higher rate providing a higher return when their NPVs are the same.

The output from the expected return formula is the discount rate to be applied in the NPV or internal rate of return formulae.

(2) NPV. This uses the discount rate for the year calculated in the expected return formula to convert future investment monies into current values. Investment projects can then be compared fairly on the basis of the cash value of a profit or loss.

(3) Internal Rate of Return (IRR). This calculates a rate of return that produces a NPV of zero. Investment projects can be compared fairly on the basis of the rate of return on an investment.

The sequence in which the discounting techniques need to be applied is the expected return, followed by the NPV or IRR techniques. The NPV and IRR techniques are alternatives once the expected return discount rate is obtained. Their merits are compared later in this chapter and one is recommended as the technique to apply for IA.

The components of the expected return, NPV and IRR formulae need to be explained in detail. Without an understanding of what the components of the formulae are, how they fit together and how to apply them the application of the formulae to the measurement of the value of projects in general, and IT projects in particular, cannot be made. What follows is a long and at times difficult explanation of the workings of these three formulae crucial to the correct valuation of investment monies in projects. At times one may ask: "Where is all this accounting theory leading me? Why am I reading about shares and stock-markets? How does this relate to the valuing of the investments I plan to make in such and such an IT project?" The reader is asked to be patient. All will be revealed. The components are rational, the formulae work, they fit together and the resultant calculations of the value of IT project investments are that much better than those from traditional CBA. When the techniques of IA are presented at seminars the frowns on delegates' faces gradually turn to smiles and nods of understanding.

3.4.2 The Expected Return Formula

The authors' opinions are that the only sound model for the setting of discount rates is the Capital Asset Pricing Model—CAPM. Whilst the CAPM is based on theory and therefore has its critics, the model can shed a great deal of light on the problem of calculating the correct discount rate.[2]

The CAPM argues that for the purposes of calculating expected returns only the market risk of the company matters. This framework is supported by empirical evidence of stock-market data. The returns required for the shares of many companies freely traded in national stock-markets have been measured and found to agree with the CAPM.

The CAPM is a major breakthrough in investment evaluation in that it quantifies a relationship which was previously only intuitively understood. It formalises and explains the relationship between risk and return in a rational way. Most importantly, however, it enables a means of calculating the discount rate to be applied to the investments of different risks so that they can be properly valued and compared.

The model shows that there is a relationship between the return that investors require for an investment and the level of risk of that investment. This relationship is based upon observation of the various stock-markets around the world, and is as shown in Figure 3.3. Given that investors expect a higher return for a higher level of risk, the next question is "What is the

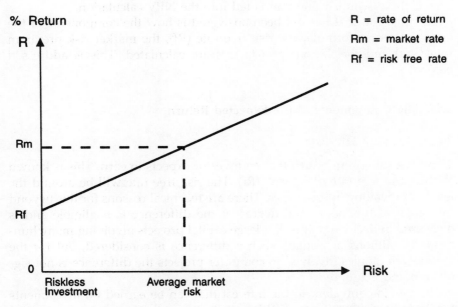

Figure 3.3 The relationship between risk and return—based on the CAPM (assumes a free capital market)

---

[2] For a rigorous treatment of this model see Brearley and Myers (1989). *Principles of Corporate Finance*, McGraw-Hill.

shape of such a graph?". As shown in Figure 3.3, there is a linear relationship between risk and return. This is the financial return to be expected when investing in something, be that something a stock-market, an industry, a company or a project. The formula is:

Expected return = Rf + *beta* value (Rm–Rf)

where Rf is the risk free rate of return, *beta* value is the company or project *beta* factor, depending on what is being invested in, and Rm is the market risk premium rate—the return for investing in a risky market.

This book only considers investments made at the company and project level. The company is considered only because it is the basis within which project investment decisions are made. The same expected return formula is relevant to both levels of investment, viz:

- The company discount rate = Rf + company *beta* factor (Rm–Rf);
- The project discount rate = Rf + project *beta* factor (Rm–Rf).

This expected return becomes the discount rate for the company or project as a whole. Of course, some of the project investments that a company makes will be above the average risk for the company and some below. This is the discount value that is fed into the NPV calculation.

The question that has not been answered is how the components of the expected return formula, the risk free rate (Rf), the market risk premium rate (Rm) and the various *beta* factors are calculated. This is addressed below.

3.4.3 The Components of the Expected Return

3.4.3.1 *The Risk Free Rate*

There is a minimum return that an investor expects to earn. This is known as the "risk free rate of return" (Rf). The risk free rate will be around the level of prevailing interest rates. There are technical reasons for this beyond the scope of this book. The degree of the difference is negligible and is measured in decimal points. For large capital projects involving many hundreds of millions of pounds such a difference is considered, but for the volumes of monies involved in computer projects the difference is not significant and is ignored.

The rate is equivalent to the interest that can be earned on investments that have no risk whatsoever. This usually means the return on government bonds, which is slightly higher than that possible in a bank or building society deposit. With such an investment the investor knows his money is safe and is certain of a return above the rate of inflation. A 10% government bond will pay the same fixed amount in times of boom or recession. There is virtually no chance of the government being unable to repay the debt or the interest. The investment therefore has a *beta* value of zero reflecting the fact that the investment is safe and certain, that is, it is riskless.

Obviously, if 10% can be earned for no risk at all then no investor would invest in a company or project which earned less than 10%. It therefore follows that if an investor were to invest in a risky project then an expected return of greater than 10% would be required. Thus Rf is the starting point for consideration of alternative forms of investment. The minimum rate of return to be achieved by a project has to be greater than Rf.

Of course, the prevailing interest rates can and do fluctuate. They tend to be slightly higher than inflation, the degree of difference depending on such factors as government policy. If the government is wanting to dampen demand and so reduce the pressure on price rises then the gap will widen, so as to make borrowing more expensive. As a result Rf that generally tracks the interest rates will also rise and fall, and this in turn affects the expected returns from the company's rate of return. Thus, if interest rates fall then so will the expected rate of return.

The return on such risk free investments is an important anchor for the model. It determines the minimum that investors expect to earn and the premium required from the more risky investments.

3.4.3.2 *The Expected Market Portfolio Return*

The second anchor for the model is the Expected Market Return (Rm). This is also known as the average market return. Rm represents the return that is obtained from investing in the stock-market as a whole, that is on a well diversified portfolio of shares—such as the FT100 Share Index in the UK market or the Standard & Poors 500 in the US market. Moreover, as the portfolio is well diversified it will be of average market risk and so have a *beta* value of 1 (by definition). By calculating Rm and plotting its value with a *beta* value of 1.0 on the graph of Figure 3.3, using Rf as the starting point of the line of risk, it is possible to construct the line shown. This is known as the "market line" and passes through the points that show the rate of return for a given level of risk: (Rf, *beta* = 0); (Rm, *beta* = 1.0).

The Rm is a readily published figure (available from the same source as the *beta* values) and is the return calculated on a portfolio of company investments which is representative of the stock-market as a whole. Of course, the returns on the stock-market do fluctuate with the economic cycle and will change with the interest rates. However, the premium that investors expect to earn on the average market portfolio, above the Rf, is largely constant. This premium is Rm–Rf, and is usually around 8% from empirical data. Thus, if the prevailing Rf is 10% then Rm would be around 18%. This is the expected return on a market portfolio of average risk (*beta* value of

1.0). By plotting these two rates on the graph of Figure 3.3 and by drawing a straight line between them it is possible to establish the expected return for any share of a given *beta* value.

Companies of below the average market risk for being in business (that is with a *beta* value of less than 1), such as utilities, food manufacturers and food retailers, have guaranteed markets that are not so vulnerable to economic cycles, particularly recessions, and would therefore have a lower risk premium and a lower return on any investments. This can be seen in the company *beta* factors listed earlier where the food manufacturer had a *beta* factor of only 0.530, half the average market risk and the lowest company *beta* in the list. They would therefore expect a return of 4% above the Rf 10%.

Companies of above the average market risk for being in business, such as high technology and leisure companies, would have a higher market risk premium and a higher return on any investments. The telephone company had a *beta* factor of 1.236, two and a half times more risky than the food manufacturer. There would be about a 10% return above the Rf 10% for these companies.

For a share of a given *beta* value the expected return can be calculated by the formula:

Expected return (Er) = Rf + *beta* value (Rm–Rf)

For example, if Rf = 10% and Rm = 18% then for a share of a *beta* value of 1.5 (the company is higher risk than the market) the expected return would be:

Er = 10% + 1.5 (18%–10%)

Er = 22% expected return

Note that because the share is above the average risk the expected return is higher than the average market return of 18%. Another 4% is required.

3.4.3.3 *The Beta (Risk) Factors*

For the purposes of project investment, the base *beta* factor is that of the company, both for the more general market *betas* and industry types and the more detailed project *beta*. This is because the more general *betas* are obtained from adding the company *betas* of the companies in the stock-market in a weighted manner, and the more detailed project *betas* are obtained from measuring the variability of the project cash flows and relating the resultant project *betas* to the company *beta*.

The market *beta* factor is set to a value of 1 for the country in which the investment is to take place and acts as a common baseline for the other *beta* types to be measured against. Both company and project *betas* are based on the principle of risk being something that is variable. If something is constant there is no risk. There are two approaches to the measurement of the risk:

(1) The plotting of two variables in relation to each other. If one variable is regarded as the base variable then the variability of the other variable in relation to the base variable is the measure of risk. This approach is used for the measurement of the company *beta*, the two variables being the value of the company and the market share values in relation to each other, the market share values being the base variable and producing a value of one.

The returns of company shares over time are plotted in relation to the average returns of market shares over time. If the returns of the company shares vary more than the returns of the market shares the company is a higher risk than the market and so has a higher *beta* value. The technique of plotting company shares against market shares does not include unique risk and it produces a diagram that can be easily interpreted for the measurement of company risk in relation to market risk.

(2) The calculation of standard deviation. Standard deviation is used to measure variability so the histogram plotting approach to establishing the risk cannot be used. This approach has to be used for the measurement of project risk. There is only one component that is at risk, the cash flow of the project. If the variability of the cash flow is high the riskiness of the project is greater and the project standard deviation goes up. Unfortunately, project cash flows include unique risk.

The use of the standard deviation technique is an excellent mechanism for obtaining a "feel" for the riskiness of an investment within a project. However, the technique suffers from two problems: not many people are familiar with the calculation of standard deviations; it includes unique risk.

3.4.4 The Plotting Measurement of the Company *Beta* Value

The standard deviation can be used as an absolute measure of company risk, that is the total risk of the company based on the spread/variability of the returns on the company's shares. However, it is not the most appropriate measure of risk as far as investors are concerned.

The reason for this is that the variable being measured for risk, the shares of the company, is unique to that company. The CAPM theory states that unique risks are not important to investors because they can be diversified away.

If one measures the absolute risk of a portfolio of shares by the standard deviation of the return on that portfolio then the risk drops as the number of different investments increases. As the number of different shares in the portfolio increases so the unique risks are diversified away. From empirical results about 15–20 different shares will eliminate all unique risks. What is left is known as market risk.

Market risk is simply defined as the risks which cannot be diversified away. For example, if an investor in the food processing industry holds shares in around 15 different food processing companies, the only risks that his portfolio is likely to be subjected to will be the risks common to all companies operating in that industry. These non-diversifiable risks will be things like commodity prices of basic foodstuffs, the level of household spending on food and so on. All food processing companies bear these risks.

As investors cannot diversify away market risks then it is these risks that matter. This is one of the most fundamental principles of the CAPM, namely that investors are only interested in the market risks of their investments, not the unique risks.

The significance of the deficiencies of standard deviation is that a new measure of market risks must be found—a measure of market risk, not the absolute or total risk. This could be a very difficult problem. Identifying all possible risks for a company, deciding which are unique and which are market risks, then measuring each would be a practical impossibility.

The answer to this problem is the equity *beta* measure of risk. This measures the riskiness of a company's shares relative to the stock-market as a whole. This is done not by calculating standard deviations but by plotting the returns of a particular company share over time against the returns on a wide portfolio of company shares which represent the stock-market average over time, for example the FT100 Share Index. A typical plot is shown in Figure 3.4. Each dot represents the returns of the company share for a period of time (usually a month) as compared with the market return, with the time spread typically over a three to five year period.

As can be seen from the plot there is often a large scatter of points. However, the underlying trend in this case is for the company returns to increase with an increase in average market returns. As an economy booms and average returns rise then so should the returns of the shares in a particular company. Similarly, when an economy goes through recession average market returns will drop and so should the returns on the shares. (There are rare cases when the shares of a company may move in opposite directions to the general economy, for example firms that work in insolvency do well when times are bad and the number of bankruptcies increase).

By the use of linear regression the line of best fit can be drawn through the points to give an overall trend line. The slope of the line is known as the company's *beta* value of the share (technically known as the company's equity *beta*, denoted by βequity), this showing the return of the company

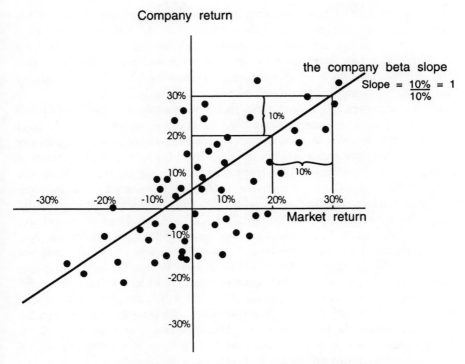

Figure 3.4 Company return versus market return

as compared with the market return. (It is this *beta* value of the share that can be obtained from companies like Datastream and the various business schools.) The angle of slope in Figure 3.4 is therefore the riskiness of the company as compared with the riskiness of the market in Figure 3.3. This is not the same line as in the CAPM market line in Figure 3.3, which is the return of all the companies in the market against their respective *beta* factors. We are now able to measure the *beta* value of the company as compared with the market *beta*. The angle of the risk slope in Figure 3.2 can be adjusted for the company plotted in Figure 3.3. The plot shown in Figure 3.4 is of a company with a *beta* value of 1, that is the variability of the company shares matches the variability of the share weighted average of all the companies in the stock-market. It just so happens that the company has the same riskiness as the market. If the angle of slope is shallower than Figure 3.4 the company *beta* value will be lower than the market *beta* value, that is less than 1, such as for the food company with a *beta* value of 0.530. If the slope is steeper than Figure 3.4 the opposite is true such as for the telephone company with a *beta* value of 1.236. Figure 3.4 shows the return to be expected from any project investment of a given *beta* value.

If the slope has a value of 1, that is where there is an equal shift of the slope on both the horizontal and the vertical axes, as there is in Figure 3.4 with the 10% change for both the market and the company returns, then the share has a risk equal to the market average and thus a βequity value of 1. In this case if the market returns increase by 10% then it is highly likely that the company share will also increase by 10%.

Some companies will have shares that give a steeper slope than that of Figure 3.4, that is a slope greater than 1. These companies tend to give greater improvements in return than the market average when times are good. If a company has a *beta* value of 1.7 then for a 10% improvement in average market returns a 17% improvement would be expected in the return of the share. If things turn out badly then the shares of such a company suffer more than the average. A 10% fall in average returns would lead to the expectation of a 17% fall in the value of the shares. These shares are high risk shares. The returns can be very high but so can the losses.

For companies whose shares have a *beta* value of less than 1 the risks are lower than the average market risk. For a share of *beta* value of 0.5 a 10% improvement in average market returns would tend to produce only a 5% improvement in returns for the share. Likewise a 10% decline will only lead to an expected 5% fall. For such low risk shares the potential improvements are low but so are the potential losses. Thus low risk shares are less volatile than average. They do not rise much when times are good, but they do not fall much when times are bad.

It is the company equity *beta* measure which is the measure of risk that is most relevant to investors. It measures the susceptibility of a company's share's return to the general ups and downs of an economy as a whole. It measures the correlation of a share's return to the return of the market average for the type of business a company is in.

This market aspect of the equity *beta* is important because there is nothing investors can do to influence the booms and recessions that economies face. The average market return is beyond the control of the investor (and the cynical may delight in saying that it is further still beyond the control of national governments). Investors and companies must live with these changing fortunes.

A good example of the difference between total risk and market risk is an oil exploration company. The odds on finding oil are not very good— the total risk is high as measured by the standard deviation. However, investors do not mind these risks. They can invest in a number of different oil exploration companies and so the good luck of some balances out the poor fortunes of others. The risks which do bother investors are the market risks of the oil industry—mainly the price of oil. This is a much lower risk than the odds of finding oil in one particular site. The market risks of oil exploration are much lower than the total risks of each individual survey.

Beta values are more relevant because they measure the exposures to market risk, and market risk is the only risk investors and companies can do nothing about.

However, an investor can control the relative risks of the portfolio of shares he holds. An investor can choose a high risk portfolio (that is high *beta* value shares) or a low risk portfolio (low *beta* value shares).

Equity *beta* values for quoted public companies are measured by banks and city institutions and are readily available from sources such as the London Business School Library and Datastream International. This saves time-consuming plotting of the market and company shares and avoids some of the technical problems in measuring returns (technical details which are beyond the scope of this book).

Given that the equity *beta* value is an appropriate measure of market risk and that investors are only concerned with market risk, the next step is to determine what extra return is required for a share of a given *beta* value, as compensation for the risk involved.

3.4.5 The Expected Return

The first point to note is that there is a minimum return that an investor expects to earn. This is known as the Risk Free Rate of Return (Rf). As explained in section 3.4.3.1 this rate will be close to the prevailing interest rates.

The other point of interest is the average market risk, where *beta* is equal to 1. This point gives an expected average market return—Rm. This represents the return required from a well diversified portfolio of shares of average market risk. The difference Rm – Rf is the premium required by investors for taking the risks of investing in a portfolio of shares of average risk rather than investing in safe and certain investments. As stated earlier this premium is typically in the region of 8%. Thus, if the Rf of interest is 10% then the average Rm would be around 18%.

The quantity (Rm – Rf) is also a measure of the return required for the market *beta* risk of 1. This means that if the beta value of a share is known (and Rf and Rm are known) then the return that investors should expect from that share can be calculated as:

$$Er \quad = \quad Rf \quad + \quad \beta equity \quad \times \quad (Rm - Rf)$$

or

$$\begin{matrix} \text{Expected} & = & \text{risk free} & + & \text{equity} & \times & \text{average market} \\ \text{return} & & \text{return} & & \textit{beta} & & \text{risk premium} \end{matrix}$$

Hence, if equity *beta* = 1.5 and Rf = 6.5% and (Rm – Rf) = 8% then the required return would be:

$$Er = 6.5\% + (1.5 \times 8) = 18.5\%$$

Suppose that a company with an equity *beta* value of 1.2 was considering an investment that expanded its current business, then the return that should be expected by the company's shareholders can be calculated. If Rf = 8% and (Rm − Rf) = 8% then the expected return would be:

Er = 8% + (1.2 × 8%) = 17.6%

When analysing an IT project under consideration for investment the company should use a discount rate of 17.6% as that is the fair target return for an investment of that level of risk. If the NPV is positive when the discount rate is set at 17.6% then the project is worthwhile, as it pays its way and the investors will be happy.

If a company has an equity *beta* value of 0.8 then the expected returns will be:

Er = 8% + (0.8 × 8%) = 14.4%

A lower target return will be required to reflect the lower market risk of the company.

3.4.6 Refinements to Company Discounting

The CAPM provides a theoretical framework for setting an appropriate discount rate for investments of a certain risk level. There are, however, a number of problems with the expected return formula defined above. They include:

- Not all companies are freely traded on the stock-market—how can the *beta* value be measured for a private company, the assets of which are not traded as shares on the stock-market?
- Companies are often composed of a set of subsidiary companies in diverse industries—conglomerates such as the Hanson group are composed of many commercial groupings (internal companies if you will) with different business activities. These internal groupings have all the hallmarks of different companies which, if traded on the stock-market, would have different *beta* values and so on. The separate investments in the internal groupings are of different risks.

Some companies do go to some lengths to calculate or estimate a suitable *beta* value for certain subsidiary companies. However, for companies with many diverse divisions, such as the Hanson group of companies, or for private companies which have no stock-market calculated *beta* values, the usual approach is to find a proxy *beta* value of a public or traded company in the same industry. The drawbacks of such an approach are in finding a "typical" company and in measuring the *beta* value of a single company's shares. That is why industry *beta* values are so much better. They smooth out any errors that can arise in the measurement of a single *beta* figure and eliminate the problems of identifying one company as typical of the industry. Industry *beta* are readily available from the same sources as company *beta* and are simply weighted averages of *beta* values of companies in the same industry.

One further refinement that must be borne in mind is that straight *beta* values of the shares of a company measure the risk of the shares, not necessarily the risk of the company. If a company finances its operations with significant amounts of debt (usually in the form of non-risk bearing bonds with the company giving the buyers of the bonds an agreed fixed rate of return) rather than equity (the shareholders paying for risk bearing shares) then there is an added risk to the shareholders. The added risk is that a fixed sum from profits must go to pay the debt holders, regardless of the level of profits. This risk to shareholders' return is due purely to a financing decision that the first call on any profits is to pay off debts and has nothing to do with the risk of the company's business *per se*.

In order to get a true measure of the company risk, the financial risk arising from the debt policy must be stripped out.

The true *beta* value of the company's assets can be estimated by:

$$\beta asset = \frac{\beta equity \times \textit{share capital} \text{ (no. of shares} \times \text{share value)}}{\text{share capital} + \text{debt capital (no. of bonds} \times \text{bond value)}}$$

where βequity is the measured *beta* value of the company's shares. If a company has an equity *beta* of 1.35, has a total market value of its shares of £145 million and has issued fixed interest bonds worth in total £50 million then the company's asset *beta* is:

$$\beta asset = 1.35 \times \frac{145}{(145 + 50)} = 1.00$$

The asset *beta* measures the market risk of the company, the debt having been stripped out. The bond holders add extra risk to the shareholders, so the equity *beta* is higher. The important point is that it is the company asset *beta* which is important, not the equity *beta*. However, for most companies the debt is negligible or non-existent, so equity *beta* is acceptable.

3.5 DISCOUNTING—PROJECT RISK

Up to this point in the book the techniques that have been described are those used in traditional CBA. However, this book is about the wider subject of IA. The wider issues are the identification and measurement of:

• Project risk;

- Event risk;
- Offsetting risk with flexibility;
- Intangible benefits;
- Project synergy.

The relationship of the techniques to each other is illustrated in Figure 1.3.

Project risk is considered in this chapter as the *beta* value of the risk calculated through an extension of the CAPM based techniques described for the calculation of the company risk. The project *beta* is included with the company *beta* to produce the overall discount rate for the project. The other risk, event risk and the ability of management to react to the events, and the other issues of investment valuation, detailed above are addressed in Chapters 5 and 6.

3.5.1 Project Risk

It was mentioned that the corporate/market approach to the allocation of discount rates to projects would create a fixed hurdle rate that all projects would be required to better in order to succeed for investment. This fixed hurdle rate will be shown to be a most unwise policy.

The opposite of the fixed hurdle rate at the corporate level is the contingent approach at the project level. The contingent approach is based on the premise that the discount rate for a project should reflect the risks of the project. If the risk of the project is lower than the company norm then the discount rate to be applied should be lower than the normal company expected return, and vice versa. The problem still remains the same as for the DCF techniques, that of assessing risk, but in this case the risks specific to the project.

There are two risks that affect the riskiness of projects that the CAPM technique is not able to support. They are:

(1) That the risks to the money flows can vary during the life of a project. The monies of a project are the revenues and the costs. Both have a fixed portion and a variable portion. There is no risk with the fixed portion, the monies are certain. There is a risk with the variable portion as regards the proportion of the total monies that are variable and the variability of the variable monies. The costs of the variable risks, the variable cash flow to the project value, need to be measured.

This is one of the limitations of the CAPM. The CAPM assumes that risk is virtually constant throughout the entire life of a project. Whilst this may be true of many industries and companies it is most certainly not a general rule of projects. In many cases it may be a sufficiently close approximation but for projects with widely fluctuating risk profiles over time it is not adequate. It is not surprising that the DCF techniques by themselves have failed to accurately value these projects.

Like CAPM, all the other DCF techniques assume that an investment is made and then that's it. There is nothing that the investor can do about it. A stream of cash flows of an average expected value will then come in year after year with a constant risk rate. A continuous flow of monies is not always a valid assumption to make for computer systems, and is not a reasonable approximation in many other project types as well. Furthermore the mix of fixed and variable revenues and costs of the projects can vary from year to year. There is therefore a degree of uncertainty for both these components of the project monies. This uncertainty requires to be reflected in the discount rate for the project.

(2) That management can react to events that affect the project during its life. When events occur that can change the monies of a project the management can take whatever action is required to exploit the change if it is beneficial or to rectify the change if it is adverse. Change is a risk. The investors in the projects are not passive bystanders. They can take action if the investment appears to be at risk. As Professor J. Kensinger puts it, "a project is not merely left to spin itself out like a toy top without any further human intervention".[3] If a project is in difficulty such that the investment could be lost, management can take actions that correct the problems. The ability of management to react to change is flexibility. The value of the flexibility needs to be measured.

These two aspects of variable risk and active project management need to be catered for when calculating the project discount rate.

The problem remains the setting of risk adjusted discount rates to suit each project. To get round this problem some companies take a simplistic approach setting different discount rates for different types of project. There may be 10% for safe earning projects, 15% for expansion projects—as risky as the current business—20% for new products and services and 25% or more for speculative investments. But this is not very scientific.

The other problem, as indicated earlier, is that projects are not traded in the stock-markets, so that there are no CAPM *beta* values for projects. There isn't a "free market" in individual projects. This is not surprising. Projects are unique to individual companies. They "operate" within companies.

A unit of risk measure other than company shares is required. Since projects are within companies an enhancement to/extension of the basic CAPM approach is required. The technique is the Bowater Scott model.

---

[3] "Adding the value of active management into the Capital Budget Equation", *Midland Corporate Finance Journal*, Spring 1987.

The CAPM holds true for projects as for the shares of public limited companies. Just because there is no easy way to measure project *beta* values does not mean that the CAPM is not relevant. Suppose that an investment project within a company can be isolated and sold off (e.g. a distribution arm of a manufacturer or an entire IT department). The project could then be bought and sold like a company. Then the project would be treated like the shares of any traded company. It would have a measurable *beta* value and target returns would be set accordingly.

In this way the projects of a company should be seen as many "mini" companies—the investing company seen as a holding company. This truism has been exploited by the Bowater Scott model technique for measuring project *beta* values.

3.5.2 The Choice of Cash as the Measure for Project Risk

The techniques for the identification and measurement of project risk have only recently been developed, within the last decade. One technique is considered of particular value and is used in the IA method; it is a technique developed by Bowater Scott. Its value is that it is based on the CAPM but takes into account the variability of money flows in a project. This variability is measured and the *beta* value of the company is adjusted to suit the project—if the cash flow variability is high relative to the company norm the *beta* value goes up for the project (the project is more risky than the company), if it is low it goes down (the project is less risky than the company).

Most textbooks on accounting practices discuss the plotting of a probability distribution of outcomes and the measurement of the variance of the outcomes as the measure of risk with the standard deviation technique. Indeed, the technique is used by business analysts in drawing up investment decisions in the CAPM. An example of this is shown in the next section. However, in dealing with capital projects such an analysis is not always easy or possible because the number of variables is usually large.

In analysing the risks of investing in the shares of a company an investor may look at only two or three key risk variables, such as the variability of total sales and the variability of the costs. The investor will not usually analyse the risk in more detail than that. In an IT capital project, however, there is much more detail that planners need to consider. There may be the software development costs, maintenance costs, support costs, training costs, all of which could be subject to degrees of uncertainty. On the benefits side there may be the size of the cost savings, improvements in quality of services and of the products, increased speed of response, all of which again may be uncertain. The number of variables is potentially large, so gathering data for probability distributions for all the variables would be a very time consuming and laborious task.

At the end of the day all the project variables generate revenue/income and expenditure/costs. Taking one from the other results in a cash flow. Given that cash flows can vary over time, that cash flow is a unit of value measure common to all the project variables and that variability of the cash flow is a good measure of risk, the use of cash flows as the measure of the riskiness of a project is the best unit of measure. In place of a detailed probability study of all the project variables, the technique developed by Bowater Scott uses the one variable of the project cash flows to measure project risk.

3.5.3 The Standard Deviation

Risk occurs where the outcomes can differ from the expected, that is where it is impossible to predict events. The outcomes could be shares or cash flows. The greater the deviation from the expected outcome the greater is the risk.

One way to measure risk *where there is only one variable* is to calculate the standard deviation of the outcomes. This well known statistical technique expresses the magnitude of the deviations from the mean value (the expected value) as a percentage of the mean value. The standard deviation is calculated by the formula:

$$\text{Standard deviation } (x) = \sqrt{\sum \frac{(X-x)^2}{(N-1)}}$$

where x represents the values of all the possible outcomes, N is the number of possible outcomes and X is the mean value of the possible outcomes. The example shown below relates to the variability of the shares of a company and is used solely to show how the technique of standard deviation works. Readers familiar with standard deviations can skip to section 3.5.4.

Suppose that x represents the expected return on the stock-market for a particular company. Figures for this can be obtained from the publicly announced company financial results (in the UK these figures can also be obtained from Companies House in London). This return is not certain and it varies from time period to time period. Suppose that the returns are measured for 10 periods and that the values are those shown in Table 3.3. The mean value (X) of the above is 17.88%, this being the sum total of the returns divided by the number of periods. In other words, whilst the returns are not certain we know that on average the returns will be 17.88% and that in any given period the values will fluctuate around this value,

Table 3.3 Sample stock-market returns measured for
10 periods

Period 1	25.4%	Period 6	23.4%
Period 2	17.4%	Period 7	18.9%
Period 3	13.2%	Period 8	16.2%
Period 4	15.6%	Period 9	17.5%
Period 5	18.9%	Period 10	12.3%

this fluctuation being the risk. If there was no fluctuation in the returns there would be no risk. It is also likely that this average will serve as a good projection of future averages too. Mean values are very useful in predicting future expected values by taking out wild fluctuations.

The standard deviation provides a measure of the degree of fluctuation around the average. *The standard deviation is therefore the measure of riskiness.* A small degree of fluctuation will have a low standard deviation and hence a low risk. A high degree of variation will have the opposite effect. In this case the standard deviation is calculated as in Table 3.4.

The result is now to be divided by the number of the possible outcomes less one, which in this case is nine. This is then square-rooted to take out the impact of the squaring to produce the standard deviation:

$$\text{Standard deviation } (x) = \sqrt{150.53/9}$$

$$= 4.09\%$$

In other words the expected value of the returns is 17.88% with a standard deviation (a riskiness) of + or − 4.09%. This is the variability of the company returns around the mean and therefore related to the riskiness of the shares.

Table 3.4 Calculation of standard deviation

Period (P)	Return (x)	($X-x$)	($X-x$)^2
Period 1	25.4	−7.52	56.55
Period 2	17.4	+0.48	0.23
Period 3	13.2	+4.68	21.90
Period 4	15.6	+2.28	5.20
Period 5	18.9	−1.02	1.04
Period 6	23.4	−5.52	30.47
Period 7	18.9	−1.02	1.04
Period 8	16.2	+1.68	2.82
Period 9	17.5	+0.38	0.14
Period 10	12.3	+5.58	31.14
Total			150.53

A statistical property of the standard deviation measure is that there is a 63% chance that any particular outcome will be in the + or − 4.09% tolerance limit. (Note: as may be seen in this example, four observations—those in periods 1, 3, 6 and 10—exceed this limit.) There is also a 95% chance that any particular outcome will be within twice the standard deviation limits (within + or − 8.18%, and in this example no observations exceed this limit). This property is shown graphically in Figure 3.5. The standard deviation acts as a confidence level measure of the variability of cash flows around a mean value. If the variability is high then the risk that the cash flows may be much lower than anticipated and that the project to be invested in will be a loss maker is high. The opposite is also true. But the risk that what is planned may not be achieved is high—that is the important point.

The Bowater Scott model for the calculation of project risk uses standard deviation technique to measure the riskiness of a project, the variable being cash.

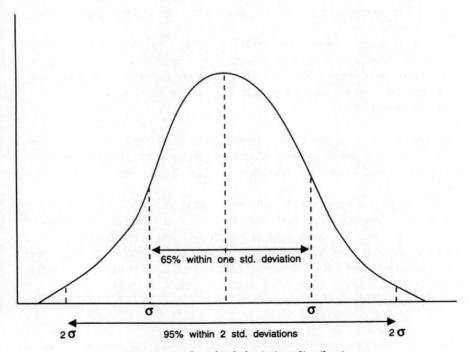

Figure 3.5 Standard deviation distribution

3.5.4 The Bowater Scott Model

Bowater Scott Ltd was formed as a joint venture company between two of the largest paper manufacturers in the world, the Scott Paper Corporation and Bowater Industries Ltd. The paper industry is both large and capital intensive, hence capital investment decisions (usually involving large volumes of money) are of crucial importance. In 1982 a working party drawn from both accounting and marketing functions was set up to develop a better method of capital appraisal. The method is described by J. Sizer in "A Casebook of British Management Accounting".[4] The main aim of the method is to set the correct discount rate for each project. As the case study quotes:

> "If a company has set its targets too low it may have undertaken considerable capital investment which may not satisfy investors' expectations. Earnings may not be high enough to cover interest payments and/or give an adequate return on equity shareholders' investment. The banks may call for guarantees and eventually refuse to lend any more. The shareholders may not wish to invest any more funds when they are already achieving an inadequate return upon their present funds. The business may contract, not be able to afford essential capital expenditures, and finally, may be taken over by someone else or closed down.
>
> If a company sets its targets too high it may turn down potentially profitable business ventures, growth might be stifled and contraction in the business may take place. It may be the case that it is satisfying its investors, however, it will certainly not be maximising its potential earnings."

The approach of Bowater Scott is to analyse risk on the basis of its component parts. They assume that project risk can be split into three parts, the first part being the company *beta* against which the project risk can be compared.

The company's market risk is the measured *beta* value of the company shares. The company *beta* is virtually static from year to year and in Bowater Scott's case it was 1.1 at the time of the study. Hence, the company was of about average market risk with the *beta* value for the paper industry being only slightly higher than the market *beta* value. Paper is judged by market analysts to be slightly more risky than the general market.

In the case study the risk free rate of return was 8.4% (Rf) and the average

---

[4] Sizer, J. (1985). *A Casebook of British Management Accounting (Vol. 1)*, Institute of Chartered Accountants of England and Wales.

market premium was 9.6% (Rm of 18% – Rf of 8.4%), giving a target return for the company as a whole of:

Expected company return = Rf + company *beta* (Rm – Rf)
Expected company return = 8.4% + 1.1 (18.0% – 8.4%) = 18.96%

The 19% represents the company discount rate. So far the Bowater Scott model is standard to the CAPM described earlier.

The remaining two parts determine whether the project is above or below this company average risk level. These parts are thus relative factors, which measure project risk relative to the company norm. The second part is the relative operational gearing. Operational gearing is defined as the level of exposure to risk. This is calculated as the ratio of variable cash flow to the total cash flows. The measure of operational gearing thus shows what proportion of the project cash flow is variable and therefore at risk. The reasoning behind this is that if the cash flow is fixed/certain then there is no risk in the cash flow—it will be achieved/it will occur. It is the variable cash flow that is the risk—it may be more or less than estimated. There is a risk that the monies anticipated may not occur. The third part is the relative revenue sensitivity, which is the measure of how variable the variable cash flows are.

Operational gearing (OG) is a term which is introduced as a measure of the exposure to risk. It is defined as the ratio of variable cash flows to the total cash flows. In the long term these cash flows would be measured by the present values of the fixed and variable costs and revenues. Thus:

$$\text{Operational gearing (OG)} = \frac{\text{Variable cash flows}}{\text{Total cash flows}}$$

or

$$OG = \frac{\text{PV (variable revenue)} - \text{PV (variable costs)}}{\text{PV (variable revenue)} + \text{PV (Fixed revenue)} - \text{PV (variable costs)} - \text{PV (fixed costs)}}$$

Suppose for a certain company that the PV of the variable revenues was £100 million, that PV (variable costs) was £50 million, that there were no fixed revenues and that fixed costs were £25 million, then the OG of the company would be:

$$OG = \frac{100 - 50}{100 - 50 - 25} = \frac{50}{25} = 2.0$$

which indicates that the variable cash flows of the company are twice the net cash flows of the company. Obviously the higher the ratio of variable cash flows to total cash flows then the higher will be the exposure to risk. Operational gearing is thus a quick and easy measure of exposure to risk.

However, operational gearing is not the whole picture as far as risk is concerned. It merely shows susceptibility to risk. The other element that needs to be considered is how risky the variable elements can be. The operational gearing of an enterprise may be high, but if the variability of the variable elements is low then total risk may not be so bad. The measure of this variability is called the Revenue Sensitivity (RS).

Strictly speaking the RS should be measured by plotting the variable cash flow against stock-market returns and then taking the slope of the line that results as the RS. In other words, it is measured in exactly the same way as the company *beta* (see section 3.4.4), the only difference being that variable cash flow is plotted on the vertical axis rather than the return on the company's shares. In this way the RS only measures the market risk of the variable elements—it measures the correlation of variable cash flow to market returns, and so ignores unique risk.

In practice, however, it can be cumbersome to plot variable cash flows against market returns. In fact it is not necessary because there is a relationship between RS and company *beta*. It can be proved that:

$$\text{Company } beta = \text{Company OG} \times \text{Company RS}$$

the proof can be found in the footnote reference below.[5] This relationship is crucial to the Bowater Scott approach. It shows that company risk has two components: OG and RS, the product of which gives the company *beta*. This relationship can be used to calculate RS, provided that the company *beta* and company OG are known. For example the Bowater Scott *beta* was measured as 1.1 and if the OG of the company were 2.0 then the company RS would simply be 1.1/2.0 or 0.55. Both the company *beta* and OG are easy to find or calculate, so time and effort can be saved by calculating company RS in this way.

This splitting of risk into two parts also gives greater detail and understanding of what causes risks within a company—the exposure to the consequences of risk (Operational Gearing) and the level of riskiness (Revenue Sensitivity). A parallel can be drawn with insurance rates. Exposure to car theft may be low if the car is alarmed and garaged every night; but risk of an attempted theft may be high if the car is in a high-risk area. The product of the two may give only a moderate risk of the car actually being stolen.

How does this apply to project risk? The answer is that the same relationship holds for project risk as for company risk. So:

$$\text{Project } beta = \text{Project OG} \times \text{Project RS}$$

If we can calculate project OG and project RS then it would be possible

[5] Brearley, R.A. and Myers, S.C. (1989). *Principles of Corporate Finance*, 3rd edn. McGraw-Hill, pp. 190–191.

to calculate project *beta* and so set the expected return for the particular project.

The project OG should be quite easy to determine, this being simply the ratio of variable cash flows of the project to the net cash flow of the project. The cash flows are measured by their PVs, so allowing for the timings of the cash flows. Each cash flow must be classified as being fixed or variable. A pragmatic approach would be to say that all cash flows that are reasonably certain in both timing and magnitude can be considered fixed whilst all other cash flows will be treated as variable.

The fixed costs will tend to be the earlier upfront costs, such as hardware and (possibly) installation costs. The variable cash flows will tend to be revenues and hence occur at the tail end of the project.

Measuring the project RS is much more tricky. Ideally the project RS should be determined by plotting the variable cash flows of the project against the returns on the market. Clearly this is not a practical option in most proposed projects. There is usually no historic data to work with and predicting future trends is difficult. In practical terms, one has to use a proxy or estimated RS. The Bowater Scott approach tackled this problem in an interesting way. They used the company RS as a starting point and then adjusted this figure upwards or downwards according to managers' assessment of the variability of the variable elements. The rationale behind this is that most projects within the company will experience much the same market risks hence a company RS is a good starting point for a project RS. The variability of the project's variable cash flows could be measured by the standard deviation of those cash flows (as calculated in section 3.5.3) and compared with the standard deviation of company variable cash flows. If the particular project had twice the standard deviation of company variable cash flows then it would be appropriate to use twice the company RS for the project RS.

It is worth stressing the assumptions that are being made here. The standard deviation measures the total variability of possible outcomes—it includes the unique risks as well as the market risks. For the purposes of setting an expected return for a project we are only interested in the *market* risk of the project not the *total* risk. We can measure, or calculate, the market risk of a company (by its RS) and the total risk of a company (by the standard deviation of its variable cash flows). We can estimate the total risk of a project by its standard deviation, but we may not be able to isolate the market risks of the project. What we can do is to assume that the market risk of a project will be in the same proportion as the total risk of the company and project. In other words, if the total risk of the project is twice that of the company, then it would be reasonable to estimate that the market risk of the project would be twice that of the company market risk. Occasionally this may not be a fair assumption, but in the main it will be a reasonable assumption to make. It must also be pointed out that the aim is to set a reasonable estimate of market risks rather than a precise figure. The accurate determination of expected returns to within a few decimal points is an unrealistic goal. If expected returns can be set to within two or three percentage points this will be a major improvement to the setting of discount rates.

The equation for project *beta* can now be expressed in terms of relative factors:

Project *beta* = Relative OG × Relative RS × Company *beta*

The three factors are multiplied together because they are relative factors. If, for example, a project has twice the OG of the norm for the company and twice the relative RS of the norm for the company then the project would be four times more risky than the norm for the company (i.e. project *beta* would be four times the company *beta*). Assume that the company *beta* = 0.5 (that is the risk of the company is half the risk of the stock-market average). If the relative OG of the project = 1 and the relative RS of the project = 1, then the project risk is exactly the same as the company risk. Therefore the project *beta* = the company *beta* = 0.5. If the relative OG of the project = 2 and the relative RS of the project = 2 then the project will be four times that of the company risk. The project *beta* = 0.5 × 4 = 2.

A worked example will illustrate how the Bowater Scott figures for project risk can be calculated and how that project risk can be related to the company risk to produce the company/project risk.

3.5.4.1 Worked Examples of the Bowater Scott Model

Two scenarios of a single business situation will be presented, one being more risky than the other. This will show how the Bowater Scott model is capable of showing project risk and how the project *beta* factor goes up and down with the riskiness of the project.

Scenario one

The first worked example is that of the contract that the authors have with an organisation for the teaching of the IA techniques described in this book. The figures are "pasteurised" but reflect the form if not the facts of the situation.

Cash flow is total fixed and variable revenue minus total fixed and variable costs. There is a fixed fee for presenting the one day seminar on the method, the fee for each of the two lecturers being £100 per day and 25% of the delegate fee of £500 for a minimum of 10 delegates. If the course is not run because there are less than 10 delegates then the fee of £100 per day per lecturer is payable only, as compensation for lost earnings. The minimum fee is therefore £200 if less than ten delegates wish to attend, or (2 × £100) + (10 × £500) 0.25 = £1450 if 10 delegates attend. There are opportunity costs of £500 per day. This is money lost to the two lecturers who could be earning consultancy fees rather than lecturing. If the course is cancelled the lecturers will lose £400 each (£500 minus the £100 fixed fee). The fixed cash flows therefore are the £200 fixed fee and the £1000 opportunity costs, so yielding a net fixed cost of £800 per seminar. This part of the costs and benefits cash flow is fixed and guaranteed and is therefore not at risk. The variable cash flow is 25% of the fee income of the delegates who attend the seminar. The running of the seminars had produced 14 delegates on average, so the average variable portion of the cash flow is (14 × £500) 0.25 = £1750.

The total cash flow of the project is the total fixed revenue (£200) and the variable revenue (£1750) minus total fixed costs (£1000) and variable costs (£0). The total cash flow is £200 + £1750 minus £1000 + £0, giving a total expected cash flow of £950 per seminar. The operational gearing is the ratio of the variable cash flows to the total cash flows. The operational gearing is therefore £1750/£950 = 1.84, which is high, but the return is also high (£950/£800 × 100 = 118% return per seminar). Suppose that the "normal" operation gearing for lecturing is 1.53 then the relative operational gearing is 1.84/1.53 = 1.20, which shows that the operational gearing is 20% higher than normal. Whilst the project has a potentially high return, it also exposes the lecturers to risk—the proportion of fixed revenue (£200) is a small part of the total revenue (£1750 + £200)—and all the costs are fixed (£1000). The costs are certain; it is the income which is uncertain. In order to compute the total risk there needs to be an assessment of how variable the variable cash flows can be.

The revenue sensitivity was based on the estimates of the number of delegates coming to the seminars. Market research had produced a profile of the likely attendance shown in Table 3.5. The variable income is calculated on the basis of the following formula: 25% × (no. of delegates × £500).

Table 3.5 Revenue variation percentage

Probability (P) %	No. of delegates	Variable income (x)	% deviation from mean (X–x)/X	$P(X-x)^2$
12.5	5	Nil	−100.0	0.125 (0.1 × 0.1 × 0.125)
17.5	10	£1250	−28.6	0.014 (0.286 × 0.286 × 0.175)
50.0	14	£1750	0.0	0.000
15.0	25	£3125	+78.6	0.093 (0.786 × 0.786 × 0.15)
5.0	30	£3750	+114.3	0.065 (1.14 × 1.14 × 0.05)
Total				0.297

For example, for the case of 25 delegates, the fee income is $0.25 \times 25 \times £500$ = £3125. The mean value of the seminar income is X (big X) = £1750, this being the sum of each income value multiplied by its probability P, the result being £nil $\times 0.125 + £1250 \times 175 + £1750 \times 0.5 + \ldots = £1750$.

The fourth column of Table 3.5 shows the percentage deviation of the income probabilities around the mean income. The columns could be used with the financial figures rather than percentages. The result would be the same and is illustrated in Table 3.6.

The square root of £910 160 is £954, which is 0.545 of the mean of £1750. This 0.545 represents the revenue sensitivity. The result is the same whether one uses the percentages for the deviation or actual figures in the fourth column. The fifth column squares the figures so as to take out the minuses and the levelling influence of the ability to earn a loss as well as to earn a profit and thereby produce a zero deviation. The number of the probabilities of all possible outcomes is 1, so that the total figure of 0.297 from the percentage deviation remains the same. The probabilities do not represent different possible outcomes but one outcome broken down into more detailed portions, each with a different probability of occurring. The probabilities sum to a total of one. The square rooting of the result of the fifth column is then used to take out the effect of the squaring so as to produce the standard deviation of the revenue. Therefore $\sqrt{0.297} = 0.545$ (the standard deviation) is a measure of revenue variation. In other words the standard deviation is plus or minus 54.5% of the expected income, which means that for approximately two out of every three seminars run, the income will be within 54.5% of the mean value £1750.

Suppose that the normal revenue sensitivity is 0.652 then the relative revenue sensitivity is $0.545/0.652 = 0.84$, which is lower than the norm.

It is now possible to calculate the project *beta*:

Project *beta* = Relative OG $\times$ Relative RS $\times$ Company *beta*

Table 3.6 Revenue variation by money

Probability (P) %	No. of delegates	Variable income (x)	Deviation from mean $(X{-}x)/X$	$P(X{-}x)^2$
12.5	5	Nil	−1750	382 812
17.5	10	£1250	−500	43 750
50.0	14	£1750	0.0	0.000
15.0	25	£3125	+1375	283 598
5.0	30	£3750	+2000	20 000
Total				910 160

The authors have assumed for the purposes of simplicity that the company *beta* for lecturing is 2.0.

The project *beta* is therefore = 1.2 × 0.84 × 2.0 = 2.01

This *beta* value can be input to the capital asset pricing formula to calculate the project discount rate required:

Company/project discount rate = 8.4% + 2.01 (18% – 8.4%) = 27.7%

This shows that the project is very risky but has the potential of very high returns. The riskiness is not in the acutal seminar—the project relative factors being about average—but in the nature of lecturing, the company *beta* factor of the company which is solely concerned with the lecturing business being twice the average. The company *beta* factor is high and reflects the hazardous nature of the lecturing business.

The risk profile of the lecturing project can be plotted. The probability distribution of the delegate income is shown in Figure 3.6, this showing that there is a 12.5% chance of earning an income of nothing at all, a 50% chance of earning a delegate income of £1750 and a 5% chance of earning £3750. This converts to a total cash flow profile for the lecturers of a 12.5% chance of making a loss of £800 if the seminar does not run (the £800 represents the opportunity costs less the £200 fixed fee), a 50% chance of earn-

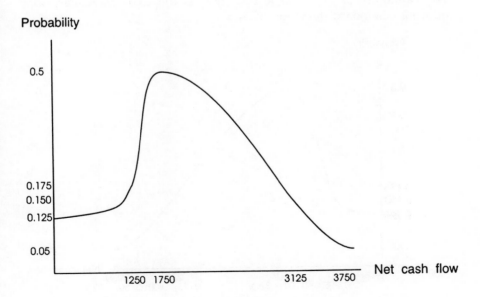

Figure 3.6 Probability distribution for delegate income: Scenario one

ing a fee of £950 on the basis of the average of 14 delegates attending, a 15% chance of earning £2325 and a 5% chance of earning £2950 (see Figure 3.7).

If these figures were real the individual project for which this book has been written would be twice as risky as lecturing as a whole! The authors are hoping to become millionaires but probably won't.

Scenario two

The second worked example is the same as the first but with the difference that the lecturers have ensured that the lecturing company advises them of any seminars two months in advance and if there is to be a cancellation one month's notice is to be given. This enables the lecturers to arrange their consultancy assignments so that there is no overlap with the seminar lecturing days. There is therefore no opportunity cost, so the cash flow of the fixed portion of the income is a benefit of £200. There is no risk with this income. The variable income is the same as Scenario one.

The total cash flow of the projects is the total fixed revenue (£200) and the variable revenue (£1750) plus the total fixed costs (£0) and variable costs (£0). The total cash flow is £200 + £1750 minus £0 + £0, giving a total expected cash flow of £1950 per seminar. Once again, the operational gearing is the ratio of the variable cash flows to the total cash flows. The operational gearing is therefore £1750/£1950 to produce an operational gearing of 0.897—the project is now much lower risk in that the proportion of the total income that is subject to variability is much less.

The variability of the variable cash flow is the same as Scenario one, producing a standard deviation of 54.5%.

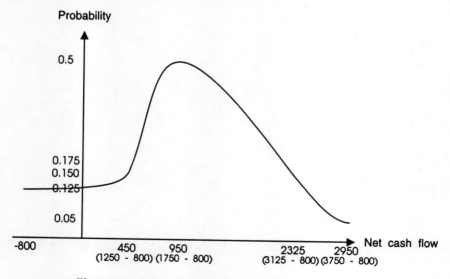

Figure 3.7 Lecturers' cash flow profile: Scenario one

It is now possible to calculate the project *beta*:

Relative OG = 0.897/1.53 = 0.586
Relative RS = 0.545/0.652 = 0.84

The authors have assumed for the purposes of simplicity that the company *beta* for lecturing is 2.0:

The company/project *beta* is therefore 0.586 × 0.84 × 2.0 = 0.98

This *beta* value can be input to the capital asset pricing formula to calculate the project discount rate required:

Company/project discount rate = 8.4% + 0.98 (18% − 8.4%) = 17.8%

This shows that the project is less risky and requires a discount rate of 17.8% rather than the discount rate of 27.7% for Scenario one.

The risk profile of the lecturing project can be plotted. The probability distribution of the delegate income remains the same as in Scenario one. The lecturers' profile is less risky in that there are no opportunity costs, this adding £200 to the variable income rather than taking off £800. This converts to a total cash flow profile for the lecturers of a 12.5% chance of making £200 income if the seminar does not run (this being the guaranteed income), a 17.5% chance of earning a fee of £1450, a 50% chance of earning a fee of £1950 on the basis of the average of 14 delegates attending, a 15% chance of earning £3325 and a 5% chance of earning £3950 (see Figure 3.8).

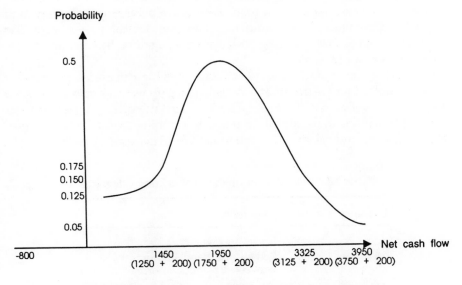

Figure 3.8 Lecturers' cash flow profile: Scenario two

Table 3.7   Definition of revenue sensitivity categories

Category	Definition
Low	< half normal RS
Medium	between half and 1.5 RS
High	between 1.5 and 2.5 RS
Very high	> 2.5 RS

3.5.4.2 *The Categorisation of the Bowater Scott Model*

Bowater Scott have devised an interesting mechanism to overcome the "hassle" of the complexity of calculating or estimating revenue sensitivity. The approach is to say that, because absolute measures of revenue sensitivity are a "hassle" to calculate, it is much easier to express these quantities in broad categories relative to the norm for the company. The task thus becomes one of prediction and categorisation and not one of calculation. For example, if the company wide revenue sensitivity was known it would be easier to say whether the revenue sensitivity of a project would be twice that of the norm or half that of the norm, rather than compute any figure. In the model built by Bowater Scott the project analysts merely had to place the project in one of four categories for revenue sensitivity—low, medium, high or very high *relative to the company norm* for revenue sensitivity. The Revenue Sensitivity (RS) categories were defined as shown in Table 3.7.

This was a much easier task than plotting probability distributions and could be done with some confidence. Four similar categories were also defined for Operational Gearing (OG), again set against the company norm. These are shown in Table 3.8.

By placing the project into one of four possible categories for each of these variables there is the ability to resolve the project risk into 16 possible project *beta*, as shown in Table 3.9. This standard calculation for project *beta* (OG × RS) can be done for all 16 possible combinations of relative operational gearing and relative revenue sensitivity. The results can then be put

Table 3.8   Definition of operational gearing categories

Category	Definition
Low	< half normal OG
Medium	between half and 1.5 normal OG
High	between 1.5 and 2.5 normal OG
Very high	> 2.5 OG

Table 3.9 The Bowater Scott matrix

	Relative OG			
Relative RS	Low < 0.5	Medium 0.5–1.5	High 1.5–2.5	Very high > 2.5
Low < 0.5	Low risk 11%	Low risk 11%	Medium risk 17%	High risk 23%
Medium 0.5–1.5	Low risk 11%	Medium risk 17%	High risk 23%	Very high risk 28%
High 1.5–2.5	Medium risk 17%	High risk 23%	Very high risk 28%	Too high? 34%
Very high > 2.5	High risk 23%	Very high risk 28%	Too high? 34%	Too high > 34%

into a matrix which can be used by general management for the quick and easy selection of a risk adjusted project discount rate. By placing a project in one category for relative operational gearing and in one category for relative revenue sensitivity the discount rate can be read off the matrix directly.

Notwithstanding the ease of the categorisation approach, the consequence of placing the projects in categories rather than calculating a value of the operational gearing and the revenue sensitivity is that precision is lost in the calculation of the project discount rate. Table 3.9 shows this effect. Instead of a range of calculated values being possible, only five discount rates are possible in this example (11%, 17%, 23%, 28% and 34%). Suppose a project is borderline between 11% and 17% discount rate. If the method were strictly applied then one of these two rates would be used rather than a more appropriate rate of around 14%. This loss of precision is a drawback. There is, however, nothing to stop an organisation increasing the number of categories to five or six and so improving the resolution. Overall, this categorisation approach is both quick and effective, with any loss of accuracy due to categorisation being made sufficiently small to ignore if the number of categories is increased.

3.6 CHAPTER SUMMARY

Discounting the monies being invested in projects is absolutely essential. Monies relating to a project over its lifetime suffer a number of features that make their accurate measurement difficult. These features need to be factored out so that future monies are brought to an accurate current value.

This factoring out is the discounting. Future monies suffer from inflation, various risks and the danger of being invested in projects other than the IT project being considered. Discounting is used to account for these factors.

Risk is more difficult to measure. The measure of risk is what is called a *beta* factor. The *beta* measure of risks measures only the market element of risk—unique risk is excluded because investors are not interested in unique risk. There is a hierarchy of risks from the general market risk to the risks of individual projects. The riskiness of the project has to be measured as the greater the risk, the greater the chance that the investment in the project could be lost.

It has been established through the CAPM that there is a linear relationship between risk and the financial return to be expected from an investment, the greater the risk the greater the return to be expected.

Risk is essentially a variability of something. If that something, and it could be a company share or a project cash flow, does not vary then there is no risk.

The market risk is measured by plotting the variability of the company's shares against the variability of the weighted average of the shares of all the companies in the market. If the company shares are more variable than the market shares then the company risk is greater than the market risk. The market risk *beta* is always given a value of 1. Given the greater variability of the company shares the *beta* value of the company would be greater than 1.

Projects occur within companies. It is not possible to use the shares as the measure of project risk as projects are not traded in stock-markets. Another measure of risk is required. This measure is the cash flow of the project. Since there is only one variable, the plotting approach used for the measurement of company risk cannot be used. The technique used for assessing the variability of the project cash flows is standard deviation. The greater the variability of the cash flow around the average/mean cash flow the greater the riskiness of the project, the greater the project *beta* value. Project risk is calculated by the Bowater Scott model. Once the project *beta* is calculated, its value is multiplied against the *beta* value of the company to produce the total project *beta* value. The multiplication reflects the fact that projects occur *within* companies.

Pitfalls, Misuse and Abuse of the DCF Techniques

This chapter is about the do's and don'ts when investing in projects. Much of the criticism levelled against the DCF techniques can be answered by showing that the techniques are misused rather than there being a fault in the techniques themselves. The leading misuses are:

- The use of excessively high discount rates;
- The use of fixed hurdle rates;
- The incorrect treatment of inflation;
- The setting of arbitrary project lives;
- Missing monies:
  - the intangible benefits;
  - project interactions/synergy and the portfolio approach;
- The setting of capital rations.

4.1 EXCESSIVELY HIGH DISCOUNT RATES

The most common criticism of DCF techniques is that they are biased against long term investments. The argument goes that only those projects that have a relatively quick return have a chance of being selected, the more distant cash returns being so heavily discounted that they cannot repay the initial outlay. This is certainly the case when very high discount rates are used. This is still common practice in most large companies today. For example, a major motor manufacturer required all its investments to return at least 30%. However, the company itself made nothing like a 30% return. They were more severe on their investments than their shareholders!

Companies often set rates much higher than their expected profit performance because:

- They want to discourage too many requests for capital;
- It provides a margin of safety so that any errors or unforeseen events do not make the project unprofitable;
- A high return has to be earned on projects with a readily measurable tangible return in order to "subsidise" those projects with little or no return, such as capital projects needed to meet new environmental or legal requirements, or for "housekeeping" type operations, such as payroll;
- They are not aware of the expected return formula.

Whatever the reason the effect is just the same. By setting these artificially high rates the company will be rejecting safe projects which yield a moderate but certain return. Projects that could genuinely provide a useful benefit to the company on all reasonable measures, on a return that correctly reflects the return expected by market investors for the type of investment, are rejected. The full profit potential of the company is lowered. The money not spent on projects that could safely earn a reasonable/expected return of 20% are sitting in the bank vaults earning lower returns. The usual results of setting artificially high rates are that:

- Proposers of projects resort to a distortion of the figures in order to gain acceptance, the extra costs later being treated as unforeseen;
- Most importantly there is a bias against long term investments; the sponsors of important strategic long term or infrastructure projects usually have difficulty in demonstrating a positive return even with their most optimistic forecast figures. The outcome is that such a project is needlessly rejected or a case may be made for it to be considered an intangible investment which must be invested in on a gut feel basis. This again forces managers down the path of the imprecise "intangible" argument and a decision is taken that is "blind".

4.2 THE FOLLY OF FIXED HURDLE RATES

The consequences of failing to set discount rates for individual projects can be serious (as discussed at length in Chapter 3). Many companies set a fixed rate of return that all projects must achieve if they are to be accepted for investment.

Suppose that a public limited company uses the equity *beta* value of its shares to set a target rate of return for all its investments. The resultant return is then set for all projects the company invests in, and if a project

Cost of capital returns

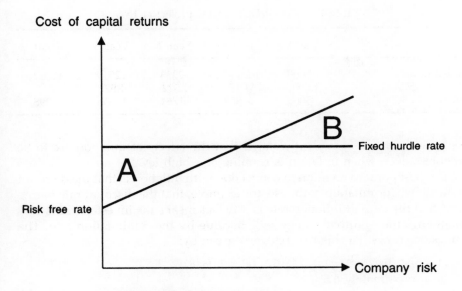

A: safe earner rejected
B: project too risky for the return, but accepted
Net effect: decisions lead to high risk portfolio

Figure 4.1 Folly of the fixed discount/hurdle rate

does not achieve the return rate set it is rejected. Whilst setting discount rates to reflect the market risk of the company may be a large leap forward it could still be a harmful policy if rigidly applied to all projects. Figure 4.1 illustrates the problem. The target rate may be 15%, say. If projects are only accepted when they exceed the 15% target, regardless of risk, then safe projects such as those in area A will be rejected. Similarly high risk projects that do not earn sufficient returns to cover the added risks, area B, will be accepted.

It is sheer folly to set a flat discount rate, a fixed hurdle rate, for all projects undertaken by a company regardless of the risk of the individual projects. The overall effect will be to increase the risks of the company's investment portfolio.

4.3 INCORRECT TREATMENT OF INFLATION

Another common abuse of DCF techniques is a failure to understand the treatment of inflation. In too many cases, particularly projects with a life

Table 4.1 Actual DCF for PC project at 15%

	Year 0	Year 1	Year 2	Year 3	Total
Cash flow	−5000	+2160	+2333	+2519	+2012
Factor (15%)	1.0000	1.15	1.322	1.521	
NPV	−5000	+1878	+1764	+1656	+298

of a few years, it is explicitly stated that the effects of inflation are to be ignored, even when inflation is running at a high level.

The first point to mention in connection with inflation is that the discount rate allows for inflation. Suppose, for example, that the discount rate is 15% and that the current inflation rate is 8%. This means the investor wants 15% knowing full well that money will devalue by the 8% inflation rate. The investor knows that his real return is given by:

(1 + real discount rate) = 1.15/1.08 = 1.06481
or approximately 6.5%

There are two options. One is to use the actual discount rate and to inflate all costs and benefits at the expected rate of inflation. The other is to use the real discount rate and to assume that all future costs and benefits will increase at the rate of inflation.

An example will illustrate the point. Suppose a PC costs £5000 as an initial investment. Suppose also that the PC will save £2000 per annum in current clerical overtime. If inflation is running at an average of 8% then the savings in the first year will be 8% higher at £2160, 8% more in the second year at £2333, and 8% higher still in the third year at £2519. The actual DCF for the project at 15% is shown in Table 4.1 The NPV is positive and so the investment in the PC is worthwhile. The 15% discount rate expects 8% of the savings to be due to inflation, so the cash flow analysis is correctly inflating the benefits in future years.

The alternative approach is to assume inflation does not exist and to use the real discount rate of 6.5%. In this case the benefits will be assumed to be inflation free at £2000 per annum. The real DCF analysis for the project will then be that shown in Table 4.2. Notice that apart from small rounding

Table 4.2 Alternative DCF analysis for PC project at 6.5% and no inflation

	Year 0	Year 1	Year 2	Year 3	Total
Cash flow	−5000	+2000	+2000	+2000	+1000
Factor (6.5%)	1.0000	1.065	1.134	1.208	
NPV	−5000	+1878	+1764	+1656	+298

errors the result is exactly the same. The two approaches give the same result.

All too often this distinction between the two methods is ignored (or not even understood) and analyses are performed using an actual discount rate of, say, 15% and then failing to inflate future costs and benefits at the expected rate of inflation. Again such a treatment will be biased against longer term cash flows (usually the benefits) and so undervalue the project.

The principle to remember is that if an actual discount rate is being used then future cash flows must be inflated at the expected rates of inflation. If real discount rates are being used then inflation must be taken out of the analysis. The two approaches must not be confused.

One drawback of the approach of using real discount rates is that it is not possible to apply differential rates of inflation to different costs and benefits. For example, it may be advisable to inflate software development costs at a higher rate, say 10%, than hardware costs, say 4%. By using the better approach of actual discount rates it is possible to inflate each of the different costs and benefits at an appropriate rate of inflation. The real discount rate assumes that all costs and benefits rise at a general rate of inflation which can be accounted for by using an inflation adjusted discount rate. This book uses the actual discount rate.

4.4 THE SETTING OF ARBITRARY PROJECT LIVES

Notwithstanding the techniques for calculating project risk there are certain aspects of the DCF technique that can adversely affect the correct valuation of projects. A common failing in the application of DCF techniques is the setting of arbitrary project lives. A company may set a policy of, say, four years to a computer system's investment life. As illustrated in Figure 4.2 any benefit after that time will not be considered for DCF analysis. This was the case with one company where the policy was that the DCF analysis could not cover a period greater than the depreciation life of the asset (in this case three years). This may be fine for PCs whose use is never certain beyond four years, but for major projects it is another cause of undervaluation.

There is always a danger to fixed guidelines, which is why a contingent approach to project lives should be used. The DCF analysis should cover the whole of the expected life of the project if a true valuation of the project is to be achieved. Of course, there is always the problem of determining just how long a project's life actually is, but some attempt must be made at assessing a reasonable life time for an investment's use.

One approach to the problem of determining the value of a project with an uncertain life is to perform a sensitivity analysis. By carrying out a DCF

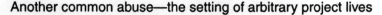

Another common abuse—the setting of arbitrary project lives

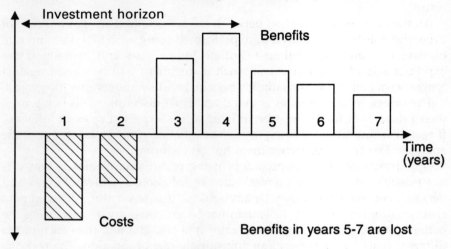

Figure 4.2 Setting the lifespan of a project

analysis on the shortest and longest lives of the project then some bounds can be set upon the project's value. For example, suppose that a PC will give annual benefits of £2000 in current terms. The uncertainty of the system is its useful life. The worst case is that it will only have a three year life, the best case is that it could last for seven years, whilst the expected life is about five years. The cash flow analysis is shown in Table 4.3. If the system only has a useful life of three years the NPV will be –702, and the investment would not have been worthwhile. If the system operates for the expected life of five years then the NPV will be +2324. If the system lasts seven years the NPV will be +4983. The breakeven point is just over three

Table 4.3 Cash flow analysis of sample PC project

Year	Cash flow	Market discount factor (15%)	PV	Cumulative PV
0	–6000	1.0000	–6000	–6000
1	+2160	1.15	+1878	–4122
2	+2333	1.3225	+1764	–2358
3	+2519	1.521	+1656	–702
4	+2721	1.749	+1556	+863
5	+2938	2.011	+1461	+2324
6	+3173	2.313	+1371	+3695
7	+3427	2.66	+1288	+4983

years, which is only just better than the worst possible outcome. On balance there seems only a slim chance of losing out. The investment is probably worth the risk.

By performing such a sensitivity analysis of the various alternatives, these options can be compared.

The sensitivity analysis approach can also be used for comparing two projects. If two projects are solutions to the same problem the expected values can be compared and the difference in the worst and best cases could then be a measure of risk. For example, project A may have an expected value of +2500 but a chance of a loss of −2000. The project B (above) has a lower expected value of +2324, but a potential loss of only −702. If you are a risk taking person adopt project A, if you are a risk averse person adopt project B.

Sensitivity analysis is discussed further in section 5.2.3.1.

4.5 MISSING MONIES

The value of the DCF technique is reduced if major parts of the project cash flows are not included in the IA process. As to be expected the most difficult to calculate monies are those that are usually left out.

4.5.1 The Intangible Costs and Benefits

The definition and calculation of intangible benefits are addressed in Chapter 6. Suffice it to say at this point that all too often a points scoring approach is used for the measurement of intangibles. The problem with this is that the points cannot be included in the monetary based IA process.

As shown in Chapter 6 the value of the intangibles is a significant part of the cash flow of most computer projects and the omission of intangibles reduces the benefit of the DCF techniques. This has led to arguments that the DCF techniques are useless in some cases. The failing, however, is not with the techniques of DCF but with management's inability to measure intangibles. Chapter 6 details a more precise way of estimating the value of the intangibles.

4.5.2 Project Interactions and the Portfolio Approach

Projects should rarely be considered in isolation. Business just does not operate that way. One performs actions because it is anticipated that there will be a reaction, the reaction generating a financial return. One makes a product so that someone else reacts by purchasing it. And so it is with computer systems. The data and processing of one system will usually have an impact on some other system's operation and efficiency. An analysis of the costs and benefits of an investment which fails to consider the impact upon other projects will most probably be flawed. A most commonly ignored benefit of interaction is the effect of synergy:

- Projects may have an opportunity to share costs, so that the benefit of the two projects taken together may be greater than the sum of the two projects taken in isolation.
- Some projects may also have a synergy of benefits. For example, a sales order processing system may provide information which can enhance the value of a market forecasting system, which in turn can provide information of value to the production schedules.
- The interactions can be cross temporal as well as the above cross sectional interactions. Both of these benefits can apply to infrastructure investments, which may have little or no net benefit in the short term but which enable other projects to happen in the future. The wide and local area telecommunications network with plenty of spare capacity may not achieve its full value for several years. Its real value may be that it enables many other systems to be developed at a future date.

This aspect of project synergy is becoming an increasingly significant factor. The cost profiles of computer projects and the benefits to be obtained from their interrelationships are being substantially altered by the emerging software development technologies.

The adoption of database technology was the first major attempt to obtain mutual benefit between computer systems, through the creation of a single pool of data (the database) for all the organisation's computer systems to maintain and access. Special design techniques of data normalisation were developed so that the data was correctly "allocated" to the records/tables to which it related. Customer Name and Address were allocated to the Customer table. Project synergy was obtained for the data, with multiple applications having access to a single and stable corporate database. But the logic in the application programs still remained at the business requirement/event level and hence specific to the applications of the business—and for each application there are often distinct computer systems, sometimes incompatible. Some real horror stories could be told here. Logic was at the application, not the corporate, level. Project synergy was thus limited to the data.

The design of logic can now also be based on the same normalisation technique as for the data. It is now realised that logic such as "If Customer has red hair then give Customer a 10% bonus" has nothing to do with an event/business requirement—with the application—but with the Customer. With object orientation such logic is also "allocated" to the object, in this case the Customer object.

It is now realised that some 80% of the code is actually not relevant to the event but to the objects. This 80% of the logic is therefore designed as additional properties of the objects in exactly the same way as data. This 80% of the logic is, like the corporate data, application independent and therefore provides full access synergy for corporate usage. Only 20% of logic is application dependent. The benefits obtained from a single database are now being achieved for the 80% of the logic. A single information base of data and most of the logic is now a reality. The full potential for project synergy is now technically available.

But the real benefit being obtained in project synergy is the ability of object oriented design to support information reuse, particularly software reuse. With new systems the design approach is to use the current information systems to a maximum extent and to add the further data and functionality as extensions to the current systems only where they are deficient in the data and the logic they contain. System development is by the process of addition to the current systems. This is maximum project synergy. What this means is that the data and functional overlap of computer systems is increasing, with different applications being able to reuse each other's data and logic.

Project synergy and the benefits to be obtained from this are now significant considerations in the cost/benefit equation. The cost profiles of projects are changing. Consider Figures 4.3 and 4.4. The first shows the typical risk/cost profile of current computer systems. The costs are low during operational running of the systems and high during design, development and maintenance. With object orientation the costs are high to begin with, as there are many more objects to design than entities with traditional systems. The beauty of the situation is that, with information reuse, new systems use the information of the current systems to an increasing extent. The core of reusable information gets larger and larger and the benefits from project synergy bigger and bigger. This can be seen with the bigger benefits in the lower costs of system development for the second and third iterations of system developments.

There can also be degrees of interaction. The spectrum of interaction can range from those projects which are strict complements (those that must be in place in order for another system to function at all) to those which are mutually exclusive (either one or the other project must be selected but not both). In between there are various degrees of complementary projects, through independent to mutually exclusive. Figure 4.5 shows the range of project interaction and gives examples of each.

Infrastructure projects in particular produce added value in that they enable other projects to be undertaken. Often these infrastructure projects do not show a net return for their base use, that is the first computer system that was installed on them. The real benefits come when the next

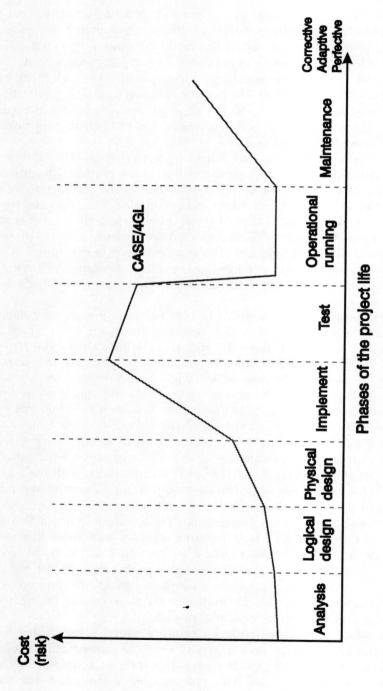

Figure 4.3 Standard IT project risk profile

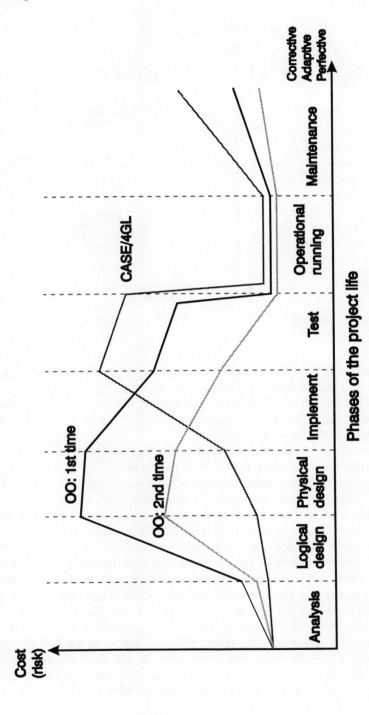

Figure 4.4   Risk changes — with object oriented technology

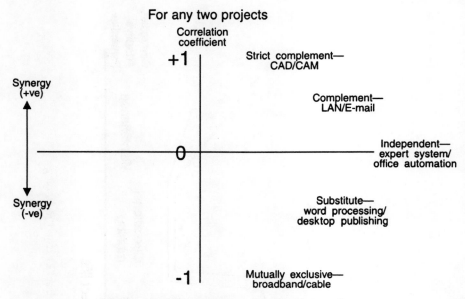

Figure 4.5   The spectrum of project interactions

stages/systems are implemented. Having installed a telecommunications network the benefit is obtained when the previously distinct systems can dynamically transfer data. It is no wonder that DCF techniques do not show the true value of such investments when the analysis is restricted to the base case use of the infrastructure.

The question is often asked as to how to ascertain the value of such infrastructure projects. The question that needs to be asked is "What can you do now with the infrastructure that you could not do before the infra-structure?". Identify, measure and value the difference.

Taking the example of a local area network (project A) and an E-mail system (project B), IA has shown that both have a reasonable return on a standalone basis, but because these two projects are complements then there is opportunity for synergy. The costs and benefits are shown in Table 4.4. Some of the costs of the network can be shared with the E-mail system, so the costs of the two projects taken together are less than the costs of the two systems invested in totally separately. In this example the costs for the systems taken separately would be £180 000, but because the two can be merged the costs taken together fall to £120 000. Some of the benefits may be lost, however, by the compromise solution. In this example the benefits fall from £250 000 when taken separately to £220 000 when the two systems are merged. However the overall effect is that the NPV is greater when the

Table 4.4 Project synergy benefits

	Project A (LAN)	Project B (E-mail)	Both
	£'000	£'000	£'000
PV (costs)	−80	−100	−120
PV (benefits)	+100	+150	+220
NPV	+20	+50	+100

two projects are merged to take advantage of the synergy (rising to £100 000 from £70 000).

Given that these impacts can be significant it makes sense to adopt a portfolio approach to investment in systems. This means that the aim is to maximise the return on the portfolio of investments that are made and not to merely select the individual projects with the highest return. The portfolio approach can be used with DCF techniques, such as with the NPV as shown in the example above. Indeed, failure to recognise the positive synergy of complementary systems will lead to undervaluing the investment portfolio. Similarly the failure to recognise the negative synergy of mutually exclusive projects will lead to the overvaluation of a portfolio. The measurement of a project's value can be a meaningless exercise if there are strong interactions with other projects and these interactions are ignored. Once more it is no wonder that CBA techniques fail to capture the true worth of investments when these synergies are excluded. Once again the fault lies in the failure to correctly analyse the problem and the benefits and not in the techniques in themselves.

Given that these interactions do occur it is of crucial importance to look for these interactions before a detailed CBA is performed. Once these interactions are understood then it is possible to predict the costs and benefits for different combinations of projects. The exercise is then to calculate the NPV of the portfolio and to select the combination of projects which maximises that portfolio. By adopting this portfolio approach to the use of the NPV technique the return on capital invested will be maximised for the range of computer investments open to the organisation. Hence one further criticism of DCF techniques can be answered if they are used with some common sense.

The task of analysing all possible combinations of projects is daunting. Anyone familiar with combinatorial mathematics will appreciate that this can quickly become impractical—for example, the number of different combinations of only six projects is 63. The only practical approach is to concentrate on those projects with an obviously high level of interaction, as indicated in Figure 4.5. Those which are independent or close to being independent can be treated in isolation—they may have synergistic relationships with other types of system but such systems may not be part of the set of investment opportunities open to the organisation, hence they can be treated separately. Where projects are obvious complements the two can be merged into one project. Where projects are obviously mutually exclusive the poorer option can be eliminated. In this way the number of combinations can be reduced. By the careful pruning and making of sensible approximations the problem of measuring the increased value of projects with synergy can be whittled down to one of manageable size.

By recognising that there can be synergy between only the top three or four projects in a portfolio, much of the added value of the portfolio can be found. This represents a new approach to IA and it gives the greatest improvements to investment decisions for relatively little effort. The monies from project synergy can be put into the DCF calculations.

4.5.3 Capital Rationing

The primary function of capital rationing is to limit the spend on capital to within planned levels. A secondary consideration is to restrict the number of requests for capital.

The common approach to capital rationing is to set a capital budget for the organisation at the beginning of a financial year. The capital budget may be set at £Xm. for the year and this is then allocated to various functions. Production may be awarded 40% of this amount, marketing 10%, systems 20% and so on. These then become the capital rations for each function for the year.

Once the limits have been set then no department may exceed its capital spending limit (other than in exceptional circumstances, such as a takeover which may require a radical restructuring). In such circumstances each function must manage its capital wisely, because if all its capital ration is spoken for then it will be hard luck if an outstanding new investment opportunity materialises. The funds will not be available.

A special consideration for capital rations is that project selection on the basis of maximum NPV breaks down. Consider the three projects with cash flows shown in Table 4.5. If the capital ration for the department is £1m., then on the basis of selecting the project(s) with the highest NPV up to a limit of £1m. capital costs, the outcome would be to select project A only. However, this would not maximise profit on capital invested. The better solution would be to select both projects B and C—this would yield an NPV of £2.8m. for an investment of £1m. This example again reinforces the message that the aim is to maximise the return of a portfolio, not to select the individual projects with the highest NPV.

Table 4.5 Illustration of how NPV based project selection breaks down under capital rationing

	PV capital Costs £'000	PV net Benefits £'000	NPV £'000
Project A	−1000	+3100	+2100
Project B	−500	+2100	+1600
Project C	−500	+1700	+1200

When capital is rationed it is best to select the projects with the highest NPV per unit of capital cost, thus providing the "biggest return bang per input buck" (NPV/PV capital costs). This measure is often known as the profitability index. The profitability indices of the three projects are: Project A—2.1; Project B—3.2; Project C—2.4. Selecting projects in order of profitability index, the order of investment priority becomes B, then C and finally A. By adopting this policy the right investment decisions will be made for a given capital ration.

The same principle applies to other constraints. If, for example, the constraint on investment is not capital but, say, software development man hours, then the order for project selection is on the basis of highest NPV per software development hour required.

Capital rations are set as a means of management control. There is nothing sacred about them. If there is an exceptional investment opportunity that could make a significant difference to a business's financial performance then it would be folly for the directors of that business to forgo such an investment simply because it exceeded the capital budget of the company for that year. If such an investment is really worthwhile then there should be no difficulty in raising the capital.

4.7 CHAPTER SUMMARY

The do's of discounting are:

- Measure project synergy. With the increasing use of object oriented technology and the ability of computer systems to use/reuse each others' objects of information, project synergy is going to become an increasingly important factor in the financial benefits to be gained. The long established use of database and telecommunications started the creation of corporately linked systems with 100% of the data and 100% of the messages to the data on a common infrastructure, the database and the network. Object orientation does the same with 80% of the logic.

- Include all monies in the valuation of projects. It is essential to include the value of the intangible benefits. These are an increasing proportion of the revenues from IT projects.

The don'ts of discounting are:

- Never set a fixed hurdle for a project to satisfy. The hurdle could be a rate of return or a fixed time limit to provide a return. Either way a fixed hurdle rate will cause errors in investment to be made. A fixed rate of return hurdle will produce a high risk investment portfolio. A time hurdle will cause some viable projects to be rejected and again result in a higher than necessary investment portfolio. Always adopt a risk adjusted discounting described in section 3.5.
- Do not use an excessively high discount rate, either as a hedge against possible problems occurring during the life of the project or as a subsidy for less profitable projects.

Chapter 5

Investment Measurement II

This chapter describes aspects that affect the value of a project investment which have not been addressed by the traditional CBA approach. These aspects are the events that were not anticipated when the calculations of the project cash flows were originally drawn up and the actions that project management can take to offset the effects of the events if they are adverse to the project and to exploit the events if they are beneficial to the project. These management actions are the flexibility aspect of project valuation. Both the impact of the events and the flexibility actions require to be valued and the project cash flows adjusted accordingly.

5.1 EVENT RISK

It is important to understand there is a risk of events occurring that can affect the financial value of a project. Such events are of two kinds, those that are unforeseen or unlikely and those that can be anticipated with a reasonable degree of probability as to their timing and impact.

The unforeseen events cannot be anticipated when project plans are drawn up. Such events are of the type known as "acts of God", such as earthquakes and storms, and human incidents such as political coups and company takeovers. Such events are of their nature unpredictable and cannot be planned for. They should therefore not be included in the investment measurements of a project.

There is another kind of event that most certainly should be included as part of the financial calculations of a project's investment. These events can be anticipated with a reasonable degree of probability. They also can be caused by natural as well as human factors. For example, there could be a project to invest in a computer system that monitors volumes of water flow in a hydro plant. The flows are based on the current water flow in the river, which is in turn based on the current weather conditions. It is known that climatic change is occurring and, based on estimates from climatologists, it is anticipated that the water flow will probably increase in water flow of X% with a probability of Y%. These increased flows and the degree of certainty of the probability (the higher the percentage probability, the higher the certainty) affect the required size of the hydro plant, the overflow channels and so on, and hence the design of the controlling computer system.

Human factors affected the design of a container ports computer system. The size of the proposed computer system was based on the anticipated volume of customer business, particularly as regards the shipping companies, certain growth factors with estimated probabilities being built in to take account of various business scenarios that could occur. In fact the estimates proved to be on the conservative side, such that the computer system required up-sizing.

In both the above examples, foreseeable events affect the project plans against which investments have been calculated and can generate a whole series of knock-on effects. It is these predictable events which could affect the investment in a project and the knock-on effects which require to be identified, measured and valued.

5.2 EVENT RISK AND FLEXIBILITY

The two aspects of risk and flexibility in the valuation of a project's financial value are considered together because they are both identified and measured using the same technique.

Risk is a cost on a project and therefore lowers its value. The greater the risk the greater the chance of loss. If there is a 50% chance that a project will fail because of a foreseeable event that adversely affects the project and the planned profit without risk (the world is perfect and all plans are fulfilled) is calculated to be £1m., then the expected profit will be £500 000. There is an event risk against the project. The financial value of a project is reduced if it is high risk, for the simple reason that the investment may incur lower than expected return, down to half the expected return. It should be mentioned here that foreseeable events may well be unique to the project, in which case they are unique risks. Whilst unique risks do not affect the desired return (see section 3.4.4) they do not affect the expected profit and hence the NPV value of the project.

Event risk can be offset by flexibility. Projects which have flexibility can reduce the impacts of event risk and so raise the value of a project. If the cost of the flexibility is less than the cost of the risk times its probability of occurring, then the value of the project will increase. In the above example the value of the project will increase if the cost of the flexibility is less than £500 000.

Flexibility enables project managers to take advantage of beneficial change and can also be used to limit the impacts of an adverse twist of fate in the project's environment. The greater the degree of flexibility built into a project's plans the greater the ability to exploit opportunities and avoid unexpected disasters, so lowering event risk. Flexibility can add value to a project.

The difficulty is in capturing this added value. A prime example of this problem is when a straight decision has to be made between a potentially high value but high risk solution and a lower potential return from a more flexible option. The dilemma is to determine which investment will give the better return in the long run. In order to do this there is a need to ascertain what the event risks are and cost them. Facts about the event risks—and there can be many of them all interacting with each other—their probabilities and impact on the cash flows all have to be ascertained. Then it must be decided how to offset the risks with flexibility and value the flexibility.

Infrastructure projects are examples of projects which bring added value through flexibility. These types of investment tend to yield a low return, but they do open up many options that would not otherwise exist. An example of this is a Local Area Network (LAN). The introduction of a network is usually in response to a specific need. In a manufacturing site, a LAN may be a solution to a materials control system, the various production managers and controllers having access to the system across the site. This becomes the "base case" justification of the system. With infrastructure projects the added value is "What is it that I can do now that I could not do before?". The network adds value in that it:

- Enables new applications to be introduced at much lower cost—the network is there already;
- Enables users to communicate online with each other.

Another example of flexibility is to choose open system hardware and software technology, that is the ability to use plug compatible hardware and message compatible software from a variety of vendors and thereby obtain the best possible price. One is not tied to specific products from specific suppliers. One can "cherry pick" the most suitable product for the best price. It is options such as these which create flexibility and enable systems to develop to meet ever changing demands without massive redevelopment.

A specialised bespoke system may perform very well for a time but it is vulnerable to changing demands—it is less flexible because of its specialisation. One of the authors witnessed a database developed for a confectionery company which was highly tuned by an intensely protective database administrator who loved to "play" with the fine tuning knobs of the database file handler—and the file handler was IMS. The response times to user queries were most impressive, but requests for change were met with stiff resistance. This is not flexibility.

5.2.1 A Classification and Measure of Flexibility

There are five types of flexibility, three base flexibilities:

(1) Product or service;
(2) Volume of business;
(3) Robustness.

And supporting these base flexibilities in that they can each be used for any of the above are the flexibilities of:

(4) Organisation;
(5) Technology.

The first flexibility is the ability to alter the product or service that the system produces. A system produces a product/service because there is a demand for such from customers. However, these demands are not constant. New products are introduced, old products are no longer required. Product/service flexibility is the extent to which the output of the system can alter the products produced to meet these changing demands. A production planning system may be set up to produce production plans on a one month planning period, so enabling its products to be supplied to a one month lead time. If the market changes and shorter lead times are required by customers (say one week) then a flexible system would be easily modified to enable planning on a one week cycle. The service that the system provides in this case is flexible and is an example of product/service flexibility.

The second type of flexibility is the ability to alter the volume of output. The customer demand may be for the same product/service, but the volume of demand may alter. The volume of demand for a sales order processing system may double, but the computer system may not be capable of expansion to that extent. Volume flexibility is the extent to which the system can support variations in the volume of demand for a system's services. In computing the perfect solution to this problem is to adopt scalable software and hardware—the ability for the software to run on the largest to the "smallest" configuration and for the hardware to be linearly expandable by plugging in additional speed and/or memory capacity on a modular basis and without limit.

The "smallest" means the ability to run on remarkably small computers. Clearly there has to be a lower limit on the processing speed and memory capacity of the computer, but the lower limit is constantly being reduced. The ORACLE relational database can run in full in the largest mainframe computer down to personal computers of less than 10 megabytes of main memory—a remarkable feat of software design.

Robustness is the ability of a system to maintain its service/output for a variation in its operating environment. For example, a bulk trading system may be able to match suppliers to buyers successfully despite a disruption to supplies. The situation of extremely limited flexibility occurs when one is dependent on a single supplier for a product/service—as Michael Porter would define, the "power" to dictate business is with the supplier. Flexibility is achieved when there are alternative suppliers to choose from— the "power" to dictate business is with the buyer. From the supplier's point of view the solution to the dilemma is to have many customers. This flexibility is best described as robustness of operation.

In summary the three base flexibilities can be described as follows:

(1) Product/service flexibility is the ability to alter the type of product or service offered to customers;
(2) Volume flexibility is the ability to alter the scale of the product or service offered to customers;
(3) Robustness is the ability to maintain the product/service to customers despite environmental disturbance.

There are other facets of flexibility which support these flexibilities. Examples of these are organisational flexibility and technological flexibility; these flexibilities are not just desirable in themselves, but are desirable in that they are able to support any one of the three "base" flexibilities:

(1) Organisational flexibility occurs where the structure of management and the roles to be played by individuals can be altered with ease. An inflexible situation is well demonstrated by the old working practice of fixed demarcation lines between workers on the production line in the car manufacturing industry. Worker A could not move from job 1 to job 2 because job 2 was within the scope of worker B. The adoption of Japanese working practices has eliminated these boundaries. Workers can now move between job types without restriction, as demand dictates. Bad management is just as much a component of higher risk as inflexible working practices. Management flexibility has been provided by a company that:
  - Requires all its managers to be skilled in more than one operational area, in order to reduce the risk to the company of key personnel leaving and to allow managers to be switched to different positions as the situation dictates;

- Has no one operational area limited to the support of only one manager.
(2) The final type of flexibility relates to technology. The computing industry has long been restricted to proprietary products, those produced by a single vendor and not able to link in with the products from other vendors. This has long been the case with the major vendors—the hardware and software from IBM not being able to link in with the hardware and software of DEC and UNISYS, and *vice versa*. Customers were tied to products of the vendors. There was therefore supplier power. Inevitably this created customer resistance and a demand for the ability to move from the "one stop shop" philosophy of the proprietary situation to a "mix and match" philosophy of open system technology, based on plug compatible hardware and message compatible software.

Each classification of flexibility needs to be provided with a unit of measure to assess whether the proposed project has flexibility built into it:

(1) The volume flexibility of a system may be defined by two figures:
- The maximum volume which can be processed. This is the capacity of the system. Above this volume expansion may be necessary or a different system altogether may be required;
- The minimum volume at which the system is economically viable. Below a certain level of transactions the benefits are less than the costs of the system. An alternative system would be necessary. At very low volumes this may even be manual processing of transactions.

Using such measures the volume flexibilities of alternative systems can be quantified and compared. A stock system which can process up to one million transactions a year before needing expansion, and which is still economically viable at 10 000 transactions a year, is more flexible than a stock system which has a maximum limit of 750 000 transactions and is only viable above 50 000 transactions. This situation is clear cut. But a balancing act would be required if one system could support more than one million transactions a year but would only be economically viable with 100 000 transactions a year, and the other could support much less than one million transactions a year but be viable on very few transactions a year.

(2) Product/service flexibility may be measured as:
- The number of different products/services that the system could provide; for example, a garment manufacturer insisted on installing a manufacturing system that could be adaptable to producing both men's and women's clothing in a wide variety of styles. Flexibility was provided such that as demand in the various markets varied, both as regards the number of products and the balance of male and

female demand (and when one was going down, the other was often going up), the system could respond.

- How quickly a new product/service can be launched; the garment manufacturer's system allowed rapid analysis of all sales throughout Europe and could spot garment trends within two weeks. The production systems were also set up to respond to these rapid changes in demand and the garments could be in the right stores within a matter of weeks. This was crucial in enabling the manufacturer to capture extra sales by responding to very quickly moving trends in fashion. Previously a manual based system would have taken six months to respond to such a trend, which is too late to catch the sales in the fashion trade.

(3) Robustness can be measured as the range of disturbances within which output of service/product can be maintained. Disturbances occur all the time in business and the ability to maintain operations in the face of these disruptions is a measure of robustness. A manufacturing resource planning system may allow the production plan to be achieved even though 10% of its supplies arrived late. This is one of the problems of the "just in time" situation favoured by many manufacturers. It will reduce stock and the monies tied up in the stock, and therefore be cost effective, but it is vulnerable to irregularities of supplies. Cost effective yes, flexible no.

(4) A unit of measure for organisational flexibility could be the number of positions different staff can fill.

(5) Technological flexibility could be measured by the number of vendors with products which are suitable for a particular task and which could be integrated into the configuration in a transparent manner.

The important thing to remember is to match the flexibility to the risk. There is, for example, little or no value in having volume flexibility if the volume of demand varies little. Similarly, it is of little value to have product/service flexibility if the system will never need to do anything other than its original task. This situation is typical of company housekeeping type computer systems, such as invoicing and pensions.

It is also important to ensure that the flexibilities across the business and systems match. It is no use designing a system which supports new products if the staff that operate the system do not have sufficient training to be flexible enough to cope with such changes. A manufacturing example illustrates the point about matching across functions. For this particular manufacturer the sales department developed a system which would analyse and forecast sales on a daily basis, so improving business planning. The production planning department however had purchased a package which could only plan production on a one month cycle, so the potential advantage of being able to respond more rapidly to demand was lost because the production systems were not sufficiently flexible to respond. The matching of flexibilities across the business is crucial otherwise all the benefits will be lost.

These issues of flexibility are often ignored. Proposed investments are often looked at in isolation, so it is not surprising that the true value of a project is not established.

A sound approach to the treatment of risk and flexibility would be to perform a risk analysis during the feasibility study stage of a project to identify the significant risks, and to look for the flexibility opportunities to counter that risk. For a rapidly growing company or department the biggest uncertainty may be volume/scale of system. For a system which deals in rapidly changing markets it may be product/service flexibility. A contingent approach to flexibility using a variety of options specific to the most significant risks of the project is the best mechanism to adopt.

In reality the number of options and flexibilities may well be huge. The range may be too great to analyse in the limited amount of time available for the feasibility stage. To analyse every single flexibility would be impossible. However to investigate the most significant risks and to develop a flexible solution based on those risks would be the approach to yield best results in the long run.

5.2.2 The Difficulty of Measuring Risk and Flexibility

Risk and flexibility have certain features that cause certain difficulties with their valuation. There are several problems:

(1) A particular problem of long term projects is that their risk is not constant. At the beginning of a computer design and development project the risk is high with current technology because the uncertainty about the projected, and potentially long-to-be-awaited, tail-end benefits may be very high, particularly if the calculation of the main benefits, the intangibles, is perfunctory or unscientifically conducted. As progress is made the risk is reduced as the uncertainty about the benefits is reduced. There is thus a general reduction of risk as the project progresses. This can be seen in Figure 4.3. When the project is completed and the full costs and benefits finally calculated, the risk is comparatively low. However, as the system grows older, and technically and commercially outdated, it is usual that system maintenance costs start to rise and new user business requirements have to be added. Further development is needed. Uncertainty increases and with it the risks.

New design techniques and development technologies are altering the risk profile of computer projects. This is particularly the case with object orientation. Object orientation will replace the widely used relational technology of today. It has several significant facilities that reduce the risk profile of computer projects—and the profile changes as the computer applications progressively develop. As the systems become more mature the risk profile for new applications becomes lower and lower. This is shown in Figure 4.4.

(2) Flexibility can also cause changes to a project's value throughout its life. If demand doubles and the scale of the project doubles to match, then the project value should also double. Like the CAPM, all the other DCF techniques assume that an investment is made and that's it. A stream of cash flows of an average expected value will then come in year after year with a constant risk rate to allow for fluctuations around this value. This may not always be a valid assumption to make for computer systems.

There are actions which can be taken to enhance a project's life part way through and to limit the impact of an unexpected adverse outcome. In this respect flexibility has two advantages. It enables us to take advantage of beneficial change in the project's environment and it also helps to limit the impacts of an adverse twist of fate.

A beneficial impact of flexibility would be where a new electronic sales ordering system is so successful that the increase in sales is double the best estimates at the implementation stage and it is possible to expand the system to take advantage of the unexpected increase in sales. A DCF view would be that the system is geared up to a certain level of sales, plus or minus a margin for risk, and if those sales exceed the upper limits allowed for risk then there is nothing that can be done about it. There is no scope in the DCF techniques to allow for expansion of the system if demand exceeds the risk limits. DCF techniques do not allow for managers to change the course of a project at certain points in its life.

Similarly if a network is installed with a particular application in mind and that application happens to be a failure then that may not be the end of the matter. There may be options to use the network for other systems and so resurrect something from the failure. In a straight DCF analysis if a project fails that is it—the investment is lost. The technique does not allow for the flexibility to do something else. The technique cannot capture the added value of flexibility.

(3) Flexibility is a vague and "woolly" attribute. What is meant by flexibility, and how can it be measured? It is a good example of the intangible benefits discussed later in Chapter 6. It is readily appreciated that flexibility is a good thing and that it has some value but we can't easily identify or measure it.

5.2.3 Techniques for Valuing Risk and Flexibility

As is common for the various aspects of valuing investments there is a variety of techniques to choose from. There are three for the task of valuing risk and flexibility.

5.2.3.1 Sensitivity Analysis

The most common technique for measuring risks and robustness to certain outcomes is sensitivity analysis. The attraction of the technique is that it is easy to apply and understand, and can present a great deal of information. Consider a mainframe processor solution to a stock control system and an alternative distributed PC solution to the same problem—see Figure 5.1. The high fixed costs of a mainframe system require a high level of transactions to make the system economically attractive. If the volume of transactions is so low that the benefits are less than the costs then a smaller lower cost solution, such as a PC system, would be better. In this case the volume of demand for transactions is a key risk variable.

A sensitivity analysis to this problem would plot the NPV of the benefits (i.e. total cost savings of the system over a manual system) and compare that with the NPV of the total costs of the system for different levels of demand. This is done for the two solutions in Figure 5.1. In these diagrams the expected outcome can be shown along with the best and worst possible outcomes for the volume of transactions. As can be seen from the diagrams, both solutions show a net benefit at the expected level of 750 000 transactions per annum, with the benefit being much greater for the distributed PC solution. The sensitivity analysis goes further than this. There is a known risk that the volume may be lower than expected and it is important to know whether the solutions still produce a net profit if the volume falls to the worst possible volume of only 500 000 transactions per annum. In this case the PC solution still shows a net return but the mainframe solution is a loss maker. The profitability of the mainframe solution is more sensitive to fluctuations in demand.

More importantly it can also show the break-even point. This is the volume of transactions at which the benefits equal the costs. In the case of the mainframe solution the volume can drop to 700 000 transactions per annum before it ceases to be viable, whilst the PC solution can still be viable at a level of 450 000 transactions. A large range between the expected outcome and break-even point will indicate a safety margin and a high robustness (i.e. a high flexibility). An expected outcome which is close to break-even may give cause for concern (as in the case of the mainframe solution). In this case it seems that a distributed PC based system might be less risky and more flexible to fluctuations in the volume of demand.

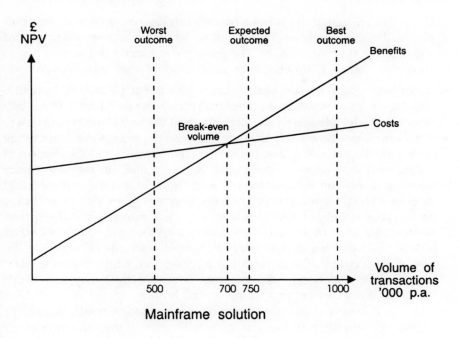

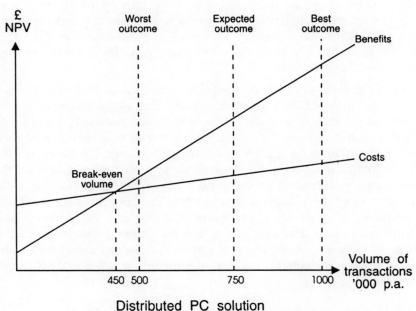

Figure 5.1 Sensitivity analysis of the value of two systems

Using this technique the various options can be compared and outcomes explored. This can easily be done for other key risk variables such as price chargeable for systems services. The principle is exactly the same.

However, there are drawbacks to the sensitivity analysis technique:

- It can only deal with one variable at a time in each diagram. In reality nothing varies in isolation. In more realistic cases one variable is not sufficient to model adequately the problem, and the technique breaks down.
- It does not show how likely the outcomes are. For example, a project may have a break-even point close to the expected outcome, but the chances of falling to that break-even point may be very small. In the case of the mainframe solution above, it may be very unlikely that the volume could drop to 700 000 transaction per annum. Conversely another project may have a break-even point far below its expected outcome, but the spread of outcomes may be so uncertain that this break-even point may stand a good chance of being reached. For example, with the PC solution, the risk for the volume of demand could increase and, whilst the break-even point is as low as 60% of the expected outcome, there may be a much increased chance of volume falling to that level.
- It does not readily show how flexibility can be used to minimise risks or exploit opportunities. It does not show how some of the value of a mainframe solution can be recovered if demand falls by using some spare capacity for an alternative use. Whilst the technique may work for simple, one variable projects it does not adequately capture the value of flexibility or risk minimisation when there are many complex options to change the use of the investment.

The most significant limitation of sensitivity analysis is that only one variable can be analysed on a graph at a time. The use of scenarios is often used in an attempt to overcome this limitation. In scenario building the analyst tries to anticipate the relationship between variables. For example, if two key variables for a project are the price chargeable for its services and the volume of demand for those services, then it may be decided that a reasonable relationship between these two variables is that for a 10% increase in price the volume will fall by 5%. By using this relationship the two variables have in effect been reduced to one and the analysis can be performed as usual. The problem is that the chosen relationship may be wrong. It totally ignores the fact that there will be some independent fluctuation of price and demand. The use of scenarios is not a real solution to the problem.

5.2.3.2 Monte Carlo Simulation

A more sophisticated technique is that of Monte Carlo simulation. This is a statistical technique developed by D. Hertz in the 1960s and has been successfully used in analysing IT investments.[1] The technique will be described only in outline here. Whilst several simulation packages exist to assist in the many calculations required by the technique, the technique should be applied with the aid of a statistician or other competent analyst for the more demanding business projects being modelled.

The simulation exercise has three stages. The first stage is to model the business situation. This involves identifying the parameters and variables that together constitute the business and project under review and establishing the relationships beteen those variables. The second stage is to set probability distributions for the variables. The final stage is to perform the simulation.

The first stage has the most significant impact upon the value of the results. It is the accurate identification and definition of the parameters and variables of the business. This is crucial to a successful simulation of the event risks and their flexibility offsets. Parameters are the fixed elements of the simulation. Typical parameters may be the life of the project, the discount rate (this is rarely variable), any fixed costs and any constraints. The variables are the uncertain factors about the project, such as costs and benefits and software development time. The parameters and variables will change from project to project. The life of a project may be fixed in project A but it may be variable in project B.

Having specified the variables, the relationships between them must be identified and modelled. A typical situation for a project could be that the development costs are a function of the known fixed costs (the purchase of the hardware and software and the installation of the configuration), the unknown software development time, the known cost of software development time and unknown support costs. A formula for the development costs can then be expressed as:

Dev. cost = fixed costs + software dev. costs + support costs

where

Software dev. costs = software dev. time × software dev. rate;

$$\text{Support costs} = \left(\begin{array}{c} \text{no. of operator} \\ \text{staff} \times \text{grade} \\ \text{rate} \end{array} \right) + \left(\begin{array}{c} \text{no. of systems} \\ \text{engineers} \times \text{grade} \\ \text{rate} \end{array} \right).$$

In this way, bit by bit, the total value of the project can be constructed.

The final value function will be basically some benefit formula less some cost formula. A typical example might be:

---

[1] Hertz, D. (Jan.–Feb. 1964). *Risk Analysis in Capital Investment*, Harvard Business Review.

Value = benefits − configuration costs − dev. costs − operating costs.

The Monte Carlo simulation technique also supports DCF techniques (although not proper risk adjusted discounting, more of this later). It is possible to introduce discounting of costs and benefits in formulae even at this early stage of the technique. To do this the variables must be split into time periods, almost invariably annual accounting periods. The periods are used to enable:

the variables in each year to be independent on a time basis;

An example could be the software development costs:

$$\text{PV (s'ware dev. cost (yr. 1))} = \text{s'ware dev. time (yr. 1)} \times \text{s'ware dev. rate/discount rate}$$

and

$$\text{PV (s'ware dev. cost (yr. 2))} = \text{s'ware dev. time (yr. 2)} \times \text{s'ware dev. rate/discount rate}$$

and so on.

The costs and benefits can vary on a period by period basis and so support cash flow analysis. The costs and benefits can then be discounted, with the possibility of different rates for each period. The cash flows can be "DCF'ed".

There will be an overall valuation equation based upon the DCF technique:

Value = PV(benefits) − PV(costs)

where the PV is calculated in the usual way.

The next stage is to specify the degree of variability of the variables. This involves constructing probability distributions for each of the variables. For example, if the software development time for year 1 is not too variable it may have a distribution as shown in Figure 5.2. From this distribution the time required will not be less than 900 hours and it will not be higher than 2100 hours. The expected value will be 1500 hours. These are the limits to the variability in year 1. In between these limits any value is possible—it is a continuous distribution. Plotting a continuous distribution is not practical. There are an infinite number of values between 900 hours and 2100 hours. Furthermore, a computer could not hold the data. The distribution must be sampled as shown in Figure 5.2. A sample of interval, of say 200 hours, may be appropriate, as in this example. Smaller sample intervals can be taken which would increase the number of samples, improve resolution and accuracy, but would also increase the amount of data to be held. A balance must be struck between accuracy and processing time.

The sampled distribution is a risk model of the likely outcomes for that

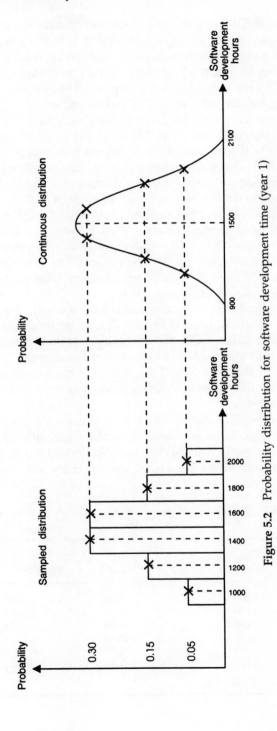

Figure 5.2 Probability distribution for software development time (year 1)

particular variable. The probability of each outcome for the software development time taken in year 1 is shown in Table 5.1. In this risk model, which is a sampled simplification of what will happen in reality, there are six possible outcomes of the actual software development time required in year 1. There is a 0.05 probability (i.e. a 5% chance) of the project requiring 1000 hours, a 0.15 probability of taking 1200 hours and so on.

Random numbers are then allocated to each outcome in proportion to its probability, as shown in the table. The outcome of 1000 hours has a 0.05 probability, so it will be allocated 5% of the one hundred possible numbers between 00 and 99. This means that it will be allocated five digits and, for simplicity, it has been allocated the five digits in the range 00 to 04. Similarly the outcome of 1600 hours has a probability of 0.30, so it is allocated 30 digits. The significance of this method of allocating numbers is that when a random number generator selects a digit between 00 and 99 then the outcome of 1600 hours has a 30% chance of being selected, 1000 hours a 5% chance of being selected and so on. The effect is to select outcomes in direct proportion to their individual probabilities. This is the crucial step in modelling the risks of the real project.

A similar distribution may be constructed for the software development time in year 2. The time needed in year 2 may be more uncertain as the scale of the project increases. In this case the lower limit may be 2000 hours but the higher limit may be 8000 hours. A similar sampled probability distribution might be that shown in Table 5.2. This must be done for all variables identified in the first modelling stage, such as support costs, hardware costs, cost savings etc.

Once these probability distributions have been set for all the variables the next step is to perform the simulation. The simulation application will take one random sample from all the variables, weighted according to the random numbers allocated as described earlier. The simulation programme

Table 5.1 Probability of outcomes for software development time — year 1

Time taken (hours)	Probability	Random number
1000	0.05	00–04
1200	0.15	05–19
1400	0.30	20–49
1600	0.30	50–79
1800	0.15	80–94
2000	0.05	95–99
Total		100

Table 5.2 Probability of outcomes for software development
time — year 2

Time taken (hours)	Probability	Random number
2000	0.05	00–04
3200	0.15	05–19
4400	0.30	20–49
5600	0.30	50–79
6800	0.15	80–94
8000	0.05	95–99
Total		100

then calculates the value based upon the valuation equations defined in the first stage of the modelling process. The simulation repeats this process many times, taking one sample at a time for all the variables defined. The results are stored and after many iterations a stable frequency/outcome histogram emerges. This frequency graph approximates to the probability distribution of the value of the project. A typical graph of value against probability (or frequency of occurrence) is shown in Figure 5.3.

A graph skewed to the right (high positive NPV) will tend to be of greater value than one skewed to the left. In Figure 5.3 the bulk of the outcomes are positive in NPV terms, which indicates a good project—it is highly likely to make a profit.

The graph also indicates some other key points:

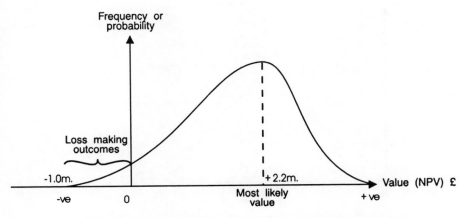

Figure 5.3 Graph of "value" versus frequency of occurrence

- The peak of the curve indicates the most likely value. In Figure 5.3 the most likely outcome is an NPV of £2.2m.
- The area to the left of the zero NPV axis indicates the chances of making a loss. The greater the area under the graph to the left of this line, the greater the chance of making a loss. In Figure 5.3 the maximum loss which is likely to be sustained is £1m., but the probability is extremely low.
- The graph also gives an indication of the risk of the project. A wide spread of possible outcomes will give a relatively flat distribution and so indicate a risky project. A narrow spread of results will give a very peaky graph and indicate a low risk project. Figure 5.4 illustrates the value graphs of two projects with the same expected outcome but of very different risks.

Monte Carlo simulation is a major improvement on basic sensitivity analysis. This more sophisticated probability analysis can give greater confidence to decision makers. It has several advantages in that:

- It forces consideration of all the major uncertain variables;
- It allows those variables to vary independently;
- It forces quantification of the risk and variability of outcomes.

The results are more meaningful because they:

- Indicate how likely the expected, best and worst outcome is likely to be;
- Indicate the chances of making a loss;
- Indicate the likely spread of results.

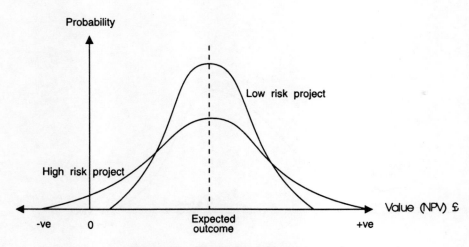

Figure 5.4 Two risk profiles compared

Despite the advantages Monte Carlo simulation has over sensitivity analysis there are two major drawbacks to the technique. The first difficulty is that of interpreting the result. For example, is it better to select a project with a low spread of results (low risk) and moderate return, or a project with a high spread of results (high risk) but with a greater expected value? The graph in Figure 5.5 shows two projects which illustrate this dilemma. There is one project that is guaranteed not to make a loss (the profile on the left) and with a high probability of making a small return, but with only a small chance of making a large profit. The other project has a small chance of making a loss, with a high probability of making a reasonable return, but some chance of making a large profit. The risk averse manager would choose the left profile and the risk taking manager the right profile. Problem decisions like that illustrated in Figure 5.5 bring out the differences in managers' preferences and can make decision making problematical. It is because different people interpret graphs in different ways that confusion can sometimes occur when the cases are not clear cut.

The other point is a more technical one that involves selection of the discount rate. As was explained in Chapter 3, the discount rate should be calculated to reflect the risk of the project. The problem in this case is that the discount rate must be selected before the simulation is run, that is before the risk of the project is known. Thus a rate must be guessed at. This means that the costs and benefits are discounted at a rate which is not the risk

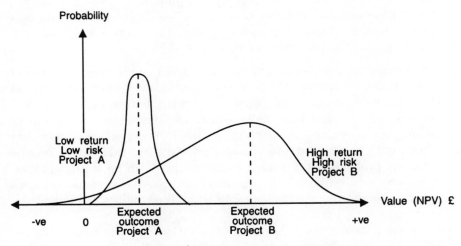

Figure 5.5 Two projects compared

adjusted rate, hence the NPV figures for valuation are "bastard NPVs", as Brearley and Myers[2] put it.

Despite these drawbacks the simulation technique is still useful and will continue to be used by analysts. Notwithstanding that the technique can be lengthy, time consuming and costly in terms of analysts' time, for large projects, the time and money invested to create the project risk profiles can bring considerable comfort to the decision making process.

5.2.3.3 Decision Tree Analysis

A cheaper and easier to understand technique for event risk and flexibility valuation is decision tree analysis. This technique was first introduced by Magee in 1964.[3] The main advantages of the technique are that:

- It supports both the identification and measurement of the value of event risk and flexibility;
- It can handle multiple events and flexibility options;
- It is easy to apply;
- It does not require software support.

Risk is handled by the use of probabilities for events that may adversely, or favourably, affect the project. Flexibility is handled by the use of options to offset these risk events. If a risk event occurs then there are options open to respond to those events. The greater the range of options, the more flexible the project. When a risk event occurs a decision must be taken as to which option is the best in response to the event occurring. These different options are known as decision branches and the point when the decision is taken is known as a decision node. By mapping out the various decision branches the costs and benefits of each can be examined and the best options selected in response to each outcome. It is a very simple and easy approach to use. The technique involves two stages:

(1) Identifying the events that can have an impact on the project. A typical event risk for a system may be the demand for the system, which could be different from that anticipated. These are outcomes that are beyond management control and are known as outcome nodes. Being out of management control, these nodes represent uncertain outcomes, but they can be anticipated and as such they are modelled by decision tree analysis probabilities. For each outcome there can be n probabilities. Two are usually modelled. Too many and the decision tree analysis model soon becomes unmanageably large. Probabilities are put on the

[2] Brearley, R. and Myers, S. (1989). *Principles of Corporate Finance*, 3rd edn, McGraw-Hill.
[3] Magee, J. (Sept.–Oct. 1964). *How to use Decision Trees in Capital Investment*, Harvard Business Review.

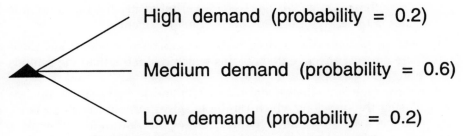

Figure 5.6 Outcome node and branches for demand

likelihood of the risk events occurring. Assume in the case just quoted there is a 0.2 probability of a high demand, 0.6 probability of a medium demand and 0.2 probability of a low demand. The sum of the probabilities must be one. This would be modelled as an outcome node with branches as shown in Figure 5.6.

(2) For each possible outcome of a risk event there is a decision node. This node represents the decision facing managers once the outcome has occurred. Unlike outcome nodes, decision nodes are under management control. For each decision node there may be several branches, each branch representing a different course of action. In Figure 5.7 the decisions open for all possible outcomes are to expand the system or

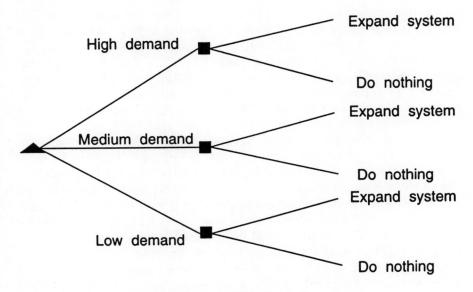

Figure 5.7 Decision nodes

to do nothing (i.e. no change scenario). The greater the flexibility, the greater is the array of options open to management.

The costs and benefits of each decision branch can be investigated and those which are not cost effective (the options which cost more than the benefits they bring) can be eliminated.

The next stage is to analyse the risks again and then repeat the process of analysing the decisions which can be taken in response to those risks. The result is a tree-like hierarchy structure of outcomes and subsequent decisions which can be taken for each outcome. The advantage of this tree structure is that it shows how a decision can impact upon future decisions. A decision not to expand early on may close off the possibility of large benefits in the future.

Decision tree analysis is unique in that it can also demonstrate the value of flexibility. The more flexible the project, the more options will be open to the managers of the project and the more valuable it will be. The use of options which branch whenever there is a risk event and the ability to value the costs and benefits of the outcomes of applying the options, adding and valuing new options if the outcomes are unsatisfactory, enable managers to assess the financial benefits of flexibility. The technique is a most power-ful tool.

Decision tree analysis—a worked example. The following case study illus-trates the power of the technique. The case study concerns a proposed stock control system for the raw materials of a large manufacturing company which was intended to be a replacement for a manual card system. The manual system was slow, inaccurate and provided very poor stock control. Stock losses were frequent and impossible to trace.

The initial plan was to develop a computer system to record receipts and issues of materials, and no more. The system would be simple, quick, cheap and easy to implement as a standalone PC solution. This solution would be attractive because it was cheap but limited in its future development. This solution will be called the "base case" solution.

There were three factors which suggested that a more flexible solution than that of the "base case" might be worthy of consideration. All these factors were subject to some uncertainty and could be considered as event risks. One of these risks was that an interface to the Finance Department's product costing database might not be possible. If the interface was possible then the option/flexibility open to the managers of the system would be that the stock control system could be extended at very little extra cost to produce material usage reports and financial accounts.

At the time there was a Manufacturing Resource Planning (MRP) package under review in a pilot site, which, if successful, was to be rolled out into all manufacturing sites within the company. The trial was not going well and it appeared that another solution would have to be found. A decision would be taken on this package in one year's time. The risk was that the trial might be a failure. If the package was to be abandoned there would be an option to develop the stock system, which already had stock figures and a basic materials database, to provide an MRP function.

There was a possibility that other manufacturing sites would close and some production might be relocated to the site in question. If this happened the range of products and materials that the system would have to handle could vary tremendously over the two to three year time span. The risk was one of uncertain volume requirements three years from thence. The flexibility reponse would require volume flexibility.

The first and very basic option was for a standalone PC based system—the "base case". This option was considered because it was a low cost option. The problem was that it would have been unable to respond to any of these events. If the events described above required any action they would have to be solved by some other means. The system could be only considered as a self contained and standalone solution.

The cost of such a system would be about £20 000 in development time and around £15 000 for the proposed hardware configuration. There would be negligible maintenance costs, so the only cost of the system would be a one off cost of £35 000 in the first year of the project.

The benefits produced included:

- Time savings, such as at stock takes (the system could produce listings of stocks by location and so save time). This was assessed at a saving of £1000 per annum in overtime payments that were usually paid for stock taking work;
- Stock losses which could be avoided because up to the minute stock levels could be produced. Materials were often over ordered because there were "hidden stocks" around the factory, which were unrecorded. As a result materials were often over ordered and subsequently surplus to requirements and later written off. The anticipated saving of this was about £10 000 per annum.

In summary, for an outlay of £35 000 the factory could expect an annual cost saving of £11 000. An NPV approach could be used to value this basic system because there were no flexibility options and the system was unresponsive to risk—the decision tree analysis approach would add nothing. Using the prevailing discount rate of 22% and assuming a six year life for the project the NPV of the project was £2570 positive. The project only just made the target return of 22%. This was hardly a startling project but it paid its way.

The alternative solution was to install the system on a network and allow sufficient capacity for expansion. The development costs of such a system would be unchanged at £20 000 but the hardware costs would be greater at around £45 000. This would allow up to four users to have access to the system and open up possibilities to respond to the uncertainties outlined above.

The particular opportunities that were identified were to:

- Extend the use of the stock system to interface with a product costing database, should the interface be possible;
- Extend the use of the system to calculate material requirements (perform an MRP function), should the trials for the other MRP package prove unsuccessful.
- Expand the scale of the system, should the extra production volume be relocated to the site in, say, three years' time.

An outlay of £65 000 would enable a networked system to be developed which could respond to all three of the above outcomes, which the initial basic PC solution could not.

These extra capabilities of the networked solution were recognised but it was not clear whether the extra £30 000 expenditure was justified, given that the three events detailed above were not certain to occur. The use of a decision tree helped to solve this problem.

A decision tree was mapped out for the project and is shown in Figure 5.8. In the tree the cash flows are denoted by $C(t,n)$ where t = the year of the cash flow and n = the number of the node in the tree for that year. The lowest node being denoted 1 and so on until there are eight nodes for year number three. So, for example, $C(2,4)$ denotes the fourth node from bottom in the column of cash flows for year number two. For simplicity, inflation has been ignored throughout.

At the root of the tree is the decision to invest. The base case is to invest in the standalone PC. The cash flow here is –£35 000 ($C(0,0)$) and yields benefit of £11 000 per annum giving an NPV of +£2570. This branch need be explored no further. The other option is to invest in a network. The cash flow resulting from this decision ($C(0.1)$) is minus £65 000 and represents the initial capital outlay. Subsequent decision nodes are denoted by squares and outcomes are denoted by triangles. The first outcome that was uncertain was whether an interface with the product costing database could be achieved. This outcome would be known within the first year. The probability of success was put at 0.8 and that of failure at 0.2.

(1) Flexibility options, year 1

In response to a favourable outcome two courses of action are possible—either the interface can be developed or one can do nothing. The costs of implementing an interface were put at £3000, but the benefits would be a

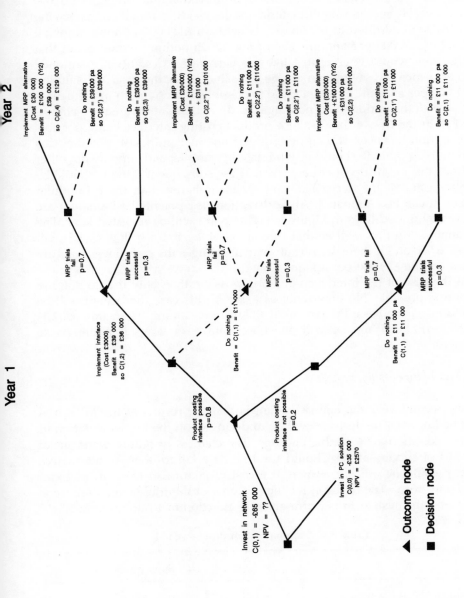

Figure 5.8 Decision tree analysis for a stock control system

saving in a costing clerk (£8000) and an estimated annual saving of £20 000 due to weekly monitoring of material usage, yielding a total annual saving of £28 000 in addition to the "basic" benefits of £11 000 per annum, giving a total of £39 000 per annum. The option to do nothing would mean that the system would operate just like the base case PC solution mentioned earlier, hence the savings would be the same as for the basic PC solution (£11 000 per annum). If an interface is possible, the option to implement is better than the option to do nothing. The do nothing option may be eliminated from the tree in the case of a product costing interface being possible (this option has been shown by a dotted line in Figure 5.8). Whether this "do nothing option" should be eliminated or not depends upon what other options this opens up or closes down. These subsequent options should be explored and if the decision to implement is better than the do nothing option it can be eliminated. All such options for potential elimination are shown by dotted lines in Figure 5.8. This point will be revisited later. The summary cash flow will be that shown in Table 5.3. Cash flow C (1,2) will be +£36 000 and if there are no subsequent changes the cash flows in future years will be £39 000 per annum.

In the case of the interface not being possible then only the do nothing option is possible. No other choices exist. In this case the benefit will be the same as the basic PC system at £11 000 per annum. Cash flow C (1,1) will be +£11 000 and so will all subsequent cash flows if nothing else changes.

(2) Flexibility options, year 2

In the second year the key risk event is that the results of the MRP trial will be known. The decision will be to decide upon the implementation of a bespoke alternative to this package. The chances of failure were put at 0.7 and of success at 0.3. Should the trial be a failure then an alternative system could be quickly written at a cost of about £30 000 with no extra hardware costs. The decision for the outcome of the trial being a failure is to extend the system to perform an MRP function or to do nothing.

Table 5.3 Summary cash flow — year 1

	Year 1	Subsequent years
Benefit of "basic" system	£11 000	£11 000
Benefit of interface	£28 000	£28 000
Total benefit	£39 000	£39 000
Less interface cost	£3000	Nil
Net cash flow	£36 000	£39 000

Table 5.4 Summary cash flow — year 2

	Year 2	Subsequent years
Benefit of "basic" system	£11 000	£11 000
Benefit of interface	£28 000	£28 000
Stock reduction benefit	£100 000	Nil
Other MRP benefits	£20 000	£20 000
Total benefit	£159 000	£59 000
Less development costs	£30 000	Nil
Net cash flow	£129 000	£59 000

The benefits for the extension of the system were put at a £100 000 one off benefit in stock reduction, due to better planning, £10 000 consequent saving per annum in interest costs, and finally £10 000 per annum saving in materials, due to better planning and ordering. Taking the branch where the product costing interface has been performed and the MRP function is implemented (resulting in cash flow C (2,4) the cash flows are as shown in Table 5.4.

This may be more beneficial than the do nothing option (which would be only the benefit of the system with an interface to the product costing database, net benefit £39 000 per annum), so the do nothing option may be eliminated from the tree C (2,3').

In the case where the product costing interface has been installed but the MRP trial is successful then the only option available is the do nothing option. In this case the cash flow will be the same as for the previous year (£39 000) and is denoted by C (2,3).

For the outcome of the product costing database not being implemented and the MRP trial failing then there is a choice open to develop the MRP function or to do nothing. The cash flow will be that shown in Table 5.5. The result will be that cash flow C (2,2) will be +£101 000 and subsequent

Table 5.5 Summary cash flow — year 2; including MRP function development

	Year 2	Subsequent years
Benefit of "basic" system	£11 000	£11 000
Stock reduction benefit	£100 000	Nil
Other MRP benefits	£20 000	£20 000
Total benefit	£131 000	£31 000
Less development costs	£30 000	Nil
Net cash flow	£101 000	£31 000

cash flows will be +£31 000. When the product costing interface is not poss-ible and the MRP trials are a success then there is nothing that can be done to the project. The cash flows will not alter from the basic systems cash flows, hence C (2,1) will be +£11 000.

Figure 5.8 maps out all these options up to year 2. As may be appreciated, the tree can quite quickly become very large (in Figure 5.8 there are nine possible outcomes in year 2 for only two risks). In order to manage the analysis the less attractive options should be taken out. In this example all the decisions and outcomes marked by a dotted line in Figure 5.8 did not uniquely open up new options nor close off others. In these cases the bene-fits were always lower than the "do something else option", hence they can in fact be eliminated. It is important to stress, however, that options which seem unattractive should not be excluded too readily until it is certain that other potentially attractive decisions are not closed off.

Further options were considered in year 3 and a simplified tree is given in Figure 5.9. The principles for modelling the decisions of year 3 are exactly the same as those described above and those who wish to accept the figures can move to the section, "Evaluation of the Tree", below. Those who wish to follow the detail can do so in the Appendix to this chapter.

Evaluation of the Tree

The worked example above was fairly straightforward and much simpli-fied. Complex risks and decisions can be modelled using this technique, but the mechanism of measurement and valuation are the same. In this example of only three risks and a small number of options the tree became big quite quickly. It may be necessary to "prune the tree" as the analysis can quickly produce a decision tree analysis structure that can become too complex. Judgement must be exercised in making any simplifying assump-tions in order to make the analysis manageable, whilst still maintaining relevance. In the worked example the do nothing options are not regarded as viable or likely and can therefore be pruned from the tree. The pruning exercise is a project specific task.

Once all the event risks and their associated flexibility options and out-comes have been mapped out over time in the tree-like structure, and the costs of the risks and the benefits of the flexibility have been calculated, the monies involved need to be discounted back to NPVs.

In evaluating the decision tree we must use the DCF principle to discount all the cash flows on the basis of their probabilities from latter years to preceding years' values. This has already been done back to year 3, in the Appendix. To work out the expected value of cash flows from C (2,4) onwards means adding the cash flow in year 2 to the expected values of discounted cash flow of all future years. Given that we are in year 2 and

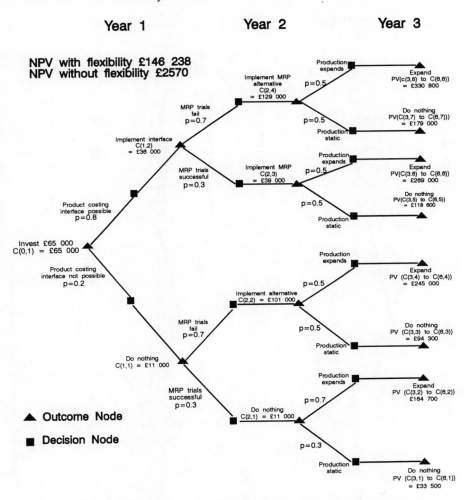

Figure 5.9 Decision tree analysis for stock control system (simplified)

that both finance and MRP systems are in place, the remaining benefit of the project is denoted by V (2,4) (the value of project at outcome 2,4):

$$V~(2,4) = C~(2,4) + \frac{(0.5 \times PV~(C~(3.8 - 6.8)) + (0.5 \times PV~(C~(3.7 - 6.7))}{1.22}$$

This is shown diagrammatically in Figure 5.10, V (2,4) is simply the cash flow in year 2, outcome 4 plus the probability weighted PVs of the future cash flows after that point. Thus V (2,4) is

$$V~(2,4) = £129\,000 + \frac{(0.5 \times £330\,800) + (0.5 \times £179\,000)}{1.22} = £337\,934$$

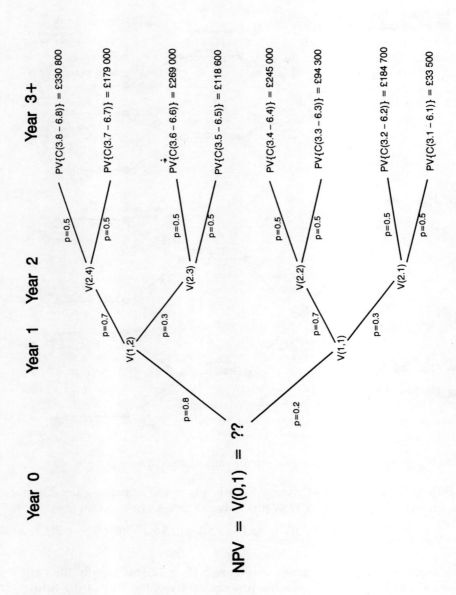

Figure 5.10 Evaluation of the decision tree

What this valuation equation is saying is that, assuming "today" is year 2 and that the current state is outcome 4, then the present value of investment in "today's" terms is £337 934. This value is made up of the £129 000 benefit of year 2 plus a 50% chance of future cash flows of £330 800 and a 50% chance of future cash flows of £179 000. In the same way the value of all other possible states in year 2 can be calculated.

$$V(2,3) = £39\,000 + \frac{(0.5 \times £269\,000) + (0.5 \times £118\,600)}{1.22} = £197\,852$$

$$V(2,2) = £101\,000 + \frac{(0.5 \times £245\,000) + (0.5 \times £94\,300)}{1.22} = £240\,057$$

$$V(2,1) = £11\,000 + \frac{(0.5 \times £184\,700) + (0.5 \times £33\,500)}{1.22} = £100\,426$$

Once the year 2 values have been calculated it is possible to calculate year 1 values. For example, $V(1,2)$ is calculated from the cash flow $C(1,2)$ plus the discounted cash flow of a 70% chance of £337 934 ($V(2,4)$) and a 30% chance of £197 852 ($V(2,3)$).

$$V(1,2) = £36\,000 + \frac{(0.7 \times £337\,934) + (0.3 \times £197\,852)}{1.22} = £278\,549$$

Similarly:

$$V(1,1) = £11\,000 + \frac{(0.7 \times £240\,057) + (0.3 \times £100\,426)}{1.22} = £173\,433$$

Finally the total value of the decision to invest in the network can be evaluated. There is an 80% chance of future values of £278 549 and a 20% chance of future values of £173 433 for an initial outlay of £65 000. Therefore the NPV of the decision to invest in the network is

$$NPV = V(0,1) = -£65\,000 + \frac{(0.8 \times £278\,549) + (0.2 \times £173\,433)}{1.22} = £146\,087$$

Finally the overall value of the project is the value in today's terms. As may be seen the expected NPV is £146 087 positive (i.e. it gives a pay-off of over two times its initial investment *in addition* to the 22% return required). The project thus has a far greater return than the basic solution to the stock control problem, this providing a return of only £2570.

The decision tree analysis technique has demonstrated how the added value of flexibility to offset the event risks which can afflict a project can be identified, measured and valued. In this worked example:

- The service flexibility was valued, that is the option to provide a financial evaluation of material usage via a product costing interface;

- Additional product/service flexibility was valued in the option to introduce an MRP facility;
- Volume flexibility was also valued, that is the ability to expand the
  throughput of the system to cope with a 60% increase in materials and
  stock items.

The technique can also support the portfolio approach in that analysis can
be done for projects individually or several projects taken together.

As can be seen from the worked example, decisions such as the option
to extend the MRP facility can depend upon the outcomes of other projects
in the future. The technique can therefore support decision making by considering project interactions. Decision tree analysis is a useful technique for
ISS, but the level of detail required in the analysis is a hindrance.

The drawbacks of decision tree analysis are that:

(1) *It can be too simplistic.* Suppose the trial of the MRP system is not a
    definite success or failure but a partial success. In this case perhaps
    some elements of a system may be used. Suppose that an increase in
    demand is not 60% but 40% or 30% or 29.52%. In the interests of keeping
    the analysis manageable the price to be paid may be simplification and
    this may not do a project justice.
(2) *A discount rate has been assumed.* Just as in Monte Carlo simulation,
    decision tree analysis therefore fails to provide risk adjusted dis-
    counting. The circular argument applies. A discount rate cannot be
    selected until the risk is known and the risk is not known until the
    analysis is done but the analysis requires a discount rate. The project
    discount rate can be calculated by the Bowater Scott model technique
    or its variants on an annualised basis. If the project discount rate has
    not been calculated an approximate rate should be used. This is just a
    distortion that has to be tolerated.

5.3 CHAPTER SUMMARY

Flexibility can be used as a powerful tool in combating the risk of unplan-
ned-for events during the life of a project. It enables exploitation of beneficial twists of fate and limits the cost of adverse twists of fate. The major
problem is in recognising the event risks. Once the possible events are
identified the necessary actions to offset and exploit those events need to
be identified and costs/benefits measured. The monies involved then need
to be discounted in the standard manner.

There are several techniques which can be used to model complex projects and their flexibilities. The one used by the IA method is decision tree

analysis. The others offer nothing that is not provided in the decision tree analysis technique and in most cases a good deal less.

5.4 APPENDIX: FLEXIBILITY OPTIONS, YEAR 3

The last uncertainty was the volume of transactions and the corresponding flexibility was the ability to expand if necessary. There was a 50% chance that a particular line of production would come to this factory in three years' time. Conversely there was a 50% chance that the volume of production would remain unchanged. The expansion in production would represent an increase in output and handling of 60%. The basic PC design would not be able to cope with such an increase, but a networked design could cope at no extra cost.

If the expansion in production did occur then the options were to expand the system or do nothing. It was assumed that if expansion did occur then the savings per annum would be 60% of the material savings already recognised per annum. This would mean a one off saving of £60 000 in the year of expansion plus an additional £30 000 per annum for that year and all future years. The option to do nothing would lead to no improvement, so it has been eliminated.

If the expansion in production did not occur then the only option open is to do nothing and in these cases the cash flow is the same as in the previous year.

The cash flows that would result are calculated for each case in Tables 5.A1 to 5.A8

Table 5A.1 Summary cash flow — year 3: Case (3,8 to 6,8)

	Year 3	Three subsequent years
Benefit of "basic" system	£11 000	£11 000
Benefit of interface	£28 000	£28 000
Other MRP benefits	£20 000	£20 000
Stock reduction benefit	£60 000	Nil
Other benefits	£30 000	£30 000
Total benefit	£149 000	£89 000
Net cash flow	£149 000	£89 000

$$\text{PV of 3,8 to 6,8} = £149\ 000 + \frac{£89\ 000}{1.22} + \frac{£89\ 000}{(1.22)^2} + \frac{£89\ 000}{(1.22)^3} = £330\ 800$$

Note that for the final three years of the project there are no envisaged changes in cash flow. Because of this the remaining benefit of the project for each of the eight possible outcomes over the final three years is simply

Table 5A.2 Summary cash flow — year 3: Case (3,7 to 6,7)

	Year 3	Three subsequent years
Benefit of "basic" system	£11 000	£11 000
Benefit of interface	£28 000	£28 000
Other MRP benefits	£20 000	£20 000
Total benefit	£59 000	£59 000
Net cash flow	£59 000	£59 000

$$\text{PV of 3,7 to 6,7} = £59\,000 + \frac{£59\,000}{1.22} + \frac{£59\,000}{(1.22)^2} + \frac{£59\,000}{(1.22)^3} = £179\,000$$

Table 5A.3 Summary cash flow — year 3: Case (3,6 to 6,6)

	Year 3	Three subsequent years
Benefit of "basic" system	£11 000	£11 000
Benefit of interface	£28 000	£28 000
Stock reduction benefit	£60 000	Nil
Other benefits	£30 000	£30 000
Total benefit	£129 000	£69 000
Net cash flow	£129 000	£69 000

$$\text{PV of 3,6 to 6,6} = £129\,000 + \frac{£69\,000}{1.22} + \frac{£69\,000}{(1.22)^2} + \frac{£69\,000}{(1.22)^3} = £269\,000$$

Table 5A.4 Summary cash flow — year 3: Case (3,5 to 6,5)

	Year 3	Three subsequent years
Benefit of "basic" system	£11 000	
Benefit of interface	£28 000	£28 000
Total benefit	£39 000	£39 000
Net cash flow	£39 000	£39 000

$$\text{PV of 3,5 to 6,5} = £39\,000 + \frac{£39\,000}{1.22} + \frac{£39\,000}{(1.22)^2} + \frac{£39\,000}{(1.22)^3} = £118\,600$$

the present value of the cash flows in years 3 to 6. The discount rate has been set at 22%, and calculations are shown in the tables.

Table 5A.5 Summary cash flow — year 3: Case (3,4 to 6,4)

	Year 3	Three subsequent years
Benefit of "basic" system	£11 000	£11 000
Other MRP benefits	£20 000	
Stock reduction benefit	£60 000	Nil
Other benefits	£30 000	£30 000
Total benefit	£121 000	£61 000
Net cash flow	£121 000	£61 000

$$\text{PV of 3,4 to 6,4} = £121\,000 + \frac{£61\,000}{1.22} + \frac{£61\,000}{(1.22)^2} + \frac{£61\,000}{(1.22)^3} = £245\,000$$

Table 5A.6 Summary cash flow — year 3: Case (3,3 to 6,3)

	Year 3	Three subsequent years
Benefit of "basic" system	£11 000	£11 000
Other MRP benefits	£20 000	£20 000
Total benefit	£31 000	£31 000
Net cash flow	£31 000	£31 000

$$\text{PV of 3,3 to 3,6} = £31\,000 + \frac{£31\,000}{1.22} + \frac{£31\,000}{(1.22)^2} + \frac{(31\,000}{(1.22)^3} = £94\,300$$

Table 5A.7 Summary cash flow — year 3: Case (3,2 to 6,2)

	Year 3	Three subsequent years
Benefit of "basic" system	£11 000	
Stock reduction benefit	£60 000	Nil
Other benefits	£30 000	£30 000
Total benefit	£101 000	£41 000
Net cash flow	£101 000	£41 000

$$\text{PV of 3,2 to 6,2} = £101\,000 + \frac{£41\,000}{1.22} + \frac{£41\,000}{(1.22)^2} + \frac{£41\,000}{(1.22)^3} = £184\,700$$

Table 5A.8 Summary cash flow — year 3: Case (3,1 to 6,1)

	Year 3	Subsequent years
Benefit of "basic" system	£11 000	
Net cash flow	£11 000	£11 000

$$\text{PV of 3,1 to 6,1} = £11\,000 + \frac{£11\,000}{1.22} + \frac{£11\,000}{(1.22)^2} + \frac{£11\,000}{(1.22)^3} = £33\,500$$

Chapter 6

Investment Measurement III

This is an area of IA that has always been poorly addressed, yet the positive cash flows from the intangible benefits are an increasing portion of the project revenues. The need to measure the value of the intangibles is therefore all the more acute. This chapter describes a technique that, while not providing a magical answer, shows how the measurement of the intangible benefits to be obtained from an IT project can be achieved more accurately than in the past.

6.1 THE INTANGIBLE BENEFITS

Conventional wisdom has been that there are two groupings of CBA techniques, each with two categories—the financial tangibles and the non-financial intangibles. The problem is that none of the methods for CBA are able to show how to measure and value the intangible benefits in financial terms and thereby enable the value of the intangibles to be included in the IA process. The best that can be offered is that a score is allocated to the intangibles based on a perceived benefit that is obtained.

The measurement and valuation of intangible costs and benefits has always been the major area of difficulty for the subject of IA. By their nature the intangibles are difficult to identify and measure, and if you cannot identify and measure you cannot calculate financial value. It is for this reason that many of the manuals, such as those issued by HM Treasury, have used other forms of measure for the intangibles, measures such as weightings and scorings. Only the tangibles have been measured in monetary terms.

It has to be said that this book will not provide a magical answer. At one of the seminars the authors presented on this subject a delegate was unimpressed by what was described and gave this part of the seminar a low mark, with the comment that "What has been described is nothing more than the science of commonsense". The authors were a bit miffed by the low mark but were delighted with the comment, because it described perfectly what is about to be described.

An intangible is anything that is difficult to measure. At face value that is not a very helpful comment. Certainly the boundary between what is tangible and intangible is at times not at all clear. If the question is asked about the value of "something" and the answer is that "something" can be measured with a high degree of precision without too much difficulty then it is not an intangible. The "something" about labour saving is easy to ident- ify—the staff in the offices and on the shop floor—and measure—the staff who are no longer there. Such a benefit is tangible.

Some intangibles are easier to identify, measure and value than others, while some, particularly those of a political and futuristic nature, are almost impossible. One civil servant on a seminar asked "How do you identify, measure and value the benefit of siting an airport in the north of England?". Apparently the project was being seriously proposed because "political clout" would be obtained. No answer was made as to the political clout. The science of commonsense was applied to the economics and not the politics. But questions were asked in terms of the economic costs and bene- fits of siting an airport in a location. "What can you do when the airport is finished that you cannot do now?" What can you do in the north as compared with what you cannot do in the south? Identify and value the dif- ferences.

Some other examples given by the delegates have proved equally difficult to crack. A consultant from a consultancy company mentioned that the company had invested heavily in computers so that clients would gain the impression that they, the consultancy, were modern and progressive! Lots of PCs were installed in the reception area and the front offices! What is the value of the investment when all that is gained is a perception of com- petence? Again we applied the science of commonsense to the application by identifying and valuing the differences. "What is it that you can do now with the computer systems that you could not do before? Can you answer questions and give advice on difficult subjects because you have created an expert systems database about the potential difficult questions?" "Yes." "OK, how often are these questions asked?" "Can you charge a fee for the new advice that you are able to give? If so how much?" The "What can you do now that you could not do before" was continuously broken down into its constituent parts, until chargeable actions from the parts were ident- ified. The frequency of the actions was measured and multiplied against the charges and a value calculated. Crude, perhaps, but certainly better than the void of before. In both cases, the delegates, perhaps not totally convinced, did appreciate the more precise approach to the identification and measurement of something that is inherently difficult to measure. All the intangibles can be broken down into the results that they can achieve—that which is measurable.

Any intangible benefit can result in any combination of the following measurables. The intangible can result in:

- A higher price for a premium product or service;
- More sales from an existing product or service;
- Retained custom;
- A saving in money by an existing or new product or service;
- New business/new sales from a new product/service.

The identifications, measurements and valuations of intangibles are all based on one or more of these five results.

Figure 6.1 shows a classification of intangibles into four groupings, two of which are for intangibles that are on-going and two of which are for intangibles which may occur in the future. The more the intangibles are in the future the more difficult they are to identify, measure and value.

The first of the on-going intangible benefits are those concerned with the internal improvement of the company's operations, that is output performance. Some have argued that these internal improvements are almost tangible benefits, certainly if precise measurements of the beneficial impact

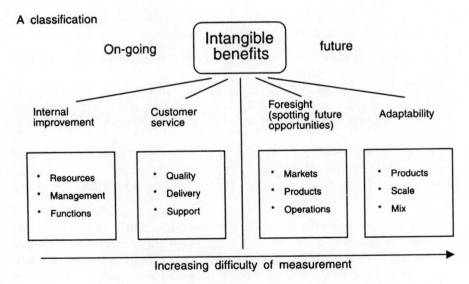

Figure 6.1 What are intangibles?

can be made. They are easy to measure and are within the control of the organisation. It can be argued they therefore fall outside the definition of an intangible. Certainly of the four groupings this is the most difficult to state definitely as intangible. For this "intangible" improvements can be made:

- in the way the equipment for the production process is used, such as less labour per item of equipment;
- in the way the management of the company operates, such as in the control and planning mechanisms used;
- in the way that operations are carried out, for example in the way that the length of the distribution line is reduced. Instead of a five-stage process it is reduced to three.

These benefits can be converted into increased output and/or lower production costs.

The second grouping is concerned with matters of value that are generally agreed to be difficult to measure, their effectiveness being decided by external forces outside your direct control; they are therefore intangibles. This grouping concerns service to customers, that is the increased utility of the product or service being provided. There can be improvements in:

- the quality of the product or service, such that customers recognise it as different from one's competitors';
- the delivery of the product or service, such that it is recognised by your customers;
- the support provided for your products and services, such that it is recognised by your customers.

These improvements can be converted into custom retained/sales not lost, increases in sales and an increase in price.

In all the above cases the quality aspect by itself is not enough. However good the customer service is *unless it is different from your competitors'*, even though it may be recognised by your customers as being high, *it has no added value*.

The groupings relating to the future are definitely within the orbit of the intangibles. Those relating to foresight are concerned with identifying opportunities for new business and thereby gaining advantage, for example by:

- spotting market trends, either in new products and services or in the volume of business that can be conducted. If these can be ascertained, particularly new products and services, then being first is an excellent way of gaining new sales (this book falls into this catagory, being the first to address the subject of full project IA);

- developing new ways in which the production process can be undertaken. There is a constant search for improvements in the efficiency of methods by which products are manufactured and services provided. If a company can be there first this can be a way of saving money ahead of competitors.

The above improvements can be converted into new sales and increase in price.

The final grouping relates to the ability to be adaptable to change, which could be by:

- adapting the product or service to market trends. If the product or service is flexible in its design then it is much easier to prolong its life within changing market conditions for the same original investment. One can see this in modern car designs. They may change their chassis/body design but the internals are the same. This is the case with all new car models, with the basic chassis being used throughout the model range, which varies from the basic model with few frills through to the luxury model with the full range of facilities. The cost of designing a totally new product for each variation of a basic through to luxury model has been saved.
- adapting the production rate of the product or service rapidly to market conditions. This is very much a requirement of businesses dealing in seasonal products and services.

These improvements can be converted into increased sales and increases in price.

6.1.1 The Importance of the Intangible Benefits

Intangibles are of growing importance in the context of computer systems. Computer systems are increasingly being developed for what, at first sight, are non-price factors and hence intangible. The benefits relating to internal improvements have already been described as the section of the business where intangible benefits are likely to be the least and are certainly of the type that the customer does not see. By contrast, intangible benefits are overwhelmingly those that the customer sees now and wants in the future, that is those that relate to customer service—foresight and adaptability. The ability to provide the required customer service today is something the customer sees. The ability to have foresight and to be adaptable are invisible, but result in the long run in the organisation being attuned to what the customer wants. Thus, by being what the customer sees and wants, the intangible benefits have an intrinsic value that may be greater than the immediate and calculable financial returns.

It is in the group of benefits relating to customer service where the major short term gains are to be obtained. The quickest and, given they are "what the customer sees and wants", probably the largest returns on investment are in this group.

Figure 6.2 shows the results of the survey conducted by the Kobler Unit. Of the six major benefits to be gained from computing, five were classified as intangibles. Not only were the intangibles more numerous than the tangibles but the benefits were also deemed to be much greater. The intangibles were very much of the type concerned with customer service and adaptability.

The diagram in Figure 6.3 shows the importance of the intangibles when seen from the point of view of the customer and the loss of business when the company's view of business is not in line with that of the customer. The customers regard speed of delivery as much the most important requirement of the business, whereas this is not considered an important component by the company, and the customers rate technical support and payment terms as less important than the company. The message of the diagram is that wherever the graphs of the customers' and the company's perceptions of what is needed are out of line, *where the company's line is higher than the customers' there is wasted effort and where it is lower there is lost*

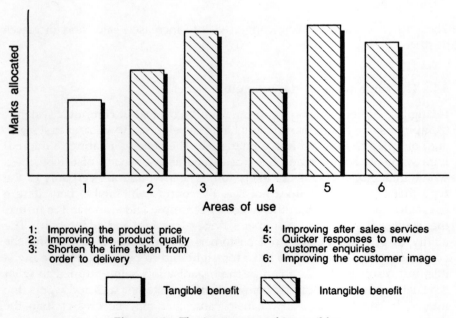

1: Improving the product price
2: Improving the product quality
3: Shorten the time taken from order to delivery
4: Improving after sales services
5: Quicker responses to new customer enquiries
6: Improving the ccustomer image

Tangible benefit   Intangible benefit

Figure 6.2   The importance of intangibles

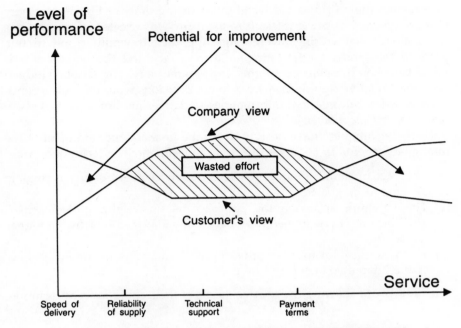

Figure 6.3   Value of intangibles — the dangers of getting it wrong

opportunity. Either way there is loss of income and a lowering of the return on any investments. *Figure 6.3 is the most important diagram in the book.*

6.1.2 The Measurement of the Intangible Benefits

A survey conducted by Ernst & Young[1] found that some 60% of all companies in the UK concerned with the manufacture of automotive components made no attempt to quantify even the intangible benefits to be gained from the use of CAD/CAM systems, that only some 20% quantified the benefits in physical terms (x staff work y hours more efficiently by z%) and that only 20% quantified the intangible benefits in monetary terms. These figures are most disturbing, particularly in that the systems being considered here are for the internal improvement of the companies, where the intangibles are likely to be the most "tangible" and therefore the most measurable and valuable.

It was argued in Chapter 2 that in order to construct a structured method for IA all business activities should be measured in monetary terms, enabling a single financial model to be developed. The usage of other forms

---

[1] Ernst & Young (1988). *The Use of CAD/CAM Systems in the UK Automotive Components Industry.*

of measure, the scorings and weightings for the units of business activity that are deemed as being difficult to measure, was rejected. If one did use the non-financial scorings/weightings approach it would result in two parts to the model for investing—the monetary and the non-monetary. Being based on different paradigms, the two measures could not be judged as to their relative significance. Investment decisions would be correspondingly based on inconsistent information—a dangerous situation. *It is essential to convert the intangibles into money.*

Three "techniques" have been used for the financial measurement of the intangible benefits to be gained from an investment. The techniques are:

(1) The "act of faith"; this approach is merely a guess of the intangible benefits to be gained.
(2) The weighting approach; this approach uses a weighting of the intangible benefits to be gained, the higher the adjudged benefit the higher the score;
(3) The quantification approach; this approach calculates the financial value of the intangible benefits to be gained.

The best way of showing the relative merits of the techniques is by example.

6.1.2.1 The "Act of Faith"

A company considered investing in an MRP system. The direct costs were £1.27 million. The tangible benefits were calculated as labour savings of £930 000 and a saving of £150 000 as a result of stock reduction through the adoption of "just in time", the holding of running stock only and no support stock. There is the obvious shortfall of £190 000. An "act of faith" estimate was made that the intangible benefits would result in a saving of, guess what, £190 000! The intangibles were used solely as a means of justifying the purchase of the MRP system by offsetting any potential loss. Not a very scientific approach to the subject of IA. Yet this is the approach followed by 60% of the companies in the Ernst & Young survey! Not an encouraging picture.

6.1.2.2 The Scoring Approach

The same business example is used again but with a different technique, that of the multiple attribute decision model. The technique was developed by C. Berliner and J. Brimson and is based on the scoring principle.[2] The

---

[2] Berliner, C. and Brimson, J. (1988). *Cost Management for Today's Advanced Manufacturing*, Harvard Business Press.

Table 6.1 Multiple attribute decision model

MRP investment benefits	Score (0–10)	Weighting (0–1)	Risk (0–1)	Total (A×B×C)
Direct benefits				
* Labour savings (930k.)	7	0.6	0.9	3.78
* Stock reduction (150k.)	1	0.6	0.9	0.54
Intangible benefits				
* Improved quality	2	0.05	0.5	0.05
* Quicker delivery	8	0.2	1	1.6
* Greater reliability	2	0.05	0.5	0.05
Net value				6.02

first step is to produce the data illustrated in Table 6.1. The figures are entirely fictional but representative of a business the authors worked on. This is based on Table 6.2, which gives the breakdown of the savings into a ranked score against the amount of the savings being made. The score in the second column of Table 6.1 represents the scoring of the benefit when based on Table 6.2. The labour saving of £930 000 produces a score of 7 on the table. The stock reduction benefit of £150 000 produces a score of 1.

The intangibles also need a table of scorings so that their "value" to the company can be measured against the financial figures. The problem faced in the example is that the intangibles are not common to each other. The improved quality cannot be measured on the same basis as the quicker delivery (the first is based on quality as judged by the number of complaints per week and the second on time), which cannot be measured on the same

Table 6.2 Multiple attribute decision model — tangible benefits table

Score	Labour saving/stock reduction
0	£0
1	£1–200k
2	£200–300k
3	£300–400k
4	£400–550k
5	£550–700k
6	£700–800k
7	£850–1000k
10	£150k

basis as the greater reliability (the first is based on time and the second on mean time between failures). There is no common basis of measure. It has therefore been necessary to use three different units of measure for the three intangibles.

A score table for the intangibles was developed by the authors and added to the technique. It is shown in Table 6.3; the score results are for the improved quality 2, quicker delivery 8 and greater reliability 2.

This is, of course, an artificial situation in that the scores for the intangibles when pitted against the tangibles would mean that the financial value of the intangibles would be worth £200 000 to £300 000 for the improved quality, over £1 million for the quicker delivery and £200 000 to £300 000 for the greater reliability. Yet the technique does not measure the financial value of the intangibles—it measures their "value" on the basis of a score. And the scores shown in Table 6.1 show that the greatest "value" is obtained from the quicker delivery.

The weighting in the third column of Table 6.1 is the importance of the benefit to the company, the higher the score the greater the importance. These figures are for illustrative purposes only, but they should be regarded with considerable suspicion. It is likely that they have been judged by a person or persons who value a "tangible buck" as more important than an "intangible bang". It is noticeable that the intangibles are not regarded as being of high importance as compared with the tangibles. Even the quicker delivery intangible that has a higher score than the labour saving is judged to have only one third the importance. There seems to be a bias against intangibles. Perhaps the person(s) applying the technique is the custodian

Table 6.3 Multiple attribute decision model—intangible benefits table

Score	Reliability (MTBF)	Quality (complaints/week)	Delivery (mean delivery time)
0	< 1 hr.	> 70	20 days
1	1–2 hrs.	60–69	12–19 days
2	3–4 hrs.	50–59	10–11 days
3	5–8 hrs.	40–49	8–9 days
4	9–16 hrs.	30–39	6–7 days
5	17–32 hrs.	16–29	5–6 days
6	33–64 hrs.	8–15	4–5 days
7	65–128 hrs.	4–7	3–4 days
8	129–256 hrs.	2–3	2–3 days
9	257–512 hrs.	1–2	1–2 days
10	512 hrs.	< 1	< 1 day

of the company's finances. It is suggested that figures like these should be questioned as to their balance.

The risk is the probability of the benefit being achieved.

All that remains to be done is to multiply the second to fourth columns to produce a compound scoring. This shows that the greatest benefit is from the tangible of labour savings and the least benefit is from the intangible of improved quality. On the basis of the findings in Table 6.1 the first place to invest the company's money is the labour saving followed by the quicker delivery.

The technique has the merits that it is easy to apply and attempts to put the "value" of the intangible benefits alongside the tangible benefits. The results, however, must be regarded with considerable suspicion. They can be misleading. Scores have little meaning unless they are based on a common unit of measure. That is not achieved here. The basis of measure of the tangible benefits is based on money and the three intangible benefits are each based on different paradigms. There is no common baseline for the measurement of any of the benefits. The technique is therefore liable to produce dangerous results, such that the investments may well be made in the wrong application. *The technique as it stands should be discouraged*. We shall see later that it has a most useful role in another way for the valuation of intangible benefits.

6.1.2.3 The Quantification Technique

This technique is the "science of commonsense", a formal way of applying a set of steps and practices that convert the intangibles into money. The technique has also been called "bridging the gap". The steps that bridge the gap from an intangible to cash are illustrated in Figure 6.4. While it is inevitable that judgement will be required with the application of the technique, so that the valuation of the intangibles will still be open to question, the technique does put the task of ascertaining intangible valuation

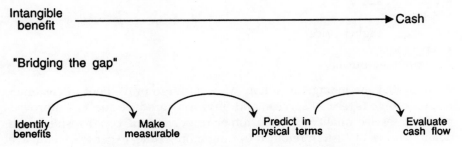

Figure 6.4 The quantification approach steps

into a formal framework of "things to do/advices to apply" which enables the valuation to be more accurate than either of the two previous approaches. The quantification technique does not provide a magic solution to the measurement of intangible benefits but it certainly helps.

6.1.2.4 *Identify the Benefits*

The first step is the identification of the intangible benefits. There are two useful sources of information for this:

(1) The CSFs are often intangibles. All that needs to be done is to make the CSFs measurable in the same way as in the multiple attribute decision model technique and then one is progressing along the steps of the quantification technique. For example, the CSFs in Figure 2.3 for "credibility as a supplier" could have been defined as the number of complaints per week from the customers and the "maintaining high quality staff" could have been defined as the number of graduates as a percentage of the employees along with the duration of their time with the company. One can put numbers to the measurables and value the numbers.

(2) Create a checklist of intangibles. This has proved to be a more fruitful approach to the problem. The checklist shown below has become very stable as it has been applied unchanged on a number of projects:

- Customer satisfaction;.
- Product/service quality;
- Product/service reliability;
- Premium service;
- Speed of service;
- Product presentation;
- Improved service.

All these intangibles can be converted in monetary terms into the ability to:

- Maintain sales.
- Sell more;
- Charge a higher price;
- Save money;
- Create new business.

Assume that the intangibles identified were an improvement in customer response time (speed of service) and improved product quality (improved product/service quality). The customer response time could result in the detail benefits of custom retained (selling more), time/expense saved (save money) and increase in revenue (sell more and/or higher price). The benefit of improved product quality could result in the measurables of custom retained (maintain sales), reduction in defects/scrap (save money/higher price), reduction in quality assurance expenses (save money), premium price (higher price) and increase in revenue (sell more). Note that the same benefit can be obtained from more than one intangible.

6.1.2.5 Make the Benefits Measurable

The above benefits can be re-expressed in measurable terms. Custom retained becomes number of customers retained, increase in revenue becomes number of extra sales/extra price, reduction in quality assurance defects becomes number of defects, premium price becomes extra price and so forth.

6.1.2.6 Predict in Physical Terms

This is the largest, most important and most difficult of the quantification steps. There are a number of ways in which the measurables can be converted into actual numbers:

(1) *Market surveys*. This is much the most fruitful and recommended approach. Market surveys have a number of attractive features about them. Perhaps the most significant is that they are:

- The best way of matching the company's perception of what the customer wants with what the customer actually wants. The company and customer lines in Figure 6.3 can be merged from the result of a good market survey. There is no lost opportunity or wasted effort.
- The surveys are able to take a forward look at likely developments. They are able to relate known customer intentions against known company achievables. The question can be asked "If we (the company) do this will you (the customer) do business with us?" It therefore leads to proactive actions—events responding to you and not the other way around. There is therefore an element of you being in control if you act on the findings of the survey. When events are reacting to your actions the risks on any project resulting from the market survey are lowered. The value of the project therefore goes up. Yet another advantage of market surveys.

  If the survey is conducted with care and professionalism, accurate answers can be obtained to a decision that if an investment is made here (the system providing the product/service) then a return can be achieved there (the customer purchasing the product/service). Decisions about future actions can be made with a much greater degree of confidence.
- The focus, scope and precision of the survey can be precisely defined by the company requiring the survey.

(2) Management estimates. These should be used where there has been no market survey. The more senior the managers making the estimates, the closer they are to the operations supported by the project and the more they are removed from the responsibility of the project the better—the estimates will have a greater authority, the knowledge used for the estimates will result in estimates of greater confidence and the estimates will be judged to be made without bias and emotion.

The managers making the estimates need to have the confidence of their peers.

The problem with management estimates is that they are based on past evidence and are therefore reactive. The advantages of proaction become disadvantages with reaction.

(3) Comparative case studies. This exercise considers a similar business which has conducted an investment in the recent past similar to the one being planned. Such studies have the merit that mistakes which may have been made can be identified and avoided. But studies of this kind suffer from a number of serious disadvantages. Any comparison is by its nature against a project that is in the past—comparative studies are always backwards looking. This means that comparative studies are of little use if the company is planning an investment in a system that is cutting edge. It also indicates that an organisation content with comparative studies cannot be cutting edge. Comparative studies by their nature are a sign of weakness.

Comparative studies are useful for avoiding the mistakes of the past— and that is where they should end.

6.1.2.7 Evaluate in Cash Flow Terms

This is a simple mathematical process, with the physical volumes from the previous step being related to the monetary value of the benefit. For example, an increase in sales is multiplied by the monetary contribution made to produce an increase in profit; the increase in price is multiplied by the sales to produce the increase in profit; and the custom retained is multiplied by the marginal revenue to produce the profit saved.

6.1.2.8 A Worked Example

A worked example of the application of the quantification technique shows the merits of the technique over the other approaches to the valuation of intangible benefits. The case study is based on a European port authority.

The port was concerned with the movement of containers. While the port had been successful in holding its market share, it faced the most intense competition from the two adjacent ports along the coastline to the east and the west. This can be seen in Figure 6.5. The port had some 25% of the business along the coastline under consideration and a turnover of around one million containers entering the port and leaving the port. Each container vessel would have some 370 containers for unloading. The competitor ports had modern online computerised container scheduling and handling systems which enabled them to offer the prime customers, the shipping companies, fast and reliable turnaround of their vessels. The case study port was in danger of losing competitive edge to these two rivals.

Figure 6.5 shows that the two competitor ports had been able to win business from the case study port in that containers which they handled were for and from destinations that were in the geographical catchment area of the case study port. This catchment area was regarded rightly as part of the case study port's "home ground", for which the port should have a business edge if only because of geographic proximity lowering transport costs. The 20% of the containers from port A and the 60% from port B (the east–west canals made the penetration of port B that much the easier) represented one million containers, or the entire case study port's current business for a year. Something had to be done.

It was decided to use technology to outdo the other ports. The case study port already had a similar online container scheduling and handling system which was assessed as being as good as the other ports, but these other ports had better geographical settings, one with one of the largest rivers in

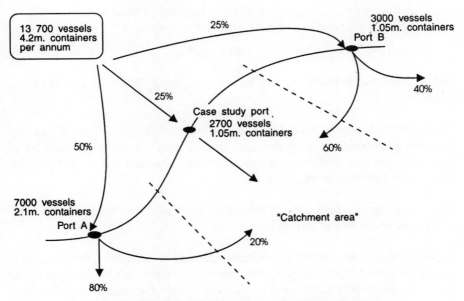

Figure 6.5 Case study: A European port authority

Europe running deep into the natural hinterland/catchment area and the other with the blessing of many canals running on the east–west axis. The decision was made to invest in a realtime container scheduling and handling system, not only for the vessels but also for all means of container transport into and out of the port, thus covering not only vessels but also barges, trains and trucks. The system was divided into two parts: the "waterside" operations, concerned with the loading and unloading of vessels and barges, and the "landside" operations concerned with the loading and unloading of trains and trucks.

Waterside operations are much more complicated than landside—the loading of several hundred containers onto a vessel is a highly complicated task, as it has to take the ports still to be visited and the buoyancy of the vessel into account. The loading of one or at most two containers onto a truck is a simple affair to plan and schedule and the more complicated loading of a train merely has to take the destinations of the train into account and group the railcars and the containers they carry accordingly. Buoyancy and containers on top of each other is not an issue. The system with which this case study is concerned is for waterside operations only.

The system would be able to:

- Provide a predictable, rapid and reliable turnaround of vessels;
- Provide a significant reduction in turnaround time;
- Provide a significant reduction in container movements;
- Handle larger vessels;
- Assist the shipping companies in the planning of their vessels;
- Provide realtime control of the container movers.

The benefits to be obtained from this would be:

(1) An improved market share (sell more); in terms of Figure 6.1 this is part of "customer service".

The improved service would enable the port to retain and even gain an increase in market share, particularly in the port's home catchment area. The intention was that the new system would enable a substantial portion of this lost business to be recovered.

(2) Reduced penalty payments for the late turnaround of the vessels (save money); this is part of "customer service".

Currently one vessel in 10 was missing the tide on which it was scheduled to sale. A vessel that is so delayed compromises the rest of the journey to the other ports it is scheduled to visit. Not only that but a vessel that is static is a vessel that is not earning revenue. The shipping company is

doubly penalised, when the vessel was not able to depart on the scheduled tide the port was required to pay a penalty to the shipping company. This issue of penalty clauses was particularly significant for the shipping companies trading in the North Sea. If the company is trading across the world and misses the tide in Japan then there is plenty of time to make up the time lost if the deliveries are to Europe. If one is leaving the southern shores of the North Sea to take containers to Norway or the Baltic to a strict time-table then missing the tide becomes a serious issue. Steaming at a higher speed increases the fuel consumption of the vessel and thereby the costs to the shipping company. The requirement was to reduce the penalty payments from one in 10 to one in 70.

(3) Reduced number of container movements that produced no revenue (save money); in terms of Figure 6.1 this is part of "internal improvement" and therefore a more easily identified and questionable intangible.

The only movements of containers that the port can charge for are the unloading and loading of a vessel. Any movement of containers within the container port for planning and scheduling purposes is a burden carried by the port. Any reduction of the internal container movements would produce a significant saving to the port. At the case study port, there were seven movements from the unloading to the loading of a container, this including the unload and the load. Five movements were internal. For each internal movement saved there would be a saving of 20% of internal costs. It was planned that the internal movements would be reduced from five to three—a 40% saving. This would be achieved by the proposed computer system containing a new yard planning container scheduling system.

(4) New types of container vessels visiting the port (new business); this is part of "adaptability".

Although following the same principles, the algorithms for unloading and loading large container vessels are much more complicated than for small vessels. The variety of vessel designs is but one of the additional problems. The new computer system therefore enabled the port to support larger vessels of a greater variety of classes, as well as the smaller vessels. The operations of the port were more adaptable. This brought in new business to the port.

(5) Premium price for premium service (charge a higher price); this is part of "customer service".

The faster and more reliable service would enable the port to charge the shipping companies a higher price for the unloading and loading of containers.

(6) New business and premium price for a premium service; this is part of "foresight".

It was known from the market survey that 40% of the shipping companies did not have an advanced vessel planning system and were thus not able to schedule their vessel operations. The new system was deliberately designed with spare data processing capacity, as the scheduling algorithms for yard planning could also be used with some modification for vessel scheduling.

(7) Labour, equipment and space savings.

The new system would enable more efficient use of the container cranes for the unloading and loading of containers, the van carriers for the picking up and movement over short distances of the containers and the service trailers for the long distance movements of the containers.

The benefit from this efficiency was *not* claimed by the system on the basis that the investment in container cranes, van carriers and service trailers made some years back when the current system was developed had been written off—on the basis of the advice offered in section 7.1.6 sunk costs should be ignored. The advice preached in this book was advice practised in reality.

It can be seen that all but one of the benefits was in the more difficult to categorise classes of Figure 6.1. The system was therefore genuinely dealing with the intangible benefits.

The approach adopted to obtain the evidence for the calculation of the intangible benefits was through a market survey and management estimates. The use of a comparison study would be a waste of time because it was planned that the new system would be leading edge—there was no comparison to be had even if it had been a good idea.

The market survey was conducted most carefully and thoroughly, with advice and support from a specialist market research company. There were interviews with the shipping companies, the train operators and the trucking companies. Individual owners of barges and trucks were not part of the survey as they, by and large, were not able to switch business to other ports. They were "safe" within the catchment area. There was also much reading of trade journals and shipping manifests.

The results of the survey were carefully recorded. The replies of the shipping companies to the question "If we do this will you do that?" were plotted and marked, with a confidence factor based on the assessment of the credibility of the company's management and trading history with the port. The results of the survey were given high confidence marks by the port's management.

The survey was able to cover three of the five intangible benefits claimed for the new system—an increase in market share, new business and an increase in price chargeable. Management estimates were used where the market survey could not be used, that is for the reduction in penalties and the percentage of sales saved.

The steps of the quantification approach produced the following results:

(1) Identify the benefits:
  - An increase in custom (A);
  - An increase in the price chargeable (B);
  - Custom retained (C);
  - A reduction in penalty payments (D);
  - A reduction in container movements (E);
  - Handle larger vessels (F);
  - Assist the shipping companies in the planning of their vessels (G). (The benefits have been marked ( ) so that a trail of their progression through the application of the technique can be made).
(2) Make the benefits measurable; the benefits become:
  - Percentage increase in the total shipping market (A);
  - Increase in price over the old price (B);
  - Percentage of sales saved (C);
  - Number of penalties saved (D);
  - Number of containers in the port not being moved more than four times from unloading to loading (E);
  - Number of new vessels by class visiting the port (F);
  - Number of shipping companies using the port container scheduling facilities for a number of times (G).
(3) Predict in physical terms:
  - *Increase in the total shipping market (A)*. The assessment of the ability to increase market share was based on the market survey. The original aim was to increase the share from 25% to 50%, a doubling of business, that is half of the containers coming into the catchment area from the other ports were to be "captured" by the port. Negotiations with the shipping companies showed that this was over-ambitious, and that the best that could be achieved would be a 50% increase in business. The market share would go up from 25% to about 37%.
  - *Increase in price over the old price (B)*. The market survey enabled a plot to be produced showing the price that the shipping companies would be prepared to pay for a given improvement in the turnaround time

of the vessels. Negotiations were held with individual shipping companies to ascertain very precisely what the premium price for the improved service could be. The result was that there could be an average 8% increase in the price charged for the unloading and loading of containers.

- *Sales saved (C)*. The number of sales saved was based on management estimates and the market survey. The marketing manager estimated that some 80% of the market currently held by the port could easily switch to the other ports and that some 10% of the current business could be lost per annum, unless improvements were made of the type envisaged by the system. The cost of landward transport of containers was not high enough to limit the ability of the competitors to penetrate the catchment area and there was not much shipping company loyalty to a port. Both the landside and the waterside sectors of the market were vulnerable. The estimate was that if the improvements were made then the potential haemorrhaging of the business would be effectively stopped. The survey had shown that the shipping companies were impressed by the other two ports' ability to offer rapid online planning of the scheduling of the vessels, this enabling the vessels to alter their ports of call at short notice and still be able to have a rapid turnaround. Turnaround time of the vessel was judged by the shipping companies as the most significant factor in their decision as to which of the three ports to call at.

- *Number of penalties saved (D)*. The figures for this were from the management estimate. The current level of delays was one in 10. The intention was to reduce this to one in 70. On the basis of the estimated increase in business the total number of penalties would be reduced from 270 to 60 per annum, this taking into account the 50% increase in trading volumes.

- *Number of internal container movements per vessel compared with previous figures (E)*. The figure for this was obtained from the yard planner, who was responsible for the scheduling of the vessels and the planning of the movement of containers in the port. His knowledge of the scheduling algorithms and his past good performance from the less capable system the port currently had gave his cautious estimates credibility. The estimate was that the number of container movements from unloading to loading would be reduced from seven to five, thus non-fee earning movements would be reduced from five to three.

- *Number of new vessels by class visiting the port (F)*. The source of information for this was the Lloyd's Register of Shipping. It was a simple case of ascertaining which class of large vessel could now be supported by the new vessel scheduling system, checking the number of vessels per class and the owning shipping companies and approaching the companies for negotiation. Three shipping companies which were not currently trading with the port agreed to use the port if the claims for the new systems proved valid. The port was provided with the average number of containers being unloaded per port visit for this part of Europe. From the evidence provided it was calculated that some 40 new vessel visits per annum would be made to the port and that the number of containers to be unloaded and loaded per visit would be around 450 rather than the usual 370.

- *Number of shipping companies using the port container scheduling facilities for a number of times (G).* The market survey provided a detailed breakdown of which shipping companies were requiring a lot of replacing of the containers on their vessels because of poor vessel planning facilities. The port also had a good idea as to which of the shipping companies needed help in this regard from the number of containers that were unloaded and then reloaded onto the same vessel. The port authority approached these companies and offered to do the scheduling for them. All that was required was for the shipping manifest to be faxed or, preferably, transmitted electronically on a daily or other basis and the port would do the scheduling and transmit the reply in whatever time span and manner was required. The port could thus offer not only the scheduling of the container placements on the vessels for visits to the case study port but for all ports the shipping companies visited.

  The total number of shipping companies which accepted the offer, mainly the smaller ones with limited computing facilities, was six. They provided the port with the total volumes of trade they were dealing with and a scheduling charge was made per container. It was necessary to ensure that the charge was less than the total costs the shipping companies were incurring because of poor placement. The price charged was the result of "bargaining".

(4) Evaluate in cash terms. This step is shown in Table 6.4. The figures are non-discounted. They occurred in the second year of the project. Their NPV is described in Chapter 9 and is obtained from Table 9.1. The figures with the ** are those that are based on the market survey and therefore have a greater degree of credibility.

What was clear was that the proposed computer system would provide a substantial source of revenue while the competitor ports were using their existing and to-be-outdated vessel scheduling systems and that, although all the revenue would be based on intangibles, 92% of the benefits value was based on the most credible measurement, the market survey. The decision was made to go ahead with the project. The result was so successful that a similar system for the landside operations was developed and

Table 6.4 Container port project evaluation in cash terms

The benefit	Calculation	Cash flows
(A) Increase in sales	525 000 containers × £20	= £10.5m.**
(B) Increase in price	1.57m. containers × £8	= £12.6m.**
(C) Custom retained	150 000 containers × £20	= £3m.
(D) Reduction in penalties	210 × £1000	= £0.21m.
(E) Reduction in internal	1.57 × 2 × £4	= £12.56m.**
container movements	20 000 containers × £20	= £4m.**
(F) New business	270 999 containers × £3	= £0.81m.**
(G) New scheduling		
	Total cash flow	= £43.68m.

the port has been able to sell the computer system to other ports which are geographically too distant to be competitive. The two competing ports responded with their own versions of the system so that the high revenues indicated above lasted for only a few years. Nevertheless the sytem was very profitable and saved the port from losing its current business. The objectives of the system were fully achieved.

What was remarkable was that the large investments were justified solely on the basis of the intangible benefits. The quantification technique proved its worth.

6.1.3 Can the Scoring and Quantification Techniques be Merged?

The question that needs to be asked of the container port evaluation exercise was "Can the figures presented, the £43.68m., have been finessed even further?". It is becoming clear that the answer is yes. The pure monetary measure was not adequate.

The figures given above of the revenues the new computer system would generate value the system solely in monetary terms. The port authority board, while pleased with the figures, also concentrated on non-monetary business benefits, for example:

• The crucial concern was to stay in business and then beat the competition, not the other way round. Therefore the benefits that would enable custom to be retained and a reduction in penalty payments had a higher business significance than, say, increase in sales and new scheduling. The benefit "custom retained" (C) was the benefit that most impressed the board, this benefit ensuring that the core of the port's business, its existing customers, would be maintained. The reduction in penalty payments (D) was also rated as important as this created the impression with the customers of an improvement in port operations. Good customer "vibes" were crucial. Without its existing customers staying with the port, the port would die. The benefit of reduction in internal container movements (E) was rated third by the board, as the savings in non-revenue earning activities would be substantial.

- The correct perception that the market survey based intangibles were proactive indicators of business opportunities and therefore had a greater and longer term intrinsic value than the reactive management estimates.
- The market survey intangibles were customer oriented rather than inward looking. The beneficial impact would therefore be more durable.

The conclusion reached was that the multiple attribute decision model technique could be used on top of the quantification approach to add the business benefit component to the overall value of the system. The financial figures showed that the proposed computer system would be profitable. This was the prime basis of the decision to proceed. But the financial figures did not show the true extent to which business objectives were being achieved. The financial figures were therefore weighted and re-expressed as a score.

The board's business objectives for the proposed computer system were to:

- Keep their existing customers $(A + D)$;
- Reduce the costs of non-fee earning activities, these being largely incurred by the internal movement of containers (E);
- Generate new business (F).

The results of the assessment of the financial figures are shown in Table 6.5. There was no need to take account of the risk component of the multiple attribute decision model approach. This had already been catered for in the market survey and the management estimates.

Table 6.5 Container port project evaluation financial figures re-expressed as a score

The benefit	Weight	"Financial" score
(A) Increase in sales	0.8	$= 8.4 \, (10.5 \times 0.8)$
(B) Increase in price	0.3	$= 3.8$
(C) Custom retained	1.0	$= 3.0$
(D) Reduction in penalties	1.0	$= 0.21$
(E) Reduction in internal container movements	1.0	$= 12.56$
(F) New business	1.0	$= 4.0$
(G) New scheduling	0.2	$= 0.16$

Information Gathering

The gathering of accurate information about a business and its operations is vital if the true value of an investment, such as in a computer system, is to be ascertained. This chapter describes and illustrates some approaches and techniques which can be used to improve the accuracy and relevance of the information used in any planning process. Some of the points made are as much to do with tried and tested tips of good accounting advice or financial commonsense as with information gathering. The reason for this is that poor accounting practices have led many companies to obtain the wrong information and from this make poor investment decisions.

Like Chapter 4, this chapter contains the do's and don'ts of IA.

7.1 THE NEED FOR THE RIGHT INFORMATION

7.1.1 What is the right information?

Whatever technique is used to value an investment the vital first step is to collect the right information. This entails knowing:

- What information to include and, just as important, what not to include;
- Whether the information is accurate.

Any technique which requires numerical information will be useless if the quality and relevance of the base information is poor. The old adage of "rubbish in, rubbish out" remains as valid for the valuation of investment projects as correct inputting of data into a computer system. Yet many organisations place great faith in elaborate techniques and systems to solve their problems, whilst neglecting simple procedures to ensure the relevance and accuracy of the basic information. The result is often highly elaborate (and expensive) rubbish.

Worse still is the false sense of value that is often placed on such results. Many managers believe that because such information has been produced by a sophisticated system then it must be of great importance. Managers may say "This data costs much to obtain and process so it must be good" without questioning the relevance or accuracy.

An incident with which one of the authors is familiar is an example of this. The stocks for a particular site of a manufacturing company were unknowingly overvalued by three times the true value. This was because stocks had been booked to the wrong code when entered to the company stock system by the poorly trained staff. The stocks should have been booked elsewhere. At a high level manufacturing meeting the stocks were quoted as being extraordinarily high and a matter of some concern to the board of directors. However the site managers knew that the stock figure quoted was an error but, despite this, the head office managers refused to believe site management and said that they would prefer to believe computer based data rather than locally kept manual data. This simple example demonstrates that if the input data is poor then the information produced can be misleading, possibly leading to erroneous decisions. The damage to corporate operations and profits can be substantial.

Another failing is that of inappropriately focused systems. A company may spend a great deal on computer systems to analyse costs on a particular operation when the costs are already under tight control, cost performance is generally good and the particular operation costs are only a small portion of the total. If cost overheads are small and cost performance is good then effort is being wasted on generating detailed cost information. It may be more appropriate for the systems to be geared to analysing sales figures if sales are a weak area. This inappropriate focusing can lead to management time and effort being directed upon relatively unimportant goals.

There are three main points to information gathering which, if properly considered, will lead to a high quality of information gathered and save valuable time in that only relevant information will be sought.

(1) Identify the costs and benefits that matter. The aim is not to waste time on data that is not relevant to the investment decision. The question is therefore what information needs to be gathered?

(2) Properly evaluate those costs and benefits which are relevant to the investment decision. These can be difficult to predict, particularly if the investment is radically different from any other project undertaken. There are techniques and practices to provide this.

(3) Continually monitor the costs and benefits. All too often decisions are taken on investments and the results are not monitored when the investment has been spent and the project completed to check whether the decision was the right one. From an investment point of view, was the information gathered on the costs and benefits correct? From the business and information design points of view, are the claimed benefits of the computer system being achieved? If the answer to these questions is not obtained then what can be learned from the mistakes?

7.1.2 The Costs and Benefits that Matter

There is often confusion as to which costs and benefits are relevant to any given problem. The real skill in starting on any information gathering exercise is to know what costs and benefits are relevant in a business situation and how much time to spend on them. It should be asked whether the investment is designed to:

- Increase income;
- Reduce costs;
- Save income that would otherwise be lost.

Any investment which does not do the above is not adding value to the investment. The balance of system benefit is shifting—the scope for cost reduction in such areas as staff savings and more efficient production is reducing, while that for better service support is increasing. Given this trend there needs to be more attention to increases in income rather than to costs.

If a proposed systems investment will generate new business, the most important information is the increase in sales that the investment will produce. A system which generates a new insurance service or home banking facilities are examples of investments which increase costs but which also raise income. In this type of investment a great deal of attention is usually paid to the costs of the project, partly because they can be easily and accurately calculated. The costs will be scrutinised and predicted to a high degree of accuracy. The more important variables should be the volume and value of extra business generated, after all that is the purpose of the computer system. There is no point in predicting costs to within 0.5% if sales figures are only accurate to within 50%. This attention to detail with figures that are easy to measure yet should not be the centre of attention and the lack of care with figures that are difficult to obtain and measure are very common failings.

If an investment aims to perform the same business but more efficiently then the income information is not so important and greater effort on the cost information becomes appropriate. New payroll or sales order processing systems are examples of such investments. The aim is not to generate new business but to cope with current levels of demand at lower cost. Hence information on reduction in numbers of people and reductions in cost per transaction is important.

Because it is difficult to predict, the income side of the valuation equation is often paid little attention and the degree of accuracy is low. Nevertheless, it would be more appropriate to spend more effort in reducing the degree of uncertainty regarding the income information rather than the cost information, particularly if the monies on the income side are larger than the cost side. And this is usually the case. Many of the costs are one-offs, such as the purchasing of the hardware and software, whereas the incomes are mostly of a recurring type, so that the longer the project life the greater the income over the costs.

7.1.3 Relevant Costs

A frequent error in the gathering of cost data is that the wrong cost figures are used. The basic principle is that only incremental cash flows are relevant. When comparing the new cash flows with the old cash flows all other costs are irrelevant.

The most important thing to remember in the gathering of cost data is that it is only changes in the cash expenses or income to the organisation that are relevant to the decision. An official document processing system for a major UK government office was justified on the basis that it would save one hour per day for all its document handling staff. The annual cost saving was calculated as the average hourly rate of its clerical staff multiplied by the number of staff and multiplied by the number of working days in the year. The problem was that there were no plans to reduce the number of staff, so the pay expenses would be no different. The actual cash cost saving was nil. All the system had achieved was to generate one spare hour a day for its staff, but there were no plans as to what to do with that extra hour per day. It may be that the time freed was used to do something else of value, or it could be that Professor Parkinson's law that the job expands to fill the time allocated occurred, but this was not measured. The result was that computer costs increased and all other costs remained static, overall a net loss.

Many projects claim time savings in terms of fractions of an operator's time. This is a common example of the kind of justification of many capital projects. The problem is that fractions of many employees' time savings cannot always be translated into reducing the equivalent number of "whole" personnel. The whole cash benefit is not realised. The point to remember is that a cost saving is not a cost saving unless it reduces the cash paid out by the business.

7.1.4 Historical Comparison

One common approach is historical comparison, that of analysing data from recent projects which are technically or functionally similar to the project under consideration and extrapolating any relevant findings from the existing project. The advantages of this approach are clear. Any findings from the existing project are based on real evidence and will therefore be likely to be much more accurate and reliable than theoretical estimates. The existing data can also be analysed statistically to test for real relationships.

This use of existing data as the basis of extrapolation of the costs and benefits to be incurred and obtained has become a science. A company called Quantitative Software Management Limited uses a software tool with parameter driven, statistical analysis algorithms for calculating the software development time of a project based upon times, skills and monies for a range of software projects, from simple PC based solutions to large mainframe applications. The algorithms look at the complexity and scale of a proposed project and compare it with a large database of similar past projects to give some indication of the expected time, skills and monies required. Benefits are not considered, which is a significant omission.

There are several dangers with the historical comparison approach. Such techniques are not good for projects which:

(1) Experience radical change.

Trends of the past do not necessarily bear close comparison with what is happening now or in the future. This can be due to a changing environment. The historical volume of demand for sales in Western Europe for a company starting to penetrate the Eastern European market will not be relevant in determining the increased capacity requirements of the sales order processing system. The purchasing habits of Eastern Europe are not the same as those of Western Europe.

(2) Are technically or functionally new and unlike anything in the past.

The design and development effort required and the cost implications for object oriented projects are quite different from those within the relational database environment. There is an upfront increase in costs as an object oriented application design is more involved than a traditional structured design, but there is a project tail-end benefit in that the development and maintenance effort can be substantially reduced, particularly if the application is able to reuse much of the existing data and logic. The cost profile is very different.

As shown in Chapter 4 the benefits from object orientation are not the same as for traditional computer systems. It is a cost reduction technology and, except for those companies providing object oriented products and support, not an income generating technology.

Current object oriented products use pre-database technology and therefore do not fully exploit the benefits of 4th Generation Language (4GL) architectures (such as the definition of the tables of data, their relationships and their data attributes in the database schema rather than the application program). The risk, time and cost profiles will change yet again when the relational vendors release their own offerings of object orientation with components of 4GL architectures built in. Historical analysis is of little use here.   On a functional basis the sales of video telephones are impossible to predict from any historical figures. They may become popular or they may not. An "act of faith" is required regarding their sales potential.

Historical data can be unreliable. In examining the profitability of an industry, an index may be constructed from the published accounts of the companies in that sector. However, if the index is based on the published accounts then it cannot take into consideration the different accounting policies adopted by each company. If the index is based on the dividends and increase in the share price then it will be accurate. Published information needs to be treated with caution according to the method of compilation.

7.1.5 Expert Advice

In the majority of cases there will be a need to resort to some form of estimate based upon expert advice and judgement because historical data is not available. In attempting to achieve this, some simple points can help:

(1) Use multidiscipline/multifunctional groups. Given the adoption of corporate databases and object oriented technology, IT applications span multiple business functions. However, the best solution for a given function is not necessarily the best solution for the business. There has to be some means of compromising between the various needs of each function in order to obtain a solution which maximises the benefits to the company as a whole. The prerequisite is therefore to obtain cross-functional expertise so as to ascertain the knock-on effects of change from one functional area to another functional area. The solution to this is to use multifunctional groups of experts, preferably with the participants having a knowledge of the other functional groups' operations.

(2) Seek the opinion of an expert whose opinion is respected. A good starting point is to seek the views of an experienced member of staff. A sales manager of some success and experience will know better than anyone else

how much more he can sell if a proposed invoicing system will cut his administration time by 10%. It is essential that the person from whom advice is sought has the respect of his/her peers, preferably having shown that advice in the past has proved valid. If the "expert" does not have respect and a proven track record then advice should not be sought.

(3) *Challenge assumptions.* Whenever an expert quotes a figure, ask why he believes in that figure. In this way it is possible to discover the basic assumptions that are made. An example could be a salesman saying that it is possible to sell 10% more for a 10% increase in selling time because there is a linear relationship between selling time and sales. This may be true for products that are in high demand but is this true for products that are *passé*? Is the salesman's claim testable?

(4) *Look at any previous estimates.* It may be possible to look at the estimating record of the "expert". Is the expert consistently an overestimator or an underestimator? This can temper the view taken on his estimates. There is a quote "if a project is badly run then it will overrun by three times the estimated costs, and if the project is well run then it will overrun by twice the original costs". This seems to apply to projects where the tasks are new to the participants and should be borne in mind if the project is different in nature from previous projects.

(5) *Look for diverse views amongst experts.* By seeking the views of as many relevant people as possible, a pattern of agreement and disagreement can be ascertained. A high degree of agreement points to a reliable estimate whilst a diverse spread of results indicates the opposite. One important point to remember in doing this is to seek opinions separately. By asking a group of experts for their views simultaneously there may be a tendency to agree with the first view expressed. By asking for estimates independently there is better scope for testing for diversity.

(6) *Try to test opinions up and down the corporate hierarchy.* Another helpful test of estimates and assumptions is to look for different views up and down the management hierarchy. A production supervisor may have a different estimate of production down time than the production manager. A view taken may be that the production supervisor is closer to the event and will hence have a more reliable estimate.

A factor which can sometimes affect this exercise is that different politics come into play at different levels of management. An example may be where the sales director is under severe pressure from the managing director to increase the volume of sales. The sales director may therefore build large sales increases into his project plans, which may be more ambitious than can be achieved. There is no substance behind the statistics, only a political drive for higher sales. Reality is different from the politics.

(7) A spread of estimates may be a measure of risk. If no consensus arises out of an information gathering exercise or meeting of experts then the spread of results may be used as a measure of risk. The mean could be used as the expected result and the best and worst estimates used as the extremes. The standard deviation of estimates could be used as a measure.

(8) Allay fear. The aim of any exercise should be to arrive at estimates that are as close to the truth as possible. Many approaches to asking for estimates can lead to defensive estimates (leaving something up the sleeve just in case things go wrong). If the questions are posed in a negative or aggressive way then negative and defensive responses will be the likely result. "The proposed computer system will be able to reduce the number of staff in your department" is not conducive to a positive attitude to it. If the question is posed in such a way as to encourage manager and user participation then a more productive result can be obtained: "Could not the proposed computer open up new opportunities for efficiency of existing operations so that we can beat our competitors and from this exploit new business opportunities? If we are successful in this would there not be a need for some reallocation of staff and resources to maximise the exploitation?".

Negative behaviour is encouraged by holding managers to the estimates they have given and imposing penalties for failure, particularly where the risk of failure is high. The process of change is often loaded with risk and it is important that risks should be taken when there seems a good chance of success.

(9) Use pilot estimating. One option that is often neglected, for cost/benefit information gathering, is piloting of projects, particularly for very large scale investments with high costs and uncertain benefits. Piloting can reduce many of the risks and uncertainties by testing just what the risks and uncertainties are and by measuring them. A major computer manufacturer was considering the introduction of a system of portable PCs for all sales staff. The PCs could be used to transmit orders from remote locations to the mainframe. It was estimated that this would lead to a 23% reduction in administration and travelling time, and so to an 8% increase in sales time with potential customers. The problem was that it was uncertain what the increase in sales revenue would be. It was decided to pilot the scheme in several regions at relatively low cost. The results were an increase in sales of over 10%, this giving a strong practical basis for projecting the likely benefits of a full scale implementation.

7.2 THE DO'S AND DON'TS

7.2.1 The Trap of Hidden Costs

The most common problem in finding the information about costs expenditures and potential cost savings is that many costs are "hidden" by accounting systems. An example (which is common to many organisations) is that all systems costs are "lumped" in a systems overhead budget. If the sales department wants a new sales order processing system it may make a request to the systems department for the development of such a system. The costs of the development, such as hardware and software development time, would be charged to the systems budget. These costs would be lumped together with all the other projects that the systems department has undertaken for other departments. The result is that it is not possible to determine the cost of each project.

The sales department may then point to a 20% reduction in its administration costs, saving, say, £100 000 per annum. On the face of it, the situation seems beneficial. However the accounting system cannot show the corresponding increase in costs for the systems department. The costs may be £120 000 per annum—the system may actually be a net loser for the business. Unless the costs of each project and system are separated, it is impossible to be sure that such a loss making system can be avoided.

Indeed, the systems department and the user departments have a vested interest in working to an accounting system that does not accurately monitor costs and savings. The user departments can easily show improvements in efficiency because they are not charged with the costs of the system. Because user departments are not charged for the expenses of systems, demand quickly grows. The systems department sees its empire and budget grow year on year in order to cope with the ever increasing demand for systems. However, the net result could be that the organisation is throwing away money.

This unsatisfactory accounting arrangement is partly historical. Many systems departments start off as quite small departments with low budgets. In these cases the sums of money invested in systems are small. The need for a detailed accounting system is not that essential to controlling systems costs. As the business grows and as systems become more and more common the costs grow rapidly year on year. The systems budget can quickly become large. In such cases there is a need to improve the accounting systems to match. This has happened in most organisations over the last 10 to 20 years. Therefore the proportion an organisation spends on IT has grown dramatically. The problem is that in many cases the original accounting systems have not been enhanced to monitor the increased complexity of costs and savings on a project or system basis. The drawbacks of this accounting arrangement are:

(1) There is no way to analyse the profitability of each system or project. There is no matching of the costs of the system/project with its monetary and intangible savings or benefits.
(2) There is no way of knowing whether the organisation is getting value for money out of its computer investments. The accounts system does not have account codes of application system by organisation/department, by type of business activity being conducted.
(3) There is no means of setting a sensible budget on systems expenditure or limiting spending on IT. Demand may expand out of control. The accounting system does not have the means of recording expenditures against budgets and providing warning and stop messages when the budgets are near to overspend or in default.

7.2.2 Opportunity Costs

The true cost of a resource is its opportunity cost. An opportunity cost of a resource is defined as the opportunity (or benefit) foregone by putting an asset to its best alternative use. For example, many large DP units operate as profit centres and sell their services to outside companies as well as to their own parent company. In such a case it may be that there are conflicting demands for some spare capacity. There may be an opportunity to use the spare capacity in processing the payroll of a medium sized company and be able to charge say £100 000 per annum for the service. If this is the case there is an opportunity to utilise the spare capacity in processing the payroll of the third party and earn £100 000 per annum. If the spare capacity is used for internal demands then this opportunity to earn £100 000 is the opportunity that is forgone. In other words £100 000 is the opportunity cost of the spare capacity. This is the relevant cost for any decision to use the spare capacity internally. If no internal user can show a net benefit when charged with the £100 000 opportunity cost then the organisation is better off by selling its spare capacity outside the organisation.

Another example is in the charging of software development time. It may seem sensible to charge software development time at the basic cost of such time (i.e. the programmer/analyst's salary plus costs and expenses). However, if such time is in short supply then the cost can be much higher. If there is a very high value project, on which an analyst can add value to the tune of £1000 per day whilst only costing £200 per day, then the opportunity cost of the analyst's time is £1000 per day and not the basic cost of £200 per day. Hence, if there is another project which requires that analyst's time then the true and relevant cost which should be applied to that project is £1000 per day.

Opportunity costs generally apply to resources that are in scarce supply or high demand. In most other cases the basic cost of the resource is the correct cost to use. One of the authors has to admit that this cost has not been included in any IAs he has done. He has reflected an error that is all too common.

7.2.3 Forget Sunk Costs

A "sunk" cost is defined as a cash expense which has been fully paid in the past and hence is irrelevant for a future investment decision. Unfortunately, often sunk costs are treated as relevant to an investment decision when in fact all sunk costs are irrelevant. Investors often get this the wrong way round in making investment decisions. The result has been that many viable investments have not gone ahead.

A large pharmaceutical manufacturer spent a considerable sum of money on a new computer centre. This cost £3m. and was to be depreciated over 10 years at an even rate of £300 000 per annum. After two years the written down value of the facility was £2.4m. and it was at this time that the company merged with another company. In looking at options to rationalise the two companies' DP resources it was established that a new facility would yield a net saving of £1.5m. over its useful life. The management decided, however, that it could not afford to do this because £2.4m. would be the expense of writing off the old computer centre. This was a big mistake. The £2.4m. write-off was irrelevant to the decision to establish the new facility because the £3m. paid for the facility was paid out two years previously. The cash had already left the business and was not part of the current year's monies. It was merely the accounting policy of depreciation which "pretends" that the cash expense of building the facility is paid out over 10 years at a rate of £300 000 per annum.

Some people the authors have talked to about this issue have commented that forgetting sunk costs is something not practised at their company and they disagree with the argument put forward. It is not easy to persuade management to abandon expensive equipment that is still working and is still capable of yielding a profit. All too often management only invest when they have to, when the equipment is on its "last legs" and is a clear candidate for replacement. What is perhaps not realised is that there are always costs to this "only invest in what has to be invested in" approach, such as the loss in profits from higher efficiency, loss in competitiveness and quality to be obtained from the new invested equipment. Given the written off nature of that which is being replaced, nothing is gained from postponing investment.

The important principle for such costs is that bygones are bygones and nothing can be done about them. They are therefore irrelevant to any future decision.

7.2.4 Include all Knock-on Benefits

In order to capture the true costs and benefits of a proposed project it is important to include all the knock-on impacts on cash. For example, in the introduction of a new flexible manufacturing system for a small engineering firm the costs and the benefits of the operators were anticipated to be substantial. The purchase costs of the system were £650 000 and as far as the users were concerned that was it. However, the downloading of the software to the robots when their operations changed cost £20, the number of downloads was 200 per day and the supervisors were now working to 105% of their time, so that overtime was being paid. The annual costs of the system were £880 000, excluding the overtime. This is an example of the many hidden and unforeseen costs that crop up in many an investment. Investments such as this often have knock-on cost implications for other departments. Knock-on impacts can be hard to recognise or predict.

A further example is the introduction of automatic cash dispensing machines by banks and building societies. If the starting costs of offering the service are compared with the benefits then the outcome is that these machines cost more than they are worth. However, the knock-on implication of not investing is that customers would be lost to other banks and building societies. The knock-on benefit in this case is the saving of customers and revenue which would otherwise be lost—revenue is saved and not gained. The benefit is to the customer rather than to the company. It is a case of investing in these facilities and staying in business or not investing and losing market share, possibly to the point of eventual nonviability. In financial terms the investment is a loss maker, in business terms it is essential.

7.2.5 Cost Dynamics

Costs and benefits change over time. Despite this fact of life many costs and benefits are assumed to be static over the life of a project. The reason for this is that it simplifies the analysis of costs and benefits and often it can be a good approximation. But in most cases this would not be appropriate. The real world does not conduct itself for the satisfaction of accountants.

If the cost savings of a payroll system were put at £100 000 per annum in clerical staff and the business was growing at a rate of 20% per annum, it would be unrealistic to put the savings at £100 000 per annum for the whole life of the system. It would be more realistic to expect the old payroll expenses to rise by 20% per annum with the savings also growing at 20% per annum.

An insurance company one of the authors worked for has purchased an early version of the ORACLE relational database product. ORACLE is an excellent product in the round, but for this particular business there were tremendous performance problems. For reasons not pertinent to this book, the version of ORACLE that was being used had a crucial weakness in the file handler, so a new version of the product had to be purchased shortly after the initial installation of the system. This added cost was not anticipated.

Maintenance costs also vary very much over a project's life. In the early stages of a system's productive life it may need a high level of support until it is "bedded down". Once the system is well established it needs little support so the maintenance costs fall. As the system gets technically old and functionally limited, the maintenance costs may rise as the existing program code is modified with threads of old logic increasingly intertwined with new code. The maintenance curve is concave rather than convex.

It is important to recognise that cost profiles change over the life of a project. The easy assumption of flat cost profiles is almost always wrong.

7.2.6 Dangers of Budgeted Overheads

Some DP departments have a policy of allocating fixed overheads to all projects so as to cover general running expenses. This is as dangerous as any fixed hurdle rate. Consider the situation of a department that installed a new flexible manufacturing system costing £1.1m. The benefits of the new system were calculated as £1.5m., producing a net benefit of £400 000. However, in addition to these project costs, a DP departmental overhead of £600 000 was charged, so the project, in reality profitable, was now loss making and was rejected. These overhead costs had nothing to do with the actual project and so distorted the "decision" to invest.

It does not matter whether the burden to be carried is a fixed sum of money or a percentage portion of the cash flow. Fixed burdens of any kind create a conservative investment structure and lower the profitability of a company. In Figure 7.1 there are five projects that yield a profit. Of these only two projects (C and F) remain profitable after the allocation of the fixed budget burdens. Three projects would be rejected (A, D and E), even though they add profit to the company.

Once again fixed hurdles in IA reduce the profitability of a company.

7.2.7 Remember Abandonment Costs

Two cosmetic companies had merged and a project that had been underway for some time was stopped. The original costs were £3m. and, to date, £2m. had been spent. To abandon the project in favour of the new project for the merged company would cost some £800 000. This £800 000

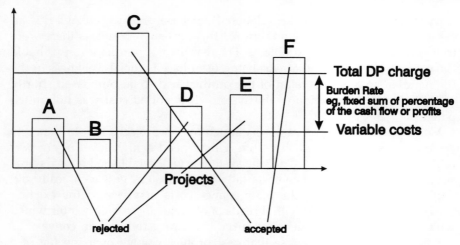

Figure 7.1 Dangers of budgeted burden rates

had to be allocated as a cost to the new project. This abandonment cost overhead on the new system is only relevant when the full costs of the original system have yet to be paid for.

7.3 THE NEED FOR CHARGEBACK MECHANISMS

Without proper monitoring of the expenditures and incomes that a computer system incurs and earns then the financial return to be obtained from an investment cannot be accurately ascertained. This is a major barrier to gathering reliable information about projects. The most popular solution is to use a system of "chargeback". Under such a system the expenses of a systems department are recorded on a project by project, system by system basis. The costs are then charged to the appropriate users of the system according to an algorithm of some kind. The advantages of such a system of chargeback are that:

- Users will give greater consideration to the adoption of a system if they are to be charged with the expenses of installing and running a system. It forces user departments to investigate the benefits and to weigh up the business benefits to be allegedly gained with the costs. The result is a likely reduction in "trivial" demands for additional computing services.
- An accurate measurement of the true returns to be obtained from a computer system can be made. Computer systems can be seen as a "business operation", having their own profit and loss accounting and the ability to provide a return on an investment just like any other investment.
- The usage of a computer system can be accurately ascertained. The allo-

cation of computer resources to user demand can therefore be better matched.

- Projects and systems undertaken by the business should be net contributors to the business. The chances of adopting a loss maker are significantly reduced.

The true value of a computer system is what the users are prepared to pay for it. A system of chargeback is one of the most important improvements that can be made in the measurement of computer systems' costs and benefits. Such systems of chargeback are becoming increasingly popular.[1] There are many ways of achieving a system of chargeback. They are illustrated in Figure 7.2 in the order of preference from top to bottom. It is not the purpose of this book to describe such accounting systems in detail, but an overview of the various approaches and their merits is given below:[2]

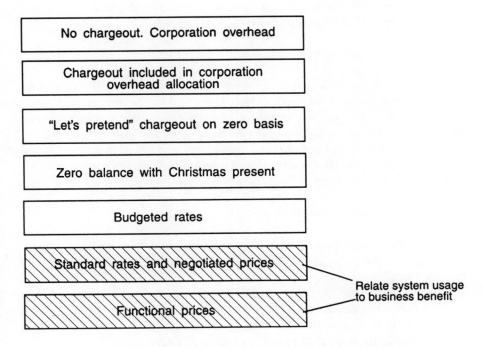

Figure 7.2 Information systems accounting practice spectrum

---

[1] Price Waterhouse (1989/1990). *Information Technology Review.*
[2] For a good introduction to the detail of chargeback systems, see:
Sen, D. (Sept. 1988). *DP: A Business within a Business,* Accountancy Magazine.
Berg, M. (1989). *Developing a Data Centre Chargeback System,* Annual Conference of UK Computer Management Group.

(1) No chargeout to the departments or users. All computing is a corporate overhead.

This approach gives no indication of the usage of the systems or the value that the users put on them. The users have nothing to lose in making the most trivial demands or requests for new systems.

(2) Charge on the basis of some fair measure, such as number of terminals or number of staff in each user department.

This is a very poor basis of charging because the development, purchase and installation costs of a system may bear no relation to the basis of cost allocation. If all DP costs are charged to user departments on the basis of the number of terminals in each user department, it would be unfair to those departments, such as payroll, with a high number of terminals but low development expenses and favourable to, say, a production department with few terminals but a high development expense.

(3) Chargeout to zero balance.

This charges the user departments on the basis of covering all computing costs. Charges rise and fall with DP expenses and so the system may seem erratic to users. No profit is sought in the operation of the computer systems. The allocation of the charges has to be on some unit of measure.

There is not much to recommend this approach. There is no concept of computing being run as a business or of relating the charges for the systems to the usage of the systems.

(4) Zero balance with a Christmas present.

The same as the above but with a built-in aim of achieving some profit. This can then be paid to the departments as a present at the end of the financial year.

This has the same demerits as the above with the modification that it tries to make the departments seem as though they are benefiting at the end of the year. Given the aim of a zero balance they are, in fact being overcharged! The feeling of benefit is entirely false.

(5) Budgeted rates.

This is the same as the above but with the aim of making a profit. Charges are fixed at agreed budgeted levels, say £X000 per month per user department. This is the first attempt to run computing as a business. Budgets for usage of the systems are planned and charged accordingly. The only problem with this approach is that there is no direct relationship between charge and usage.

(6) Standard rates for system usage.

Standard charges are set for DP resources, such as £X per CPU use, £Y per software development per hour. This approach is designed for the increasing use of windows technology. Charging per online transaction triggered from the menu screen is becoming increasingly irrelevant with windows technology, where there is much greater unplanned and undesigned for interaction between the user and the terminal. There is now a dialogue between the user and the computer, with possibly *n* windows being used as the user accesses the computer to obtain the information required. There is no longer a one-to-one relationship between the pressing of a transaction enter key and a computer processing the business requirement—one input request to access the data required and a string of information output in response. The typical user will now open a variety of windows on the screen, possibly from different products at a time (a word processor to obtain some text, a graphics package to obtain a picture and a voice image to go with the text and the picture) and will open and close the windows *n* times in a seemingly random manner.

Standard rates for system usage are widely used as a chargeback mechanism and have the benefit that there is a close relationship between usage/costs and the business benefit of the output of the system.

(7) Functional charging.

Here the charges are based on a user-deliverable rather than a DP resource. The system of charging is related to what the user "gets". In such a system the cost of each service is established and a cost per batch or online transaction is agreed. For example, there may be a cost of £1000 per payroll run, £21 per report printed and so on. It is important however that these charges are understood and agreed.

With batch run charging it is a relatively easy affair to see the business benefit and from this come to a charging agreement—so much for a specific report, the monthly departmental accounts £X, the quarterly tax position £Y. Online transactions that support a business requirement can be similarly charged.

Another solution for online access to the computer system is charging for the time the user is logged on. It is then up to the user to maximise the usage of the computer. If benefit is not obtained that is the fault of the user.

Charging on the basis of usage is a popular approach but the problem with it is that there is not a clear relationship between usage and benefit.

Functional charging is widely used and has the benefit that there is a close relationship between usage/costs and the business benefit of the output of the system.

The most attractive approaches being adopted therefore are functional charging for batch runs and online triggering of the business transactions from the menu screen (charged on the basis of the business requirement being supported) and usage charging for system development and general windows technology, on the basis of the logged on time per user and the number of messages between the user and the computer. Both approaches have the benefit of relating the charge to the purpose of the computer usage. There is therefore a clear relationship between usage and business benefit.

The DP department may in effect become a competitively priced service provider with user departments free to seek services outside the organisation if they can obtain those services more cheaply elsewhere. This means that the DP department becomes its own business and opens up the possibility of being a profit centre rather than just a cost centre. This is becoming a feature, particularly with the very largest DP organisations.

Two companies that are becoming a force to be reckoned with in the consultancy and systems development market in the United Kingdom are a large international photocopying company and a large national telecommunications company, which are now charging external clients for the services their DP departments can provide. Those departments are profit centres, run as a business.

The subject of chargeback is only lightly addressed. The book is not about how to charge for your services (that is a huge subject on its own) or about how to charge for your services via a computer program; it is about how to calculate the profit or loss from the charges, whether the revenue from the products/services adds value to the business. This book is about investment measurement, about the value of the investment, not about the different ways of charging for the investments in products/services. Charging brings in revenue and as such the results of the charging need to be measured, as this, along with the costs, produces the NPV of the projects. Should any reader wish to know more about computerised charging, two references are given in the footnotes on page 233 for a detailed understanding of the issues involved.

7.4 ON-GOING REVIEW

One of the most frequent questions asked of IT is "Are we getting value for money?". In large part the reason for the inability to answer this question lies in the fact that few projects are ever monitored after the implementation. Such reviews as there are, are often a one-off post-implementation review and seldom on-going. In a survey of major projects undertaken by large firms, over 50% had no monitoring system at all after the implementation and in those cases where there was monitoring, it was usually one-off and superficial.

The importance of on-going monitoring as opposed to a post-implementation review is that conditions are constantly changing. It is only by such monitoring that the system can be kept in tune with business needs. And a time will come when a system should be abandoned. This time is when the costs of running a system outweigh the benefits of the system or when an alternative solution yields a better return. Often systems are only replaced when it is obvious that they can no longer be maintained, the point at which an alternative solution became more attractive having been reached long ago. The profitability of the company thereby goes down. Unless there is continuous measurement this point will not be realised. There is natural reluctance to abandon an expensive project but, as explained in section 7.1.6 on ignoring sunk costs, it is a false economy to "hang on" to projects just because they have not been financially written off.

Finally, the most important argument in the authors' view for the practice of continuous monitoring is that in the long term it will improve the ability to forecast and estimate. One of the problems in measuring the costs and particularly the benefits of IT is that the technology is so new and there is very little experience. To date there has been little effort in trying to measure the actual costs and benefits after systems implementation with the claimed costs and benefits of the planning and valuation process. By adopting the regular discipline of measuring costs and benefits and comparing them with the original estimates, lessons will be learned and the standard of cost/benefit estimation will improve. How to do this is discussed in Chapter 8.

7.5 CHAPTER SUMMARY

From the above examples of relevant costs and benefits, the following guiding principles for investment in a project can be distilled:

- "A cost saving is only a cost saving if it saves cash flowing out of the business or if it saves cash that would otherwise flow out of the business";
- "A benefit is only a benefit if it increases the cash into a business or saves cash in flow which would otherwise be stopped";
- "The true cost of a resource is its opportunity cost";

- "Bygones are bygones, hence sunk costs are irrelevant";
- "The true value of a system is what the users are prepared to pay for it".

Two forms of chargeback should be used—a computer usage algorithm of some kind for the dialogue type processing used for interface between the user and the computer, and a functional based charging for traditional batch run type processing and online transactions triggering business requirements.

Chapter 8

Benefits Realisation

This is an aspect of assessing the ultimate value of a project that has only recently begun to be addressed in any detail. Some studies have been conducted recently in the UK into the development of a mechanism for measuring the real value of a project once it has been implemented and is earning its keep, as against the claims made for it as part of the planning process, claims that may well have been based on the techniques so far described in this book. As far as the authors are aware, nothing has been published on the results of the study.

This chapter describes an approach that integrates the claims of the benefits of a computer into the very design of the application system itself, so that the computer system can monitor itself as to the benefits it produces.

Investments in computer systems have been made on the basis of claims that the benefits outweigh the costs and that there is a positive NPV. The systems have been duly implemented and it has been assumed that the claimed benefits will flow as planned. Post-implementation reviews, and particularly the measurement of the actual benefits against the claimed benefits, have been rarely considered and even less included in the information systems life cycle.

Computer systems are expensive and must justify themselves. It is not just a case that the systems have a job to do, helping the organisation become more efficient and profitable. They must justify that job. But the justification can only be done if proper measurement practices and procedures are available. It is these that are missing. Fortunately the ability to measure the claimed benefits of a computer system is now becoming an issue and thought is being given to the matter. This is perhaps reflected in that the issues involved now have a title, that of "benefits realisation".

Neither of the authors have witnessed a conscious decision and, even less, any formal effort to measure whether the benefits claimed for a computer system are being achieved once the system is installed and running. This omission is due to the following facts:

- As stated in Chapter 1, 60% of IT managers invest in systems on the basis of a "hunch" ("It seemed a good idea at the time" was a comment once heard at a post-implementation review of a disaster). You cannot measure a hunch.
- There has been no consideration of what to do for a post-implementation review and how to go about it. Just as with the need to do an IA of a proposed computer system, the subject of benefits realisation has been ignored by the developers of structured methods used for designing computer systems. None of them include advice as to what needs to be done or how to do it. These methods initially were developed for the forward engineering of information from analysis to design to development to installation. More recently they have addressed the issue of reverse engineering from the current physical system back to a logical design.[1] They are being constantly refined and extended. But for benefits realisation there has been nothing.

There is general consensus that computers are "a good thing" and that to stay in business one needs to computerise company operations. But how much of a good thing? Much money is invested in the computer system's claims that the benefits are greater than the costs and the company's revenues will increase. But which of the claimed benefits actually provides the claimed return? Very few can answer this question. And yet the question is a valid one. The solution is to be found by the following means:

(1) Using the computer system itself. It is the computer system that records/controls the operations for which the benefits are claimed and therefore generates the benefits to be gained. The tragedy is that no mechanisms for business requirements are built into the design of the computer systems that conduct the operations. Structured methods are primarily responsible for this. These methods advise the analyst to obtain from the users of the proposed system the business requirements which they need to satisfy. This information is provided, recorded in a

---

[1] The ANSI-SPARC model for information modelling has three levels of information abstraction—the conceptual, the logical and the physical. The conceptual is the production of an information model that takes no account of the physical constraints of hardware and software; the logical is the conversion of the conceptual model into a design that is based on the physical facilities generic to file handlers and programming languages—the design is therefore a "universal" design; the physical design is a product specific design appropriate to the target environment on which the system will run. The term logical has long been used in the UK for what ANSI-SPARC calls the conceptual. The term logical in this book is used in the ANSI-SPARC context of conceptual.

requirements catalogue, and the data and the processing to support the business requirement is modelled. The problem is that these users are not concerned with the broader management issues of overall benefits provided to the company by the system but with specific day-to-day business operations. Most computer systems are developed for operational/production processing for the day-to-day running of the organisation and are not designed from the outset to include information specifically for management.

One of the authors recently worked on the development of a huge telecommunication system covering virtually all areas of the telecommunications company. The users being interviewed as to their requirements were the operators of the business and not the planners. When the question was asked "How do we know that the system is furthering the business objectives and CSFs of the organisation?" the answer was "Oh, don't worry, somebody is giving it some thought". But nowhere in the requirements catalogue of the business were the business objectives and CSFs, the *raison d'être* of the organisation, included. And no consideration whatever was given to whether the computer system was justifying the enormous expenditure. Which parts of the system were giving the best value for money? Legitimate questions like this were not even considered. Thus the benefits were also not included in the requirements catalogue.

(2) The introduction of procedures and working practices that makes benefits realisation as much part of the system design culture as the user requirements.
(3) The introduction of teams that monitor and measure the reality of the achievement of the benefits claimed and take corrective action as appropriate.

These three requirements to achieve benefits realisation are discussed below.

8.1 INCLUDING BENEFITS REALISATION IN THE SYSTEM'S DESIGN

The best way to explain this is by example. The example is based on the port authority case used in Chapter 6.

The benefits claimed for the port were those shown in Table 6.4. All the benefits are classified as intangible. The board of the port authority had accepted the financial figures for the benefits because of the care taken in the market survey and management estimates, and the application of the quantification technique for the measurement of the intangibles. But there were lingering doubts. The computer system was central to the successful operation of the port. Failure would cause serious damage to customer confidence. So it was essential that the benefits claimed were being achieved— they therefore needed to be closely monitored.

The computer system was the place to do the monitoring as it was the computer system that was conducting the operations from which the benefits could be obtained. *The solution to the first of the needs to achieve benefits realisation was to include the benefits in the design of the computer system from the very beginning, as if they were just another set of user requirements, and let the system provide the evidence of success or otherwise.*

The relevant entities that required modification will be identified and described as they are modified to support the claimed benefits. Any additional processing will also be identified and described. The first three benefits are used to show how the design of the vessel scheduling and container handling computer system was modified:

(1) Increase in sales (A). This benefit was achieved by the general ability of the system to offer a more reliable and faster turnaround of vessels.

All that required to be done was to include the appropriate data attributes in the following entity: number of container loadings and unloadings per (Shipping) Company per month both before and after the date of the system's installation. The dates after the installation date would be a rolling figure for the year as the months passed by, while those before the system's installation would be fixed. There were two sets of rolling figures to cover two years of business, with annualised figures thereafter, this to obtain trends. The Company entity therefore had the attributes:

- Company Name;
- Company Type (such as shipping, trucking, train);
- Trading only after system installation date*;
- Monthly Totals for container unloadings for year before system installation date*;
- Monthly Totals for container loadings for year before system installation date*;
- Monthly Totals for container unloadings for two years after system installation date*;
- Monthly Totals for container loadings for two years after system installation date*;
- Annual Totals for container unloadings for three years after system installation date*;
- Annual Totals for container loadings for three years after system installation date*.

Those attributes with an * are those specifically included to monitor the

(A) benefit. The processing for this benefit was an enquiry that accessed this entity and summed up the asterisked attributes as appropriate.

(2) Increase in price (B). This benefit was the 8% increase in price that could be charged for the faster service. Not all companies had agreed to this and a very careful monitor had to be made so as not to charge those companies with the premium surcharge.

All that required to be done was to include the following data attributes in the company entity:

- Surcharge allowed*;
- Surcharge percentage*;
- Date Surcharge Begin (old and new)*;
- Date Surcharge End (old and new)*.

Those attributes with an * are those specifically included to monitor the (B) benefit. The processing for this benefit was an enquiry that accessed the Company entity to find the surcharge percentage and then accessed the unloading and loading movement instructions for the vessels of the shipping company that had visited the port between the dates specified in the query. The number of movement instructions was multiplied by the surcharge percentage.

(3) Custom retained (C). This benefit was achieved by the general ability of the system to offer a more reliable and faster turnaround of vessels.

All that was required to be done was to include the following data attributes in the Company entity: Date company first traded with port.

The processing for this benefit was a simple matter of ascertaining which of the port's existing customers continued to trade with the port after the system start date.

All the benefits were designed into the system. They were defined as enquiry business requirements and the supporting information was modelled using the traditional techniques of a structured design method. Enquiries were raised on a monthly basis and reports submitted to the port management. It was now the task of the management to take whatever actions were appropriate to the information contained in the reports.

8.2 BENEFITS REALISATION

The monthly reports provided the raw measurement information that management needed to know whether the benefits claimed for the system were being achieved. The reports were assessed by the port authority board, conclusions drawn and the appropriate actions decided and taken. But before any of this could be done the benefits realisation organisation had to be created.

The organisation for monitoring the benefits was considered carefully. The benefits were reviewed as to their classification and it was ascertained that they fell into three categories:

(1) Those that were in the port's operational control.

These benefits were internal to the port and for which no customer/external factors were in play. The benefits falling into this category were the reduction in container movements between the unloading and loading of vessels (E), a reduction in penalty payments (D) and the handling of larger vessels (F).

(2) Those where the port had only a passive role to play as regards all the external forces (the shipping companies) and therefore could not influence the result once the planned project actions had been taken.

These benefits were of the type where the port authority could do everything that was required of the system and yet have no control over the achievement of the benefits. Once the required project plans had been achieved it was a case of sitting back and seeing if the benefit achieved what was hoped. The benefits were to be obtained from the general container shipping market trading within the catchment area of the port. No approaches had been made to specific shipping companies. If the benefits were not being obtained there was nothing that the port could do other than carry out a general reassessment of its operations and the container market. The benefits falling into this category were an increase in custom (A) and custom retained (C).

(3) Those where the port had an active role to play as regards specific external forces (specific shipping companies with whom verbal and contractual agreements about trading with the new system had been reached) and could influence the companies if the benefits were not being obtained.

These benefits were of the type where the port could approach the shipping companies which had entered into verbal or contractual agreements with the port. They were the companies who had been approached in the market survey and when asked the question "If we do this will you do that?" had given a favourable answer. The answer may not have been a commitment but there had been an understanding of a *quid pro quo*. Some of the shipping companies had entered into contractual agreements, such as for the payment of a higher price for the premium service and letting the port do the container planning for them. If the monthly benefits reports showed that these shipping customers were not living up to the verbal assurances or contractual agreements then the port could approach the shipping company for discussions. The benefits falling into this category were an increase in price chargeable (B) and assisting the shipping companies in the planning of their vessels (G).

On consideration of these different types of benefit it was clear that different mechanisms of monitoring and control were required, one for each type of benefit.

For the first type of benefit all that could be done was for a team to ponder the reasons for the failure to achieve the targets and make recommendations. Bearing in mind the benefits, the team was composed of the yard planner, the harbour master and the manager of the container movers.

The second benefit type required a different monitoring team. The team was composed of different skill types—a marketing person and one person from each of the port operational departments (yard planning, vessel scheduling and so forth). A marketing person was best qualified to assess why the container market was not behaving as anticipated and the operational managers were best able to assess whether the port was failing to achieve the project plans. The third benefit type required the sales department as the monitoring team. While the marketing department played a role in the market survey prior to the computer project being undertaken, it was the responsibility of the sales department to act as account managers with the shipping companies. Thus if a shipping company was not trading as expected by verbal agreement or as required by contract then it was the sales department's responsibility to approach the company for discussion.

What became apparent during the planning for the benefits realisation process was that *benefits realisation is a contingent mechanism*. The team structure and composition and the actual way that the benefits are monitored are contingencies of the type of benefit and the operations and structure of the business. To this end, and as described above, different monitoring teams were set up, each composed of the persons responsible for ensuring that the benefits were being achieved. The organisation and team membership for benefits realisation cannot be of fixed form. Both are contingent.

8.3 CHAPTER SUMMARY

The claims made about the benefits that a computer system can provide should be treated as business requirements. The claim that it will improve customer satisfaction and that this will generate £nn per annum needs to be converted into a business requirement that shows the number of satisfied customers before the system was developed *versus* the number of satisfied customers after the system was developed. The difference is the benefit. The data to support the monitoring of satisfied clients and the processing to access and present the relevant information about satisfied clients needs to be included in the design and specification of the system.

Chapter 9

Worked Example of
the IA Method

All the techniques described for the full IA of a decision to invest in a computer system are illustrated in the costs and benefits obtained from the port authority. The monies involved are listed in Tables 9.1–9.6 and Figures 9.1–9.3. These monies and associated figures are hypothetical so as to protect client confidentiality, but are based on a real world situation. They match those for the valuation of the intangible benefits in section 6.4. The unadjusted costs and benefits for the first four years of systems development and operational running are given in Table 6.4. The first year is one of loss for the simple reason that the system was being designed and developed and the hardware and software purchased and installed. The benefits were highest in the second year because the competitor ports had not been able to respond with their own upgraded systems and the benefits forecasted in the market survey and management estimates were being achieved. Thereafter the benefits declined as the competitor ports improved their own performance and stabilised at a higher level of profit. On the basis of the non-discounted monies the project would yield a profit of £72.11 million over its four year life.

9.1 THE MEASUREMENT OF THE COSTS AND BENEFITS

The costs incurred by the project were those for the purchase of the hardware and software and for the setting up of the computer system support and training. They are listed in Table 9.1. There is no comment of signifi-

Table 9.1 Container port cost/benefit figures (not discounted)

Port authority revisited Unadjusted/non-DCFs	Years			
	0	1	2	3
Costs (£m.)				
* Hardware	10	0	0	0
* Software	4.7	0.5	0.7	0.7
* Maintenance	2.5	1.8	2.3	2.3
* Training	2	1.5	0.8	0.5
* Support	0	0.2	0.2	0.2
	19.2	4	4	3.7
Tangible benefits regarded as sunk costs				
Intangible benefits (£m.)				
* Increase in sales	0	10.5	8	6
* Increase in price	0	12.6	5	2
* Custom retained	0	3	3	2.5
* Reduction in penalties	0	0.2	0.2	0.2
* Reduction in container movements	0	12.56	11.52	10.72
* New vessels	0	4	4.2	3.9
* New scheduling	0	0.81	1.1	1
	0	43.67	33.02	26.32
Total cash flow (3m.)	−19.2	39.67	29.02	22.62

cance relating to the identification and valuation—the purchase and support costs were obtained from the vendors.

The benefits of the proposed realtime computer system for the container port were all identified as intangible. Some seven intangible benefits were identified and the steps for their valuation are fully described in section 6.4.

The calculations of the non-discounted values of the intangibles produced a benefit to the project of £43.67 million for the first year of operation. Their values for the subsequent three years are shown in Table 9.1.

9.2 THE CALCULATION OF THE MARKET DISCOUNT RATE FOR THE CONTAINER PORT COMPANY

The market conditions of company risk were assessed from the general rates for container port operations from the CAPM. The market risk *beta* factor for port operations in general was 1.0, for general cargo was 1.1 (general cargo is a declining proportion of sea-borne trade and is therefore higher risk through declining returns) and container port operations was 0.9—they were regarded as a safer investment because the business was

Table 9.2 Container port costs/benefits of expansion in year 3 (probability = 0.2)

Port authority revisited Unadjusted/non-DCFs	Years			
	0	1	2	3
Costs (£m.)				
* Hardware	10	0	15	0
* Software	4.7	0.5	1.7	1
* Maintenance	2.5	1.8	3	3
* Training	2	1.5	1.5	0.7
* Support	0	0.2	0.2	0.2
	19.2	4	20.4	4.9
Tangible benefits regarded as sunk costs				
Intangible benefits (£m.)				
* Increase in sales	0	10.5	23.1	25.4
* Increase in price	0	12.6	6.4	2.2
* Custom retained	0	3	3	3
* Reduction in penalties	0	0.2	0.2	0.2
* Reduction in container movements	0	12.56	16.8	16.8
* New vessels	0	4	4.6	4
* New scheduling	0	0.81	1.2	1.1
	0	43.67	50.2	52.7
Total cash flow (3m.)	−19.2	39.67	29.8	47.8

Table 9.3 Container port costs/benefits of sales/marketing system with "do nothing" (probability = 0.8)

Port authority revisited Unadjusted/non-DCFs	Years			
	0	1	2	3
Costs (£m.)				
* Hardware	1	0	0	0
* Software	0.7	0	0	0
* Maintenance	0	0.2	0.2	0.2
* Training	0.4	0.2	0.2	0.2
	2.1	0.4	0.4	0.4
Tangible benefits regarded as sunk costs				
Intangible benefits (£m.)				
* Cost savings	0	1.1	1.1	1.1
* Increase in sales	0	2.3	3.3	3.3
	0	3.4	4.4	4.4
Total cash flow (£m.)	−2.1	3	4	4

Table 9.4 Container port costs/benefits of sales/marketing system with expansion in year 3 (probability = 0.2)

Port authority revisited Unadjusted/non-DCFs	Years			
	0	1	2	3
Costs (£m.)				
* Hardware	1	0	0	0
* Software	0.7	0	0	0
* Maintenance	0	0.2	0.2	0.2
* Training	0.4	0.2	0.2	0.2
	2.1	0.4	0.4	0.4
Tangible benefits regarded as sunk costs				
Intangible benefits (£m.)				
* Cost savings	0	1.1	1.4	1.4
* Increase in sales	0	2.3	5	5
	0	3.4	6.4	6.4
Total cash flow (£m.)	−2.1	3	6	6

Table 9.5 Container port costs/benefits of both systems with "do nothing" in year 3 (probability = 0.8)

Port authority revisited Unadjusted/non-DCFs	Years			
	0	1	2	3
Costs (£m.)				
* Hardware	10	0	0	0
* Software	4.7	0.5	0.7	0.7
* Maintenance	2.5	1.8	2.3	2.3
* Training	2	1.5	0.8	0.5
* Support	0	0.2	0.2	0.2
	19.2	4	4	3.7
Tangible benefits regarded as sunk costs				
Intangible benefits (£m.)				
* Increase in sales	0	11.4	13	11.7
* Increase in price	0	12.6	5	2
* Custom retained	0	3	3	2.5
* Reduction in penalties	0	0.2	0.2	0.2
* Reduction in container movements	0	12.56	11.82	11.18
* Costs saved	0	0	1	1
	0	4	4.2	3.9
	0	0.81	1.1	1
	0	44.67	39.32	33.48
Total cash flow (£m.)	−19.2	40.47	35.32	29.78

Table 9.6 Costs/benefits of both systems with expansion in year 3 (probability = 0.2)

Port authority visited Unadjusted/non-DCFs	Years			
	0	1	2	3
Costs (£m.)				
* Hardware	10.1	0	14	0
* Software	5.2	0.5	1.7	1
* Maintenance	2.5	1.9	3.1	3.1
* Training	2.4	1.6	1.6	0.8
* Support	0	0.2	0.2	0.2
	20.2	4.2	20.6	5.2
Tangible benefits regarded as sunk costs				
Intangible benefits (£m.)				
* Increase in sales	0	11.4	30.6	32.6
* Increase in price	0	12.6	6.4	3
* Custom retained	0	3	3	3
* Reduction in penalties	0	0.2	0.2	0.2
* Reduction in container movements	0	12.56	17.2	17.4
* Costs saved	0	0	1.4	1.4
* New vessels	0	4.1	4.3	4
	0	0.81	1.2	1.1
	0	44.67	64.3	62.7
Total cash flow (£m.)	−20.2	40.47	43.7	57.5

Discounted Cash Flow

$$NPV = -£19.2m. + \frac{£(43.67-4.0)m.}{1.1} + \frac{£(33.02-4.0)m.}{1.1^2} + \frac{£(26.32-3.7)m.}{1.1^3}$$

(year 0) (year 1) (year 2) (year 3)

$NPV = £56.75m.$

Figure 9.1 Container port cost/benefit figures (discounted)

increasing, particularly in the part of Europe where the port was located where the full potential of containerisation had not been obtained.

The expected return from the container port operations was Rf + *beta* value (Rm − Rf) where Rf is the risk free rate and Rm is the market rate. The inflation rate for the country was 8% and stable for the life of the project. Allowing for a return of 2%, also for the life of the project, the Rf

■ Major uncertainty is the volume of demand
■ Capacity of the system is 1.8m. containers per annum

NPV = £77.29m. (£60.61m.)—non-discounted figures (discounted figures)

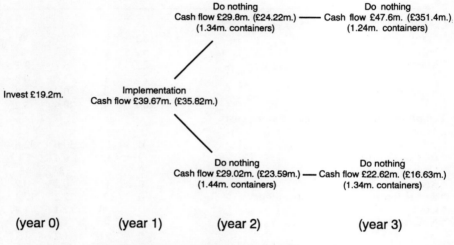

Figure 9.2   Container port decision tree analysis

of investment for the container port was 8% plus 2%, to give 10%. The industry rate for the company was 17%. The company discount rate for container port operations to be applied to the non-discounted monies of Table 9.1 was therefore 10% + 0.9 (17 − 10) = 16.3%.

9.3 THE CALCULATION OF THE PROJECT RISK FOR CONTAINER PORT OPERATIONS WITH THE BOWATER SCOTT MODEL

The next task is to measure the project risk; this entails ascertaining the operational gearing of the benefits cash flow (that is the proportion of the cash flow that is variable and therefore at risk) and the revenue sensitivity (that is the variability of the variable cash flow, the riskiness of the risk).

The project risk was based on the proposed cash flow that was fixed as opposed to that which was variable. Taking year 1, the total benefits cash flow is £43.67m. The costs are ignored simply because they are not a risk— they have to be spent for the project to proceed. Each of the benefits to be obtained was reviewed and that portion of the benefit that could be safely assumed to be achieved was judged to be a fixed cash flow. The reviewed

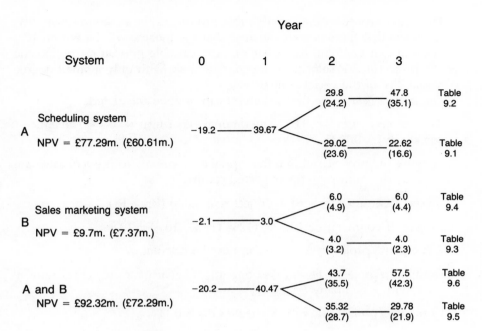

Figure 9.3 Container port project synergy

assessment is shown in Table 9.7. This produces an operational gearing of 0.65, that is the variable cash flow (£28.344m.) divided by the total cash flow (£43.67m.). Over half of the revenue cash flow was subject to risk. It must be appreciated that the greater the proportion of the revenue cash flow that is variable the greater the project is subject to risk. The container handling project was therefore regarded as risky as regards operational gearing.

The variable income portion, the £28.344m., was taken to the sales manager and the persons who had conducted the market survey for re-appraisal as to the variability of the cash flow of each variable, so as to ascertain the revenue sensitivity. In reality each of the variables were put through the exercise of calculation of the standard deviation. To do this in the book would be a huge task and very repetitive. The task of calculating the standard deviation of the variable income will be done for the entire £28.344m. rather than for each of the variables.

The split of the overall variable income was that there was a 25% chance that the income would be only £20.0m., a 50% chance that it would be £28.344m. and a 25% chance that it would be £35m. This produces a mean of £27.92m. (X) from the calculation of $((20.0 \times 0.25) + (28.344 \times 0.5) + (35.0 \times 0.25))$.

Figure 9.8 shows the calculation of the project sensitivity.

The square root of 0.036 = 0.190, this producing the revenue sensitivity. This means that there is a 63% chance that the income will be within 19% of the value of £27.92m. It is clear that the variable portion of the income of the project is not subject to considerable risk, with only a small degree of variability of the variable income.

The project *beta* value (the riskiness) can now be calculated:

The project *beta* = 0.65 (operational gearing) × 0.19 (revenue sensitivity) = 0.1235

This figure can now be put into the capital asset pricing formula to calculate the project discount rate/the expected return:

Project discount rate = Rf + project *beta* value (Rm – Rf)

Project discount rate = 10% + 0.1235 (17% – 10%) = 10.86%

The company/project *beta* value can now be calculated:

Company/project *beta* = project operational gearing × project revenue sensitivity × company *beta*.

Company/project *beta* = 0.65 × 0.19 × 0.9 = 0.111

This figure can now also be put into the capital asset pricing formula to calculate the company/project discount rate/the expected return:

= Rf + company project *beta* value (Rm – Rf)
= 10% + 0.111 (17% – 10%) = 10.78%

It is clear that the project is not high risk. Although there is a higher than desirable proportion of the income that is variable, it is not subject to much variability. The project is much lower risk than the nature of the company's business and this is reflected in the much lower discount rate to be applied to the project (11%) than for the container port operations as a whole (16.3%). A company/project discount rate of 11% was therefore applied to the non-discounted investment figures for the proposed computer system for the container port operations. This produced a net present value of £56.75m. for the project at the end of year 3 (see Figure 9.1). The non-discounted cost and benefit figures are taken from Table 9.1.

The project risk was calculated for each year of the project—the balance of the fixed and variable cash flows changing year by year. It would be an impossibly long task for this book, so the rate for the first year has been applied for the duration of the project for simplicity.

In this example there has been no relating of the individual project risk to the market average of all projects of similar type to calculate the relative project risk, the project *beta*. In this case the unique risk of the project is going to be taken into account in the investment decision. As described in section 3.5.4 some investors are more interested in investing in types of project and so would prefer to obtain the relative project *beta* not the absolute project *beta* of the individual project being invested in. Whether to use the relative project *beta* of all projects of a type rather than the absolute project *beta* of an individual project is a matter of personal preference.

9.4 THE CALCULATION OF EVENT RISK

The major uncertainty was the total volume of demand that would come from the project, particularly the speed of response from the competitor ports. The computer system was designed to support a turnover of some 1.8 million containers coming in and out of the port per annum. The original plan was for a virtual doubling of demand from the current 1.05 million containers per year to nearly 1.5 million. The capacity of the proposed computer installation was designed with these plans in mind with the usual additional processing power to cater for contingencies. However, if the competitor ports did not respond as quickly as anticipated then the capacity would be inadequate. It was judged that there was a 20% chance that the competitor ports would not respond as anticipated within two years of the system going live and that the capacity of the computer would therefore be inadequate to cater for the additional container business.

Table 9.7 Container port project cash flow

Benefit	Certain (fixed cash flow)	Uncertain (variable cash flow)
Increase in sales	25% £2.625m.	75% £7.875m.
Increase in price	30% £3.783m.	70% £8.827m.
Custom retained	75% £2.25m.	25% £0.75m.
Reduction in penalties	90% £0.18m.	10% £0.02m.
Reduction in container movements	30% £3.768m.	70% £8.792m.
New vessels	50% £2.0m.	40% £2.0m.
New scheduling	90% £0.73m.	10% £0.08m.
	£15.336m.	£28.344

Table 9.8 Container port project revenue sensitivity

Probability (P)%	Variable income (x)	% Deviation from mean (X−x)/X	P(X−x)²
25	£20.0m.	−28.4%	0.020
		(27.92−20.0)/27.92 = 0.284	(0.284 × 0.284) = 0.081 × 0.25 = 0.02
50	£28.344m.	+1.5%	0.0
25	£35m.	+25.3%	0.016
			0.036

There were therefore the options of a "do nothing" scenario or an "expand" scenario. Notice that with the do nothing scenario the volume of trade was declining as the competitor ports were responding and taking away some of the trade that had moved to the port while it had a strong competitive edge. The expansion of the computer installation would cost £15m. and would increase the capacity of the system to some 2.1 million containers per annum, pretty much the full capacity of the port. The figures of the non-discounted costs and benefits of taking project events into account are shown in Tables 9.2–9.6. A simple case of multiplying the expand and do nothing scenario non-discounted costs and benefits by the percentage chances of the scenarios occurring, then discounting back as normal produced an increased NPV of the project of £60.61m. in Figure 9.2 (the discounted figures are in brackets). Thus by planning for event risk to the project, its value had increased by £3.86m. (£60.61m.–£56.75m.).

The last task was to ascertain the benefits to be obtained from project synergy. As part of the results of the market survey, the yard planners, who would be using the new vessel scheduling system, had close discussions with the marketing and sales department regarding the use of each others' information. The yard planners needed to know of new shipping companies who were planning to use the port, in addition to those identified from the market survey, as news of the improved operations of the port spread. Action could be taken to adjust the scheduling algorithms to cater for increased throughput. The marketing and sales department were keen to know if the objectives of the vessel scheduling system were being achieved, so as to be able to use this information in the marketing of the new services being offered between departments. The shipping companies identified in the survey as sceptical of the claims being made were those for whom specific approaches were planned, as and when the objectives were being achieved. Using the quantification approach to the possibilities of increased trade it was ascertained, as shown in Figure 9.3, that the swapping of information through the creation of a corporate database, would yield a net present value of £4.3m. additional benefits to the port (£72.28m. − (£60.61m. + £7.37m.)).

Chapter 10

The Other Techniques

This chapter considers a number of techniques that have addressed the subject of valuing investments in projects, particularly IT projects, but which have not proved appropriate to the structured IA method.

In constructing the IA method the authors considered numerous techniques, both for the identification of investment opportunities and the valuation of projects. There are a large number of techniques to choose from. Many of the techniques overlap in the areas of IA which they address, as illustrated in Figure 1.2. The large numbers and degree of overlap mean that some of the techniques are "losers" as far as the method is concerned, even if they have merit in their own right. Analysis of the techniques also showed that some would be difficult to integrate into the IA method, perhaps because they are not pitched at the project level or because they do not contain a monetary component. Even when a technique does identify and plan for investment opportunities and measure investment returns, the subjects may not be addressed at the project level. Unless the technique does not overlap significantly with the other techniques considered, does address one of the two issues of investment identification and measurement and is at the project level, it will be a "loser" as far as the method is concerned.

The techniques described in this chapter are those worthy of serious consideration by persons interested in the valuation of IT but are "losers" as regards the IA method. However, this is no reflection on the validity of the techniques within the context for which they were developed.

10.1 RETURN ON MANAGEMENT (RoM)

This technique was invented by Paul Strassmann in the late 1980s and has been the subject of many articles and seminars. Strassmann's high standing in the world of computing alone is reason enough for devoting some time to his technique, but, personal respect aside, the RoM technique is so different from any other approach to the valuation of IT that it deserves some attention in its own right. For a description of this technique, see the reference below.[1]

The basic thrust of Strassmann's argument is that it is not capital which is a scarce resource but management. If something is in short supply it is more valuable—the simple laws of supply and demand. The argument goes that if a project is worthwhile and shows that it can yield the necessary returns then it will always be possible to find someone with some capital to invest in it. The difficulty is in finding the right management to implement and control any changes that need to be made. Management is therefore the component of greatest value. The consequence of this is that we should not be measuring the return on capital but that somehow we should be measuring the return on management.

The point that Strassmann then makes is that the main benefit of IT is that it improves the productivity of managers. It provides the information for the executive information systems with their "how much?" type questions and the decision support systems with their "what if" type questions, the answers to which enable managers to spot opportunities, control resources, monitor results and take corrective action. Rapid access to relevant information is thus seen as the lubricating oil of the management machine. Without it, management would not function properly. IT is there to improve the leverage of management, that is to improve the return on management. By investing in better technology and systems then better results can be obtained with the management that is available.

It has long been accepted that IT provides benefit to business, but the problem is in defining and measuring the return on management. Strassmann has devised a technique for measuring the return on management for a given organisation. The first step is to calculate the "value added" of a business or organisation. This is simply done by taking the revenue of a company and subtracting the purchases of the company. What is left is the value added of the organisation. This value added represents the added benefit to the organisation's consumers by the workforce and capital employed by the organisation. For example, the value of confectionery to a consumer is higher than the value of the raw materials that make

[1] Strassmann, P. A. (1985). *Information Payoff: the Transformation of Work in the Electronic Age.* Free Press, New York.

the product. If the raw materials and bought in services of a confectionery manufacturer are £200m. and the sales value of the sweets it produces are £300m. then the value added by the company's employees and resources is £100m.

Strassmann then argues that this "value added" comes from three sources: the value added of operations labour, the value added of capital and finally the value added of management. Operations labour value added is the added value due to the employees who are directly involved in the manufacture of the organisation's products or the provision of its services to its customers. In traditional terms this may be considered as the direct labour force. Strassmann says that because labour is plentiful then the value added of labour is merely the cost of that labour. This may be a point of contention but for the moment it is considered valid.

Secondly the value added of capital arises from the capital assets employed by a company. These assets include plant, machinery and buildings. Again, Strassmann argues that because capital is plentiful then the value added of capital is merely the cost of capital, that is the expected returns on the capital employed.

Finally, the residue of the value added is due to management. This is because it is the management which spots the opportunities, buys the labour and capital resources to exploit those opportunities, monitors the results and takes the necessary corrective action. According to Strassmann it is only right and proper that the residual value added is attributed to the management of that organisation. Thus the value added of management is a good indicator of the management's performance.

A model of the above value added approach is shown in Figure 10.1.

The return on management is simply the value added of management

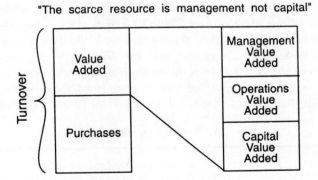

"The scarce resource is management not capital"

Return on management = Management value added/costs of management x 100%

Figure 10.1   Return on Management (RoM)

Table 10.1 RoM — example 1

	1972	1982	1992
Labour value added (£000)	7878	8989	9123
Labour costs (£000)	4717	5993	6292
Labour productivity	1.67	1.50	1.45

Table 10.2 RoM — example 2

	1972	1982	1992
Labour value added (£000)	7878	8989	9123
Operations costs (£000)	3165	2997	2759
Management value added	4713	5992	6364
Management costs (£000)	1552	2996	3533
Management productivity	3.04	2.00	1.80

divided by the costs of management. The costs of management are defined as the management salary costs plus all their incidental costs and expenses, the costs of all administrative and clerical functions which support management and the information systems which support the management. By relating value added return on management to the cost of the information systems employed, then a suitable measure for the effectiveness of the IT systems can be made.

Strassmann's argument is supported by some examples of the cost profiles of some businesses. Table 10.1 shows the costs of labour divided into the revenues from the sale of the products produced by the labour. It shows that, despite an increase in automation over the last two to three decades, there is a drop in labour productivity. Table 10.2 shows that, when the costs of direct labour are extracted from the figures in Table 10.1 to leave the value added revenue of management, and the costs of management are similarly extracted and divided into the management added value, again, the productivity of management has fallen in spite of the investment in automation. Table 10.3 shows that when the costs of IT are extracted and

Table 10.3 RoM — example 3

	1972	1982	1992
Management value added (£000)	4713	5992	6364
Technology costs (£000)	386	444	433
Productivity of IT	12.2	13.5	14.7

related to the management value added figure, the IT has a beneficial impact on management productivity. The argument therefore goes that investment in IT suitable for management, such as office automation and executive information systems, provides a benefit on management. IT is therefore beneficial for management.

The RoM technique has shortcomings:

- Too much value added is attributed to management. There is no consideration of outside influences, the factors of *force majeure*. The oil price may rise due to a war in the Gulf. In such a case, is it fair to attribute the resultant rise in the value added of oil extraction to the managers of the oil companies? Obviously not. Any changes in the national tax rates on companies and the cycles of world trade are factors of *force majeure* on which management has no influence. Such factors can substantially alter the value of a company; to what is the added value to be allocated — to the capital value added, the operations value added or the management value added?

- It may be that capital and labour are scarce resources. The early 1990s are times of high interest rates in several countries of the European Community and, given the lending excesses of the boom times of the 1980s, the banks are very cautious about lending. The value of money is that much higher because of these conditions. Furthermore, labour in Japan has long been a scarce resource and Japanese work practices make the division of labour from management a much more difficult feature to identify.

Whilst the technique may be a measure of past performance it does not help in predicting which information systems investments will deliver the greatest benefits in the future. It does not pretend to be a tool of IA or investment decision making. This is probably the major reason why the technique has not really caught on in IT circles.

Strassmann's findings are based on the PIMS database. What Strassmann has done is to use a database of companies' financial performance and from this compute each company's return on management. He then offers a service to clients which entails comparing a client's return on management with a similar organisation in his database. The aim is to spot trends and offer advice on a company's information systems investment plan. There are several dangers to this approach:

- The use of the performance information of companies in similar lines of business as the basis of advice is a dubious practice. This is fine so long as there is an industry norm of "behaviour". Cross industry comparisons of similar operations and the creation of a "universal" best practice constitute a doubtful strategy. The purchasing practices of the Boeing Aircraft Company are a very different operation from those of a corner shop —

the former does lots of little and the latter a little of lots. Their financial profiles will be very different.

This industry norm is very much out of line with the contingent style of management that is most widely practised. Contingent management assumes that each company has its own unique problems and business characteristics, and hence requires unique solutions. The PIMS database can be used to establish a norm against which other companies can draw conclusions but the norm conclusions should only be regarded as the "framework" in which corporate specific decisions are taken.

- The PIMS database is based on the performance profile of some 3000 companies in the United States, with the accounting conventions of US companies taken as typical. No attention is paid to the accounting conventions of companies in different countries. For example, capital assets can be valued on an historical basis, that is the assets are valued at their original purchase costs without bringing them to current values, or are valued at a replacement value, that is the cost to replace the assets at current prices. The effect of this is to reduce the current value of past projects/assets. The consequence of this, in turn, is that the return on these assets is artificially high, because the value of the assets is artificially understated. This is but one example of the many ways in which the costs and benefits of monies can be unrepresentative of their current value. This makes comparison between similar projects in different companies difficult, if not impossible.
- The RoM techniques are not at the project level, but at the business operations level. IA is about the value of investment in projects over time. RoM is therefore not suitable to the aims of the book.

10.2 CUSTOMER RESOURCE LIFE CYCLE

A number of writers argue that a CBA cannot properly value a project. They say that the strategic concerns are too difficult to measure accurately. Some of these writers go on to argue that because these strategic concerns cannot be measured then we should use different means of thinking about this type of investment.

Ives and Learmonth have collaborated on a number of such approaches to assessing strategic value. One particular model is the Customer Resource Life Cycle model. Ives and Learmonth use this model to explore radically new ways in which IT can give an organisation competitive advantage. This is done by examining each stage in a customer's cycle of buying, using and disposing of a given product or service.

The cycle is split into four stages—appraisal/requirements, acquisition, utilisation/ownership and finally disposal/retirement. There are several steps that a customer goes through in each of the phases of this cycle. In the requirements phase a customer will first establish a need that requires satisfying. The requirements are specified, even if only informally in the mind, followed by the selection of the supplier and so on. In the acquisition phase the customer places an order for the selected resource, pays for it, acquires the resource and tests and accepts it. While the resource is owned it is integrated in the company operations, upgraded as necessary, monitored as to its performance and maintained. Finally it is disposed of when its usefulness declines to an unacceptable level.

Ives and Learmonth quote the example of General Motors in the US. After using this Customer Resource Life Cycle approach GM decided that its customers needed help in specifying exactly which automobile model best suited their needs. The company introduced a customer support system in many of its showrooms which asked questions about a customer's driving habits, family size, budget and so on. The system would then produce a list of models which would suit the customer's needs. These models could be viewed via laser disc images of each model with details of all the options available. Not only could this system help in selecting a model for a customer but it could also advise on delivery dates and availability. The system was very successful and did much to help capture market share for GM.

Ives and Learmonth believe that it is this kind of imaginative forward thinking that yields the biggests benefits of IT, rather than analysing projects on a cost-benefit approach. This is the real benefit of the Ives and Learmonth ideas. There are no techniques as such, more a way of thinking. The approach offers a staged and operational breakdown of the life of a resource and its use by customers, the fee paying users of the resource. For each operation, the question is asked "How can IT give competitive advantage?". The important point to realise is that the Customer Resource Life Cycle model leads to a thinking process that has the following advantages:

- It is customer oriented—this is the crucial feature of an investment profile for a company;
- The thinking is proactive. One is thinking about investments that can exploit a business opportunity as well as increase competitive edge, one is looking to the future and not trying to catch up based on the past performance of one's competitors. And when one makes proactive decisions to invest then events are reacting to you and not the other way round—you are in control. Event risk is reduced. The value of the project goes up.

These are not minor issues in favour of the Ives and Learmonth approach. The life cycle approach is certainly a useful aid for the identification of the use of IT. The technique is therefore very useful in the investment identification module of the method. But the results of such an analysis do not give any measure of the size or likelihood of success, nor is there any measure of the value of an IT project. The Customer Resource Life Cycle technique is at its best as a front-end thought process and ideas generator to the techniques for the identification of investment opportunities.

10.3 CHAPTER SUMMARY

There are several techniques that have attempted to address the issues of the value of investing in information systems. The problem is that either they are not pitched at the project level or they consider aspects of identifying opportunity rather than measuring value.

Index